Sing God's

About the compilers:

Alan Luff has ministered in both parish and Cathedral settings; he is a composer and writer, focusing particularly on Welsh hymns; he is also co-editor of HymnQuest.

Paul Ferguson worked as an organist and teacher before being ordained. He served in Chester, at Westminster Abbey (where he succeeded Alan Luff as Precentor) and at York Minster before becoming Archdeacon of Cleveland in 2001.

Until 1995 Christopher Idle was in full-time parish ministry. Since then he has had varied church, school, writing and editing commitments; his own hymns appear in several books.

Canon Charles Stewart trained first as a teacher and professional singer, and was ordained in Chester in 1987. Since 1994 he has been Precentor and Sacrist of Winchester Cathedral, and also chairs the Winchester Diocesan Liturgical Committee.

Alan Dunstan was Canon and Precentor of Gloucester Cathedral from 1978 to 1993, is a former chairman of the Hymn Society, and has a particular concern for the use of hymns in worship – on which he has written two books and various articles.

Sing God's Glory

Hymns for Sundays and Holy Days,
Years A, B and C

New enlarged edition

Compiled by
Alan Luff, Alan Dunstan, Paul Ferguson,
Christopher Idle and Charles Stewart

CANTERBURY
PRESS
Norwich

© in this compilation Alan Luff, Alan Dunstan, Paul Ferguson,
Christopher Idle and Charles Stewart, 1997, 2001

Originally published under the title *Sing His Glory* in 1997 and reprinted
in 1998 and 1999 by the Canterbury Press, Norwich (a publishing
imprint of Hymns Ancient & Modern Limited, a registered charity).
This new edition published in 2001 by the Canterbury Press, Norwich
St Mary's Works, St Mary's Plain
Norwich, Norfolk, NR3 3BH

The compilers have asserted their right under the Copyright, Design
and Patents Act, 1988, to be identified as the Compilers of this Work.

British Library Cataloguing in Publication data

A catalogue record for this book is available
from the British Library

ISBN 1–85311–415–4

Printed and bound in Great Britain by
Biddles Ltd, Guildford and King's Lynn

Contents

Collation of lists, preparation and layout of originals by Paul Ferguson and Alan Luff.

The compilers express their gratitude for financial assistance from the Pratt Green Trust and Hymns Ancient and Modern in preparing this publication.

The convenor acknowledges his indebtedness in the final stages of checking the lists for comprehensiveness and accuracy to *HymnQuest, A Dictionary of Hymnody volume One* (The Pratt Green Trust 1997) in both its printed and CD-ROM versions, and for the work on *Sing Gods Glory* to *HymnQuest 2.1,* the CD-ROM data-base of Hymnody (The Pratt Green Trust 2001).

FOREWORD

The turn of the century and of the millennium set many of those responsible for the production of hymnbooks to work in preparing new editions, or indeed, completely new hymnbooks. This new Edition reflects that by including the successors to the books that appeared in the First Edition of this volume, *Sing His Glory*. Few churches will immediately purchase new stocks of books, and so we have retained the references to the older books, and have indeed enriched many readings with new suggestions.

As in *Sing His Glory* suggestions have been made from books not in the main list. In particular *Praise!* has provided many useful new metrical psalm versions.

It is clear that the First Edition is serving a considerable need in the churches, and this new Edition is offered in the hope that this will add to its usefulness.

ALAN LUFF

Autumn 2001

PREFACE

Choosing hymns

This book is meant to help all those who have to choose hymns for worship. The compilers believe that this is a task of considerable importance – for at least two reasons. First, many people absorb their theology from, and are nurtured in the faith by, the words which they sing, and the tunes to which they sing those words. Secondly, although hymns can facilitate and adorn an act of worship, they can also be impediments and distractions within it.

Hymns need to be appropriate to the points at which they are sung – in any form of liturgy. This ought to be obvious, but it is still possible to find churches where the congregation is invited to sing 'O enter then his gates with praise' just as it is about to go home. And if hymn-singing is not to be monotonous, the choice for any service must reflect variety. There needs to be variety in such matters as the metre and subject-matter of the hymns and the style of the tunes. Further variety is achieved if the hymns range over the centuries – so that not all come from the eighteenth, nineteenth or twentieth centuries. And there has to be a balance in the delicate matter of what is well known and what may be new to the congregation.

The purpose of this book

It has seemed important to make these general points about hymn-choosing before stating the purpose of this book which is more specific. It is meant to be one companion to the Revised Common Lectionary in the form in which it has been accepted by the Church of England.

This lectionary follows a three-year cycle, and for each Sunday and Holy Day, three readings and a psalm are provided. Sometimes there are alternatives. The Easter season, for example, has no Old Testament readings, but an additional table of such readings is provided for those who require them. In the Sundays of 'Ordinary Time' there is a choice of two Old Testament readings, each paired with a psalm. We have taken into account these and many other options built into the lectionary, but have confined ourselves to the readings appointed for the principal Sunday service. We have tried to suggest hymns based upon, or in some way reflecting the message of, these readings. We do not suppose (or recommend) that a hymn is sung after every reading; we seek instead to offer suggestions about what is sung *when* it is needed.

Although the Revised Common Lectionary does not allocate themes for Sundays, there are sometimes connections between the readings, and hymns proposed for one might well be suitable for another. Sometimes a single reading is sufficiently varied in its content to evoke at least two hymns of different character, and the choice must therefore depend upon how the whole service for that day is planned. We have tried to be realistic about what is *likely* to be chosen – for example, rejecting Christmas hymns for some summer Sunday when one of the readings has a strongly incarnational thrust.

We have offered metrical versions for some of the psalms – recognising that there are congregations in which this is the only way in which psalms are likely to be *sung*. Where no suitable metrical version can be found, we have followed the principle applied to other parts of Scripture – that is, suggesting hymns which seem to reflect the message of the psalm in question.

The most obvious use of the hymns listed here will be before, between or after readings. Hymns so used can expound or interpret Scripture, and enable worshippers to make some response to what has been read. But the lists will be of particular use to preachers, and, again, hymns based upon the sermon will enable its hearers to make their response.

The selection of hymn books

For reasons of space, it has been necessary to restrict the number of hymn books from which material has been selected. In general, we have chosen the standard hymn books of the main Christian denominations. We have chosen the most recent versions of them so that the books mentioned here have been published in the last twenty years. An exception is the *Church Hymnary Third Edition* (1973) – in process of revision during the compilation of our book – which we thought right to include because the Revised Common Lectionary is printed in the current *Book of Common Order*. Because of its widespread use across the denominations, we have included *Mission Praise* (1990) and we have found a place for the new Anglican edition of *Hymns Old and New* (1996). We have not included the many collections of freer hymns and worship songs that are on the market, because the rapid turn-over of repertoire and editions would quickly cause these lists to be out of date. Nor have we included Roman Catholic hymnals – partly because of their number, and partly because the contents of the Roman Catholic lectionary differ somewhat from that on which we have based our work. Most of the hymns suggested here are found in more than one book, but we have made exceptions when a hymn found in only one collection seems particularly appropriate to a reading. It is surely desirable for congregations sometimes to sing hymns from a collection other than their own. If such hymns are presented on a sheet or on a screen, the rules of copyright must be observed.

The impetus for this work has been the authorisation of this lectionary for use in the Church of England from Advent 1997. But we hope that the value of this book will not be restricted to Anglicans or necessarily to those who use a lectionary on these lines. Hymns based upon this large selection of Biblical passages could be of wider service to Christian communities and encourage them to make additions from the hymn/song books which they use.

Using this book

It will be obvious that this book differs from what might be considered its predecessors in this field. In recent years, ecumenical hymn-guides and Sunday lists at the back of hymn books have concentrated on the themes originally proposed by the Joint Liturgical Group and amended slightly in the *Alternative Service Book 1980*. Earlier guides to individual hymn books not only provided what was suitable for particular Sundays, but sought to ensure a wide coverage of the hymns in the book.

We recognise that many people will consult these lists in order to find four or five hymns for a Sunday service. They may indeed be able to make such a selection from what is provided here, but we must emphasise again that the lists are based upon the readings in the lectionary. The points in worship at which hymns are sung is a matter of liturgy rather than lectionary. In the final editing an attempt has been made to include most of the hymns that are common to us all – in so far as that can be determined. But how and when they are used must be a matter for local parishes and congregations.

Choosing hymns for a particular service needs care and time; this book is intended to aid, not replace, that process. But we hope that the choice of hymns for worship will increasingly be regarded as a creative and refreshing exercise rather than as a chore to be endured. To facilitate this choice, we offer in conclusion two suggestions. First, we recommend that every church keeps a careful record of *what* is sung and *when*. This will avoid undue repetition and sometimes counter the complaint 'We don't know it'. Secondly, we believe that among all the considerations affecting the choice of hymns, there is an over-riding question: What is a hymn *meant* to do at *this* point in the worship of *this* church? If that question is faced, it will go some way towards securing a good selection and a positive use of hymnody.

How the list is set out

The hymn selections are set out according to the Sundays in the Lectionary, the three years being grouped together. In addition some Sundays or groups of Sundays have a list of hymns that might be considered for any of the years. We give the title of the Sunday in the new Church of England version of the lectionary, *The Christian Year: Calendar, Lectionary and Collects* (1997), but to aid users of other denominations we add the title as it appears in the original version of the Revised Common Lectionary. Where the title of a Sunday is different in the two lectionaries, the abbreviations CLC and RCL are used to distinguish them. This is particularly important in the weeks preceding Lent where the numbering of Sunday Propers does not correspond between the two lectionaries.

The hymns have been chosen with one, on a few occasions two, of the lections in mind and that is indicated by the letters:

o   Old Testament (or Apocrypha)

a   Acts (in Easter season)

p   Psalm

c   Canticle

e   Epistle or Revelation

r   Revelation (Dedication Festival Years A & B)

g   Gospel

Where there are alternative lections the letter may be followed by a numeral.

In addition there are added:

s   Hymns that may be used because of the season

| Hymns which have a claim to be used for liturgical reasons or which need care in placing at a particular point in the liturgy.

Hymn texts have always been subject to editorial change and to the selection of verses by editors. We do not give the full variants but trust that the opening words given make the texts sufficiently recognisable for the user to wish to look up the number in the book in use and discover the variant offered there. In a number of cases what appear to be different hymns but which are translations of the same original texts are grouped together. A particular difficulty in selecting hymns to match lections is that in a number of cases (*All hail the power of Jesus' name* is a notable example) a hymn book may lack the verse that gave rise to the choice. All the appearances of a hymn are, however, noted and the user will need to decide whether to use the hymn as it is or to reproduce a more suitable version.

Certain fairly obvious differences between versions are not noted. Throughout the list 'Jesus' is used for both 'Jesus' and 'Jesu'. One version only of 'Alleluia' is used. Punctuation varies between books as does the use of capital letters; these have been kept to a minimum consistent with intelligibility.

The law of copyright has already been mentioned. Texts now remain copyright for 70 years after the death of the author. It should be noticed that some editors claim copyright for their revision of the texts of older hymns: this should be respected, but problems that this causes may be circumvented by using a different version of the text from another book.

The hymn books

The main selections are from the following hymn books:

AMS — Hymns Ancient and Modern New Standard Edition 1983 (This incorporates an abridged version of Hymns Ancient and Modern Revised 1950 and the whole of the two supplements Hundred Hymns for Today 1969 and More Hymns for Today 1980)

NEH — New English Hymnal 1986

HTC — Hymns for Today's Church (Second Edition) 1987

HON — Hymns Old and New (New Anglican Edition) 1996

MP — Mission Praise (Combined Words Edition) 1990

H&P — Hymns and Psalms 1983

R&S — Rejoice and Sing 1991

BPW — Baptist Praise and Worship 1991

CH3 — Church Hymnary (Third Edition) 1973

CP — Common Praise (A new edition of Hymns Ancient and Modern 2000)

SG — Sing Glory (Hymns, Psalms and Songs for a new Century; Jubilate Hymns) 1999

ONC — Complete Anglican Hymns Old and New 2000

MPC — Complete Mission Praise 2000

In addition individual hymns particularly suitable for a given reading have been selected from:

AFJ	Always from Joy 1996 (Hymn texts 1991-1996 by Alan Gaunt)
AHB	Anglican Hymn Book 1965
AMR	Hymns Ancient and Modern Revised 1950
BHB	Baptist Hymn Book 1962
BL	Borrowed Light (Hymn Texts, prayers and poems by Thomas H. Troeger) 1999
BWF	Piece Together Praise (Brian Wren) 1996
CFW	Church Family Worship 1991
CHH	Christian Hymns 1977
EH	English Hymnal 1933
FF	First Fruits (A worship anthology on generosity and giving) 2001
GH	Grace Hymns 1977
HF	Hymns of Faith 1964
HSN	Heaven Shall Not Wait (Wild Goose Songs 1) 1987
LEH	Lift Every Heart (Timothy Dudley-Smith Collected texts 1961-1983) 1984
LFB	Love From Below (Wild Goose Songs 3) 1989
LPB	Let's Praise, Book 2 1994
LUTR	Light upon the River (Hymn texts by Christopher M Idle) 1998
NSC	New Songs of Praise Book 3 1987
PFT	Praise for Today 1974
PR	Praise! (Psalms, Hymns and Songs for Christian Worship) 2000
SHF	Songs and Hymns of Fellowship 1987
SS	Story Song 1993
STG	Singing to God 1971
WAM	Worship Songs Ancient and Modern 1992
WOV	With One Voice (Australian Hymn Book) 1979

ALAN LUFF *Convenor*   CHRISTOPHER IDLE
ALAN DUNSTAN   CHARLES STEWART
PAUL FERGUSON

Isaiah 2: 1-5; Psalm 122; Romans 13: 11-14; Matthew 24: 36-44

		AMS	NEH	HTC	HON	MP	H&P	R&S	BPW	CH3	CP	SG	ONC	MPC
s	Creator of the earth and sky		152											
s	Creator of the starry height / stars of night	23	1		102						25		135	
s	Hark, a herald/thrilling voice / Hark, a trumpet call	24	5	192	196						26	436	263	
s	O come, O come, Emmanuel	26	11	66	358	493	85	126	144	165	32	338	480	493
s	The advent of our King/God	25	14		470						36		633	
s	Wake, O wake / Sleepers, wake	32	16	199	529		249	132		315	39		703	
o	Behold, the mountain of the Lord						50	130	617	312				
o	Christ is the world's true light	346	494	323	78		456	601	618	505	396	432	100	
o	Crown him with many crowns	147	352	174	103	109	255	262	37	298	166	321	137	109
o	For the healing of the nations	361			139		402	620	621		427	261	186	
p	How pleased and blest was I						497	563	10					
p	I joyed when to the house of God / Pray that Jerusalem		441				510	727		489				
p	I rejoiced to hear them say										6			
es	O heavenly word of God on high		2											
e	Awake, awake, fling off the night	342			49				404		334		57	
e	Lord, hear our prayer for this new year/day						357							
e	Lord, save thy world; in bitter need	397					425							
e	Oft in danger, oft in woe / Christian soldiers, onward go	210	434	524	396	533	715				547		487	533
e	Stand up, stand up for Jesus	221	453	535	457	617	721			481	578	644	617	617
e	Wake up, O people											704		
gs	We shall stay awake											722		
g	Christ is coming! Let creation									313				
g	Come, thou/O long-expected Jesus	31	3	52	98	102	81	138	139	320	24	335	128	102
g	Earth was waiting, spent and restless			54						141				
g	Hark what a sound, and too divine for hearing						236	660		314	28			

continued on next page

		AMS	NEH	HTC	HON	MP	H&P	R&S	BPW	CH3	CP	SG	ONC	MPC
g	Lo, he / Jesus comes with clouds descending	28	9	196	307	424	241	656	185	316	31	438	405	424
g	O day of God, draw near/nigh In beauty	405						632	635	511	33			
g	O quickly come, dread Judge of all		13											
g	Sing we the King who is coming to reign				602		244			318				602
g	The day of the Lord shall come							637						
g	The Lord will come and not be slow	29	15		489		245	128		321	37		655	
g	Thou Judge of quick and dead						247							
g	Waken, O sleeper, and rise											702		

Year B
The First Sunday of Advent

Isaiah 64: 1-9; Psalm 80: 1-7, 17-19; 1 Corinthians 1: 3-9; Mark 13: 24-37

		AMS	NEH	HTC	HON	MP	H&P	R&S	BPW	CH3	CP	SG	ONC	MPC
s	Creator of the starry height / stars of night	23	1		102						25		135	
s	Hark, a herald/thrilling voice / Hark, a trumpet call	24	5	192	196						26	436	263	
s	O come, O come, Emmanuel	26	11	66	358	493	85	126	144	165	32	338	480	493
s	The advent of our King/God	25	14		470						36		633	
s	Wake, O wake / Sleepers, wake	32	16	199	529		249	132		315	39		703	
o	Jesus, where'er thy people meet / Lord Jesus, when your people	162	390	371	282		549	476			492	16	367	
o	Lo, he / Jesus comes with clouds descending	28	9	196	307	424	241	656	185	316	31	438	405	424
o	Spirit of God within me			243			294	304	296		196	677	612	
e	All praise to our redeeming Lord					19	753		401		371			19
e	As sons of the day and daughters of light			490								570		
e	March on, my soul, with strength						716	546		614			440	
e	O Lord, I would delight in thee							593					510	
gs	We shall stay awake											722		
g	A safe stronghold/fortress/refuge	114		523		2	661	585	375	406/7				2
g	All for Jesus!		272	469	10		251		332		277	661	13	

continued on next page

g	Christ is coming! Let creation									313				
g	Christian, seek not yet repose			355										
g	Come, thou/O long-expected Jesus	31	3	52	98	102	81	138	139	320	24	335	128	102
g	Earth was waiting, spent and restless			54					141					
g	Hark what a sound, and too divine for hearing						236	660		314	28			
g	How firm a foundation			430	216	243		589	380				292	243
g	O day of God, draw near/nigh In beauty	405						632	635	511	33			
g	O quickly come, dread Judge of all		13											
g	Sing we the King who is coming to reign					602	244		318					602
g	Sometimes a light surprises	108						571	595			572		
g	Songs of praise the angels sang	196	451	350				512	667	38	574		608	
g	The day of the Lord shall come							637						
g	The Lord will come and not be slow	29	15		489		245	128		321	37		655	
g	Thou Judge of quick and dead						247							
g	Will your anchor hold				561	770	689	598	549	412			753	770

Year C
The First Sunday of Advent

Jeremiah **33**: 14-16; Psalm **25**: 1-10; 1 Thessalonians **3**: 9-13; Luke **21**: 25-36

		AMS	NEH	HTC	HON	MP	H&P	R&S	BPW	CH3	CP	SG	ONC	MPC
s	Creator of the starry height / stars of night	23	1		102						25		135	
s	O come, O come, Emmanuel	26	11	66	358	493	85	126	144	165	32	338	480	493
s	The advent of our King/God	25	14		470						36		633	
s	Wake, O wake / Sleepers, wake	32	16	199	529		249	132		315	39		703	
o	Come, O thou / O come, our all-victorious Lord			441			418							
p	All my soul to God I raise PR25													
p	Remember, remember your mercy, Lord										154			
p	Show me thy ways, O Lord									74				
p	To you, O Lord, I lift up my soul											545		
e	My hope is built on nothing less			462		473				411		537		473

continued on next page

		AMS	NEH	HTC	HON	MP	H&P	R&S	BPW	CH3	CP	SG	ONC	MPC
gs	Hark, a herald/thrilling voice / Hark, a trumpet call	24	5	192	196						26	436	263	
gs	We shall stay awake											722		
g	Christ is coming! Let creation									313				
g	Come and see the shining hope			188		86			271			454	110	86
g	Come, thou/O long-expected Jesus	31	3	52	98	102	81	138	139	320	24	335	128	102
g	Earth was waiting, spent and restless			54					141					
g	Great God, what do I see and hear			189										
g	Hark what a sound, and too divine for hearing						236	660		314	28			
g	Jesus, priceless treasure			461	262		259				484	535	344	
g	Lo, he / Jesus comes with clouds descending	28	9	196	307	424	241	656	185	316	31	438	405	424
g	O day of God, draw near/nigh In beauty	405						632	635	511	33			
g	O quickly come, dread Judge of all		13											
g	Sing we the King who is coming to reign					602	244		318					602
g	The day of the Lord shall come							637						
g	The Lord will come and not be slow	29	15		489		245	128		321	37		655	
g	Thou Judge of quick and dead						247							

Year A

The Second Sunday of Advent

Isaiah **11**: 1-10; Psalm **72**: 1-7, 18-19; Romans **15**: 4-13; Matthew **3**: 1-12

		AMS	NEH	HTC	HON	MP	H&P	R&S	BPW	CH3	CP	SG	ONC	MPC
o	Behold the saviour of the nations											63		
o	Holy Spirit, power of God AFJ													
o	My heart and voice I raise						268							
o	O come, O come, Emmanuel	26	11	66	358	493	85	126	144	165	32	338	480	493
o	O day of God, draw near/nigh In beauty	405						632	635	511	33			
o	O day of peace that dimly shines										259			
o	Spirit divine, attend/inspire our prayers		240		614		327	303		107	195			614
o	Spirit of wisdom, turn our eyes						385							
o	The day of the Lord shall come							637						
o	Who would think that what was needed			558							78		750	
p	A king on high is reigning PR72													
p	Hail to the Lord's anointed	142	55	190	193	204	125	127	142	317	87		259	204
p	His large and great dominion shall									167				
p	Jesus shall reign where'er the sun	143	388	516	277	379	239	269	313	413	490	45	359	379
p	The Lord will come and not be slow	29	15		489		245	128		321	37		655	
e	Dear Christ uplifted from the earth										453	142		
e	God who spoke in the beginning	468						60						
e	God, who has caused to be written thy word	467					472							
e	How beauteous/gracious are their feet	301					449	133			220			
e	Lord, I have made thy word my choice	490					475	316			504			
e	Lord, thy word abideth / Lord, your word shall guide us	166	407	251	318	446	476	317	102	130	515		420	446
e	Rise and hear! the Lord is speaking	509									321			
e	Thanks/Praise to God whose word	423	439	255			483	319	106		584	229		
e	The prophets spoke in days of old	513									327			
e	When Christ was lifted from the earth	525		335				655					142	

continued on next page

		AMS	NEH	HTC	HON	MP	H&P	R&S	BPW	CH3	CP	SG	ONC	MPC
gs	On Jordan's bank the Baptist's cry	27	12	601	401	538	84	134	147	208	34	339	527	538
gs	The advent of our King/God	25	14		470						36		633	
g	Christ, when for us you were baptized	442					129		405		92			
g	Come, Holy Spirit, come inflame				93						179		119	
g	Hark, a herald/thrilling voice / Hark, a trumpet call	24	5	192	196						26	436	263	
g	Lo, from the desert homes	316												
g	Lo, in the wilderness a voice	384	170											
g	Sing we the praises of the great forerunner / On this high feast day	315	168								234			
g	The Kingdom of God is justice and joy			333		651	139	200	321		591	184	646	651
g	When he was baptized in Jordan								234					
g	When Jesus came to Jordan	526					132				93			

See also Bible Sunday, pages 200-204

Year B
The Second Sunday of Advent

Isaiah 40: 1-11; Psalm 85: 1-2, 8-13; 2 Peter 3: 8-15a; Mark 1: 1-8

		AMS	NEH	HTC	HON	MP	H&P	R&S	BPW	CH3	CP	SG	ONC	MPC
s	Before all time the Word existed									162				
s	Earth was waiting, spent and restless			54							141			
s	Hail to the Lord's anointed	142	55	190	193	204	125	127	142	317	87		259	204
s	Hills of the north, rejoice	470	7		209		237		311		29		282	
s	Long ago, prophets knew	484	10				83				58		406	
s	The great Creator of the worlds	511									588			
s	The voice of God goes out to all the world						140	131						
s	Ye/You servants of the Lord	150	18	598	566		248			319	40		757	
og	Now is the time, the time of God's favour										341			
og	Prepare the way for the Lord										342			
o	Judge eternal, throned in splendour		490	329	285	395	409	626	627	519	356	600	372	395
o	March on, my soul, with strength						716	546		614			440	

continued on next page

		AMS	NEH	HTC	HON	MP	H&P	R&S	BPW	CH3	CP	SG	ONC	MPC
o	O comfort my people											481		
o	Thou Shepherd of Israel and mine						750							
p	Lord, thine heart in love hath yearned							704		75				
p	The Lord will come and not be slow	29	15		489		245	128		321	37		655	
p	We have a dream										715			
p	When this land knew God's gracious love outpoured CFW55													
e	Creating God, we bring our song of praise											134		
e	Great is the darkness that covers the earth										264			
e	Here is love vast as the ocean										174		987	
e	How firm a foundation			430	216	243		589	380				292	243
e	Love divine, all loves excelling	131	408	217	321	449	267	663	559	437	516	179	428	449
e	O/Our God, our help in ages past	99	417	37	366	498	358	705	389	611	537	542	494	498
e	On all the earth thy Spirit shower						321							
e	The universe was waiting											669		
gs	On Jordan's bank the Baptist's cry	27	12	601	401	538	84	134	147	208	34	339	527	538
gs	The advent of our King/God	25	14		470						36		633	
gs	We shall stay awake											722		
g	Christ, when for us you were baptized	442					129		405		92			
g	Hark, a herald/thrilling voice / Hark, a trumpet call	24	5	192	196						26	436	263	
g	Lo, from the desert homes	316												
g	Lo, in the wilderness a voice	384	170											
g	Sing we the praises of the great forerunner / On this high feast day	315	168								234			
g	The Kingdom of God is justice and joy			333		651	139	200	321		591	184	646	651
g	We have a gospel to proclaim	431	486	519	532	728	465		585		612	331	716	728
g	When he was baptized in Jordan								234					
g	When Jesus came to Jordan	526					132				93			

See also Bible Sunday, pages 200-204

Year C
The Second Sunday of Advent

Baruch **5**: 1-9 or Malachi **3**: 1-4; (Canticle) Benedictus; Philippians **1**: 3-11;
Luke **3**: 1-6

		AMS	NEH	HTC	HON	MP	H&P	R&S	BPW	CH3	CP	SG	ONC	MPC
c	God has spoken by his prophets			248			64		100		225		831	
c	In a world where people walk in darkness									476				
c	O bless the God of Israel			599										
s	Before all time the Word existed									162				
s	Earth was waiting, spent and restless			54					141					
s	Hail to the Lord's anointed	142	55	190	193	204	125	127	142	317	87		259	204
s	Hills of the north, rejoice	470	7		209		237		311		29		282	
s	Long ago, prophets knew	484	10				83				58		406	
s	The great Creator of the worlds	511									588			
s	The voice of God goes out to all the world						140	131						
s	Ye/You servants of the Lord	150	18	598	566		248			319	40		757	
o	God is in his temple					186	494	32	7					186
o	Love divine, all loves excelling	131	408	217	321	449	267	663	559	437	516	179	428	449
e	All praise to our redeeming Lord					19	753		401		371			19
e	Father, we thank thee, who hast planted / you now for planting	357	284					444	434	586	298			
gs	We shall stay awake											722		
g	Christ brings the kingdom where barrenness blooms										430			
g	Christ, when for us you were baptized	442					129		405		92			
g	Hark, a herald/thrilling voice / Hark, a trumpet call	24	5	192	196						26	436	263	
g	Lo, from the desert homes	316												
g	Lo, in the wilderness a voice	384	170											
g	O Spirit of the living God			513			322	577	579	496	190	605		
g	On Jordan's bank the Baptist's cry	27	12	601	401	538	84	134	147	208	34	339	527	538

continued on next page

		AMS	NEH	HTC	HON	MP	H&P	R&S	BPW	CH3	CP	SG	ONC	MPC
g	Sing we the praises of the great forerunner / On this high feast day	315	168								234			
g	The advent of our King/God	25	14		470						36		633	
g	The Kingdom of God is justice and joy			333		651	139	200		321	591	184	646	651
g	When he was baptized in Jordan								234					
g	When Jesus came to Jordan	526					132				93			

See also Bible Sunday, pages 200-204

Year A
The Third Sunday of Advent

Isaiah **35**: 1-10; Psalm **146**: 5-10 or (Canticle) Magnificat; James **5**: 7-10;
Matthew **11**: 2-11

		AMS	NEH	HTC	HON	MP	H&P	R&S	BPW	CH3	CP	SG	ONC	MPC
s	Blest are the saints/is the man / How blest are they						670	541		324				
s	How beauteous/gracious are their feet	301					449	133			220			
s	O day of God, draw near/nigh In beauty	405						632	635	511	33			
s	The race that long / The people that in darkness	52	57	71	491		89	129		168	38		656	
s	Thy/Your kingdom come, O God	177	499	334	519		783	638	644	322	607	269	691	949
o	A great and mighty wonder	43	21	49	2		90		140	192	41		4	
o	Let the desert sing			198										
o	The day of the Lord shall come							637						
o	The Saviour will come, resplendent in joy											664		
o	When the King shall come again			200										
p	I'll praise my Maker while I've breath			20		320	439	734	127		473	84		320
e	Great God, what do I see and hear			189										
e	Judge eternal, throned in splendour		490	329	285	395	409	626	627	519	356	600	372	395
e	Rejoice! the Lord is King	139	443	180	432	575	243	657	317	296	563	440	580	575
e	Teach me, my God and King	240	456		466		803	538		692	583		629	

continued on next page

		AMS	NEH	HTC	HON	MP	H&P	R&S	BPW	CH3	CP	SG	ONC	MPC
e	Tell out, my soul, the greatness of the Lord	422	186	42	467	631	86	740	391	164	362	62	631	631
e	Wait for the Lord (Taizé)				528			148					949	
e	When our God came to earth				552								740	
g	Christ brings the kingdom where barrenness blooms										430			
g	Hark, a herald/thrilling voice / Hark, a trumpet call	24	5	192	196						26	436	263	
g	Jesus the name high over all			213		385	264					323	364	385
g	Lo, from the desert homes	316												
g	Lo, in the wilderness a voice	384	170											
g	O for a thousand tongues to sing	125	415	219	362	496	744	285	59	371	534	55	485	495
g	Sing we the praises of the great forerunner / On this high feast day	315	168								234			
g	The Kingdom of God is justice and joy			333		651	139	200	321		591	184	646	651

Year B
The Third Sunday of Advent

Isaiah **61**: 1-4, 8-11; Psalm **126** or (Canticle) Magnificat;
1 Thessalonians **5**: 16-24; John **1**: 6-8, 19-28

		AMS	NEH	HTC	HON	MP	H&P	R&S	BPW	CH3	CP	SG	ONC	MPC
c	Tell out, my soul, the greatness of the Lord	422	186	42	467	631	86	740	391	164	362	62	631	631
s	Blest are the saints/is the man / How blest are they						670	541		324				
s	How beauteous/gracious are their feet	301					449	133			220			
s	O day of God, draw near/nigh In beauty	405						632	635	511	33			
s	The race that long / The people that in darkness	52	57	71	491		89	129		168	38		656	
s	Thy/Your kingdom come, O God	177	499	334	519		783	638	644	322	607	269	691	949
o	Go in Jesus' name										611			
o	God has chosen me										612			
o	God is working his purpose out		495	191	172	189	769	573		303	444	451	221	189
o	Hail to the Lord's anointed	142	55	190	193	204	125	127	142	317	87		259	204

continued on next page

		AMS	NEH	HTC	HON	MP	H&P	R&S	BPW	CH3	CP	SG	ONC	MPC
o	He's given me a garment of praise										120		986	
o	I'll praise my Maker while I've breath			20		320	439	734	127		473	84		320
o	Inspired by love and anger				252								325	
o	Jesus shall reign where'er the sun	143	388	516	277	379	239	269	313	413	490	45	359	379
o	Rejoice, O people, in the mounting years						657							
o	The Saviour will come, resplendent in joy											664		
o	The voice of God goes out to all the world						140	131						
o	Thou/God whose almighty / Father your mighty word	180	466	506	514	699	29	38	591	494	267	684	597	699
p	I will sing, I will sing a song			S15		313		279						313
p	Out of our failure to create							88					549	
p	The Lord restored us - we were freed PR126													
p	When Sion's bondage God turned back									393				
e	As sons of the day and daughters of light			490								570		
e	Be thou my vision / Lord be my vision	343	339	545	56	51	378	489	521	87	386	669	70	51
e	Father, who on man dost shower						341			515				
e	Holy Spirit, ever dwelling/living		141				303	324	290	334				
e	Lord of the Church, we pray for our renewing			499		442			486			577		442
e	Shepherd divine, our wants relieve	228					558				566			
e	Soldiers of Christ, arise	219	449	533	449	604	719	370	580	441	571	643	606	604
e	Spirit divine, attend/inspire our prayers			240		614	327	303		107	195			614
e	When circumstances make my life										540			
g	Hark, a herald/thrilling voice / Hark, a trumpet call	24	5	192	196						26	436	263	
g	Lo, from the desert homes	316												
g	Lo, in the wilderness a voice	384	170											
g	On Jordan's bank the Baptist's cry	27	12	601	401	538	84	134	147	208	34	339	527	538
g	Sing we the praises of the great forerunner / On this high feast day	315	168								234			

Year C
The Third Sunday of Advent

Zephaniah **3**: 14-20; (Canticle) Isaiah **12**: 2-6; Philippians **4**: 4-7; Luke **3**: 7-18

		AMS	NEH	HTC	HON	MP	H&P	R&S	BPW	CH3	CP	SG	ONC	MPC
c	Christ's Church shall glory in his power			522										
c	To God be the glory			584	522	708	463	289	566	374	609	71	695	708
s	Blest are the saints/is the man / How blest are they						670	541		324				
s	How beauteous/gracious are their feet	301					449	133			220			
s	O day of God, draw near/nigh In beauty	405						632	635	511	33			
s	The race that long / The people that in darkness	52	57	71	491		89	129		168	38		656	
s	Thy/Your kingdom come, O God	177	499	334	519		783	638	644	322	607	269	691	949
o	Christ is the King! O friends rejoice	345	345	492				571	475	474	165	31		
o	Glorious things of thee/you are spoken	172	362	494	158	173	817	560	480	421	435	35	205	173
o	Jesus is Lord of all the earth			53	24	30	250	234	31					
o	Praise God today: his glories never end CFW180													
o	Rejoice! the Lord is King	139	443	180	432	575	243	657	317	296	563	440	580	575
e	I will rest in Christ										549			
e	Like a mighty river flowing			32		419			632			51	400	419
e	May the mind of Christ my Saviour			550	334	463	739		537	432	521	671	447	463
e	Rejoice in the Lord always (1v chorus)				430	577		286					578	577
e	We praise you, Lord, for all that's true and pure							516						
e	What a friend we have in Jesus			373	541	746	559	413	603			646	727	746
e	Within the busy rush of life										648			
gs	We shall stay awake											722		
g	Christ, when for us you were baptized	442					129		405		92			

continued on next page

		AMS	NEH	HTC	HON	MP	H&P	R&S	BPW	CH3	CP	SG	ONC	MPC
g	Hark, a herald/thrilling voice / Hark, a trumpet call	24	5	192	196						26	436	263	
g	Lo, from the desert homes	316												
g	Lo, in the wilderness a voice	384	170											
g	O Spirit of the living God			513			322	577	579	496	190	605		
g	On Jordan's bank the Baptist's cry	27	12	601	401	538	84	134	147	208	34	339	527	538
g	Sing we the praises of the great forerunner / On this high feast day	315	168								234			
g	The advent of our King/God	25	14		470						36		633	
g	The Kingdom of God is justice and joy			333		651	139	200	321		591	184	646	651
g	When he was baptized in Jordan								234					
g	When Jesus came to Jordan	526					132				93			

Year A
The Fourth Sunday of Advent

Isaiah **7**: 10-16; Psalm **80**: 1-7, 17-19; Romans **1**: 1-7; Matthew **1**: 18-25

		AMS	NEH	HTC	HON	MP	H&P	R&S	BPW	CH3	CP	SG	ONC	MPC
s	Behold, the mountain of the Lord						50	130	617	312				
s	Hark the glad sound! The Saviour comes	30	6	193	198	210	82	137	143	160	27	435	265	210
s	Joy to the world, the Lord is come			197	283	393	77	135	315		57	340	370	393
s	Lift up your heads, ye/you mighty gates	483	8				240			12	30			
s	O come, O come, Emmanuel	26	11	66	358	493	85	126	144	165	32	338	480	493
s	The Lord will come and not be slow	29	15		489		245	128		321	37		655	
s	There's a light upon the mountains					679	246		149		198			679
s	Thy kingdom come! on bended knee	178	500		520					323	608		690	
og	O Trinity, O Trinity			6								291		
o	A Virgin most pure, as the prophets do tell						93							
o	And art thou come with us to dwell						415							

continued on next page

		AMS	NEH	HTC	HON	MP	H&P	R&S	BPW	CH3	CP	SG	ONC	MPC
p	Great Shepherd of thy/your people, hear	164		363			490	387			454	238	250	
eg	What Adam's disobedience cost	524					430							
e	Gracious God in adoration											244		
e	Long ago, prophets knew	484	10				83				58		406	
e	May the grace of Christ our Saviour	181		370	333		762		110	634	520	579	446	
gs	Mary blessed teenage mother				352								442	
g	All hail the power of Jesus' name	140	332	587/ 203	13	13	252		29	382	163	24	16	13
g	Come and join the celebration					83	97	166	160					83
g	Earth was waiting, spent and restless			54				141						
g	Glory be to God on high						101				361			
g	Had he not loved us			57										
g	Jesus, hope of every nation			58								336		
g	Let earth and heaven combine						109	190						
g	The darkness turns to dawn			68								363		
g	The hands that first held Mary's child BL66													
g	The race that long / The people that in darkness	52	57	71	491		89	129		168	38		656	
g	To the Name of our / that brings salvation	121	470	222	523		80	291		373	610	72	698	
g	Where do Christmas songs begin								180					
g	Where is this stupendous stranger	527	41					174						
g	Within a crib my Saviour lay			70										

Year B
The Fourth Sunday of Advent

2 Samuel **7**: 1-11, 16; (Canticle) Magnificat or Psalm **89**: 1-4, 19-26; Romans **16**: 25-27; Luke **1**: 26-38

		AMS	NEH	HTC	HON	MP	H&P	R&S	BPW	CH3	CP	SG	ONC	MPC
c	Tell out, my soul, the greatness of the Lord	422	186	42	467	631	86	740	391	164	362	62	631	631
s	Behold, the mountain of the Lord						50	130	617	312				
s	Hark the glad sound! The Saviour comes	30	6	193	198	210	82	137	143	160	27	435	265	210
s	Joy to the world, the Lord is come			197	283	393	77	135	315		57	340	370	393
s	Lift up your heads, ye/you mighty gates	483	8				240			12	30			
s	O come, O come, Emmanuel	26	11	66	358	493	85	126	144	165	32	338	480	493
s	The Lord will come and not be slow	29	15		489		245	128		321	37		655	
s	There's a light upon the mountains					679	246		149		198			679
s	Thy kingdom come! on bended knee	178	500		520					323	608		690	
o	Amazing grace			28	27	31	215	92	550		375	26	29	
o	Behold the servant of the Lord						788							
o	Lord, you need no house			546					349					
p	For ever, Lord, I'll sing your love PR89													
p	O greatly blest the people are								390					
p	Timeless love! we sing the story			47		707	60					100		707
e	God of God the uncreated			56								337		
e	May the mind of Christ my Saviour			550	334	463	739		537	432	521	671	447	463
e	Of the Father's love/heart begotten / God of God	33	33	56	395		79	181	145	198	64,65		486	
e	The universe was waiting											669		
gs	Mary blessed teenage mother				352								442	
g	At the name of Jesus	148	338	172	46	41	74	261	370	300	380	317	54	
g	Come all you good people			80										
g	Gabriel's message does away		4											

continued on next page

		AMS	NEH	HTC	HON	MP	H&P	R&S	BPW	CH3	CP	SG	ONC	MPC
g	Jesus, the name high over all			213		385	264					323		385
g	Long ago, prophets knew	484	10				83				58		406	
g	Now tell us, gentle Mary						142							
g	The angel Gabriel from heaven came				471		87	139	177		242		634	
g	To the Name of our / that brings salvation	121	470	222	523		80	291		373	610	72	698	
g	We thank you, God almighty										365			
g	When our God came to earth				552								740	

Year C
The Fourth Sunday of Advent

Micah **5**: 2-5a; (Canticle) Magnificat or Psalm **80**: 1-7; Hebrews **10**: 5-10; Luke **1**: 39-45 [46-55]

		AMS	NEH	HTC	HON	MP	H&P	R&S	BPW	CH3	CP	SG	ONC	MPC
c	Tell out, my soul, the greatness of the Lord	422	186	42	467	631	86	740	391	164	362	62	631	631
s	Behold, the mountain of the Lord						50	130	617	312				
s	Hark the glad sound! The Saviour comes	30	6	193	198	210	82	137	143	160	27	435	265	210
s	Joy to the world, the Lord is come			197	283	393	77	135	315		57	340	370	393
s	Lift up your heads, ye/you mighty gates	483	8				240			12	30			
s	O come, O come, Emmanuel	26	11	66	358	493	85	126	144	165	32	338	480	493
s	The Lord will come and not be slow	29	15		489		245	128		321	37		655	
s	There's a light upon the mountains					679	246		149		198			679
s	Thy kingdom come! on bended knee	178	500		520					323	608		690	
o	Bethlehem, of noblest / Earth has many	48	48		113		122			199	85		152	
o	From east to west, from shore to shore		20				99	172		189			193	
o	O little town of Bethlehem	40	32	88	377	503	113	145	170	172	63	358	508	503
eg	Let earth and heaven combine						109	190						
e	The universe was waiting											669		

continued on next page

		AMS	NEH	HTC	HON	MP	H&P	R&S	BPW	CH3	CP	SG	ONC	MPC
gs	Mary blessed teenage mother				352								442	
g	A great and mighty wonder	43	21	49	2		90		140	192	41		4	
g	All hail the power of Jesus' name	140	332	587/ 203	13	13	252		29	382	163	24	16	13
g	Come and join the celebration					83	97	166	160					83
g	Earth was waiting, spent and restless			54					141					
g	From heaven above to earth I come						100	154			51			
g	Glory be to God on high						101				361			
g	Had he not loved us			57										
g	Jesus, hope of every nation			58								336		
g	Once to every generation										605			
g	The darkness turns to dawn			68								363		
g	The race that long / The people that in darkness	52	57	71	491		89	129		168	38		656	
g	This child, secretly comes in the night					690						371		690
g	To God be the glory			584	522	708	463	289	566	374	609	71	695	708
g	To the Name of our / that brings salvation	121	470	222	523		80	291		373	610	72	698	
g	What Adam's disobedience cost	524					430							
g	When came in flesh the incarnate word		17											
g	When our God came to earth				552								740	
g	Where do Christmas songs begin								180					
g	Where is this stupendous stranger	527	41					174						
g	With God all things are possible										248			
g	Within a crib my Saviour lay			70										

Years A, B, C
Christmas Midnight

For readings see Christmas Day

		AMS	NEH	HTC	HON	MP	H&P	R&S	BPW	CH3	CP	SG	ONC	MPC
sg	Christians, awake	36	24	78	84	80	96	158	159	190	48	347	94	80
sg	While shepherds watched their flocks / While humble shepherds	37	42	94	554	764	120	155	182	174	76	367	745	764
s	A great and mighty wonder	43	21	49	2		90		140	192	41		4	
s	All hail and welcome, holy child				12								15	
s	Angels from the realms of glory	39		77	34	35	92	163	155	182	44	344	36	
s	Away in a manger		22	72	51	47	94	146	157	195	45	345	776	
s	Cloth for the cradle				86								107	
s	Come, thou Redeemer of the earth		19								49			
s	Hark! the herald angels sing	35	26	59	199	211	106	159	165	169	53	352	266	211
s	In the bleak midwinter	42	28	600	248	337	107	162	166	178	55	353	326	337
s	O come all ye/you faithful	34	30	597	357	491	110	160	169	191	62	357	479	491
s	O little town of Bethlehem	40	32	88	377	503	113	145	170	172	63	358	508	503
s	Of the Father's love/heart begotten / God of God	33	33	56	395		79	181	145	198	64,65		486	
s	Once in royal David's city	46	34	67	403	539	114	167	172	193	66	359	521	539
lg	Silent night / Still the night		35	95	444	597	112	147	176	176	69	362	597	597
l	All my heart this night rejoices			76			91	143			43			
l	Before the world began							180				318		
l	Come and sing the Christmas story			81					161			348		
l	Come, thou/O long-expected Jesus	31	3	52	98	102	81	138	139	320	24	335	128	102
l	It came upon the midnight clear	41	29	87	253	345	108	144	168	170	56	354	330	345
l	On Christmas night all Christians sing				400	537	115	153		181			523	537
og	The darkness turns to dawn			68								363		
og	What if the one who shapes the stars										364			
o	Who would think that what was needed			558							78		750	
g3	The Word was very God PR333													
g	Here is the centre: star on distant star											351		
g	This child, secretly comes in the night				690							371		690

Years A, B, C: Christmas Day

Set I: Isaiah **9**: 2-7; Psalm **96**; Titus **2**: 11-14; Luke **2**: 1-14 [15-20]
Set II: Isaiah **62**: 6-12; Psalm **97**; Titus **3**: 4-7; Luke **2**: [1-7] 8-20
Set III: Isaiah **52**: 7-10; Psalm **98**; Hebrews **1**: 1-4 [5-12]; John **1**: 1-14 (to be used at some service)

		AMS	NEH	HTC	HON	MP	H&P	R&S	BPW	CH3	CP	SG	ONC	MPC
sg	See him lying on a bed of straw			91	440	589	118	151	174		68	361	589	589
s	Away in a manger		22	72	51	47	94	146	157	195	45	345	776	
s	Child in the manger			51	75	71		150	158	180			93	71
s	Cloth for the cradle				86								107	
s	Cloth for the cradle				86								107	
s	Dost thou in a manger lie									50				
s	Hark! the herald angels sing	35	26	59	199	211	106	159	165	169	53	352	266	211
s	It came upon the midnight clear	41	29	87	253	345	108	144	168	170	56	354	330	345
s	O come all ye/you faithful	34	30	597	357	491	110	160	169	191	62	357	479	491
s	O little one sweet, O little one mild		31		376		111						507	
s	O little town of Bethlehem	40	32	88	377	503	113	145	170	172	63	358	508	503
s	Of the Father's love/heart begotten / God of God	33	33	56	395		79	181	145	198	64,65		486	
s	Once in royal David's city	46	34	67	403	539	114	167	172	193	66	359	521	539
s	The first Nowell		36	93	477	644	119		178	173			641	644
s	Thou who wast rich / Lord, you were rich			63		700					72	356		700
s	What child is this?		40		542	749		170			74		729	749
s	What kind of greatness can this be										221		959	
s	While shepherds watched their flocks / While humble shepherds	37	42	94	554	764	120	155	182	174	76	367	745	764
lg	Christians, awake	36	24	78	84	80	96	158	159	190	48	347	94	80
l	Born in the night, Mary's child				65	62	95	188	156				80	62
l	Come and join the celebration					83	97	166	160					83
l	Good Christian men / Good Christians all, rejoice	85	107	154	181		191	238	250	183	145	404	240	
o1	A great and mighty wonder	43	21	49	2		90		140	192	41		4	
o1	The darkness turns to dawn			68								363		
o1	The race that long / The people that in darkness	52	57	71	491		89	129		168	38		656	
o1	To us a child of royal birth	45		64										

continued on next page

		AMS	NEH	HTC	HON	MP	H&P	R&S	BPW	CH3	CP	SG	ONC	MPC
o1	Unto us a Child / boy/ Jesus Christ the Lord is born		39	83	526	714	127	169	181	187	73	355	700	714
o2	Make way, make way, for Christ the King				329	457		141					438	457
o3	How beauteous/gracious are their feet	301					449	133			220			
o3	How lovely on the mountains are the feet of him				219	249			310				295	249
on	Wonderful Counsellor												965	
p1	O sing a new song											89		
p	O praise ye the Lord	203	427	354	388	518		49			543	96	534	518
e1	The grace of God has dawned upon the world							741						
e3	No other prophet ever spoke										325			
e3	The brightness of God's glory			221								332		
g1	Infant holy, infant lowly			86	251	342		149	167	186			320	342
g3	Before the world began							180				31		
g	Come, come, come to the manger				89								112	
g	When our God came to earth				552								740	
g	Who would have dreamed it										366			

Year A
The First Sunday of Christmas
Isaiah **63**: 7-9; Psalm **148**; Hebrews **2**: 10-18; Matthew **2**: 13-23

		AMS	NEH	HTC	HON	MP	H&P	R&S	BPW	CH3	CP	SG	ONC	MPC
s	A great and mighty wonder	43	21	49	2		90		140	192	41		4	
s	Angels from the realms of glory	39		77	34	35	92	163	155	182	44	344	36	
s	Before the world began							180				318		
s	Behold the great Creator makes	44	23	50	58			171		197	46		62	
s	Child in the manger			51	75	71		150	158	180			93	71
s	Child of the stable's secret birth		43	53			124				47			
s	Go tell it on the mountain				165	179	135	164	571				243	179
s	God from on high hath/has heard	38					102	176						
s	God rest you merry, gentlemen		25	84	176		103		163	184		350	229	
s	Had he not loved us			57										
s	Holy child, how still you lie			60		236								236
s	In the bleak midwinter	42	28	600	248	337	107	162	166	178	55	353	326	337
s	Jesus, hope of every nation			58								336		
s	Lord, who left the highest heaven			97										
s	Love came down at Christmas			62	320	451	105	614	171	194			427	451
s	O little one sweet, O little one mild		31		376		111						507	
s	O sing a song of Bethlehem	413						201		220	545		536	
s	Of the Father's love/heart begotten / God of God	33	33	56	395		79	181	145	198	64,65		486	
s	Once in royal David's city	46	34	67	403	539	114	167	172	193	66	359	521	539
s	See him lying on a bed of straw			91	440	589	118	151	174		68	361	589	589
s	See, amid the winter's snow / in yonder manger low			90	439		117	157	173	179	67	360	588	
s	The first Nowell		36	93	477	644	119		178	173			641	644
s	The growing limbs of God the Son / The heavenly child	50	45											
s	Thou didst leave thy throne	250	465		513	697	154	192	179		601		683	697
s	To us a child of royal birth	45		64										
s	What child is this?		40		542	749		170			74		729	749
s	Who would think that what was needed				558			178			78		750	
p	Praise the Lord, his glories show			345			14	102		359				
e	A man there lived in Galilee	334			3								28	
e	Christ is the world's true light	346	494	323	78		456	601	618	505	396	432	100	
g	Unto us a Child / boy/ Jesus Christ the Lord is born		39	83	526	714	127	169	181	187	73	355	700	714

Year B
The First Sunday of Christmas

Isaiah **61**:10 — **62**:3; Psalm **148**; Galatians **4**: 4-7; Luke **2**: 15-21

		AMS	NEH	HTC	HON	MP	H&P	R&S	BPW	CH3	CP	SG	ONC	MPC
s	A song was heard at Christmas			75										
s	Angels from the realms of glory	39		77	34	35	92	163	155	182	44	344	36	
s	Before the world began							180				318		
s	Child in the manger			51	75	71		150	158	180			93	71
s	Child of the stable's secret birth		43	53			124				47			
s	Go tell it on the mountain				165	179	135	164	571				243	179
s	God from on high hath/has heard	38					102	176						
s	God rest you merry, gentlemen		25	84	176		103		163	184		350	229	
s	Had he not loved us			57										
s	Holy child, how still you lie			60		236								236
s	How brightly shines/beams the morning star		27					182		202	88		291	
s	In the bleak midwinter	42	28	600	248	337	107	162	166	178	55	353	326	337
s	Infant holy, infant lowly			86	251	342		149	167	186			320	342
s	Jesus, hope of every nation			58								336		
s	Lord, who left the highest heaven			97										
s	Love came down at Christmas			62	320	451	105	614	171	194			427	451
s	Once in royal David's city	46	34	67	403	539	114	167	172	193	66	359	521	539
s	See him lying on a bed of straw			91	440	589	118	151	174		68	361	589	589
s	See, amid the winter's snow / in yonder manger low			90	439		117	157	173	179	67	360	588	
s	The first Nowell		36	93	477	644	119		178	173			641	644
s	The growing limbs of God the Son / The heavenly child	50	45											
s	The Maker of the sun and moon		38					173			71			
s	Thou didst leave thy throne	250	465		513	697	154	192	179		601		683	697
s	To us a child of royal birth	45		64										
s	Unto us a Child / boy/ Jesus Christ the Lord is born		39	83	526	714	127	169	181	187	73	355	700	714
s	What child is this?		40		542	749		170			74		729	749
s	Who would think that what was needed				558			178			78		750	
p	Praise the Lord, his glories show			345			14	102		359				
e	Father God, I wonder how I managed to exist				119	128						107	159	128
g	O come all ye/you faithful	34	30	597	357	491	110	160	169	191	62	357	479	491
g	While shepherds watched their flocks / While humble shepherds	37	42	94	554	764	120	155	182	174	76	367	745	764

1 Samuel 2: 18-20, 26; Psalm 148; Colossians 3: 12-17; Luke 2: 41-52

		AMS	NEH	HTC	HON	MP	H&P	R&S	BPW	CH3	CP	SG	ONC	MPC
s	Angels from the realms of glory	39		77	34	35	92	163	155	182	44	344	36	
s	Before the world began							180				318		
s	Behold the great Creator makes	44	23	50	58			171		197	46		62	
s	Child in the manger			51	75	71		150	158	180			93	71
s	Child of the stable's secret birth		43	53			124				47			
s	Go tell it on the mountain				165	179	135	164	571				243	179
s	God from on high hath/has heard	38					102	176						
s	God rest you merry, gentlemen		25	84	176		103			163	184		350	229
s	Had he not loved us			57										
s	Holy child, how still you lie			60		236								236
s	I cannot tell why/how he whom angels worship			194	226	266	238	265	381		54	437	303	266
s	In the bleak midwinter	42	28	600	248	337	107	162	166	178	55	353	326	337
s	Jesus, hope of every nation			58								336		
s	Lord, who left the highest heaven			97										
s	Love came down at Christmas			62	320	451	105	614	171	194			427	451
s	Of the Father's love/heart begotten / God of God	33	33	56	395		79	181	145	198	64,65		486	
s	Once in royal David's city	46	34	67	403	539	114	167	172	193	66	359	521	539
s	See him lying on a bed of straw			91	440	589	118	151	174		68	361	589	589
s	See, amid the winter's snow / in yonder manger low			90	439		117	157	173	179	67	360	588	
s	The first Nowell		36	93	477	644	119		178	173			641	644
s	The great God of heaven		37								70			
s	The growing limbs of God the Son / The heavenly child	50	45											
s	The Maker of the sun and moon		38					173			71			
s	Thou didst leave thy throne	250	465		513	697	154	192	179		601		683	697
s	To us a child of royal birth	45		64										
s	Unto us a Child / boy/ Jesus Christ the Lord is born		39	83	526	714	127	169	181	187	73	355	700	714
s	What child is this?		40		542	749		170			74		729	749

continued on next page

		AMS	NEH	HTC	HON	MP	H&P	R&S	BPW	CH3	CP	SG	ONC	MPC
s	Who would think that what was needed				558			178			78		750	
p	Praise the Lord, his glories show			345			14	102		359				
g	His Father's house is where the Son must be LUTR 88													
g	Our Saviour's infant cries were heard									552				

New Year

		AMS	NEH	HTC	HON	MP	H&P	R&S	BPW	CH3	CP	SG	ONC	MPC
s	Be thou / O Lord, my/our guardian	217	64	374	55	385		68			385		68	
s	Be thou my vision / Lord be my vision	343	339	545	56	51	378	489	521	87	386	669	70	51
s	Beyond all mortal praise		340										71	
s	Breathe on me, Breath of God	157	342	226	69	67	280	295	282	103	174	554	84	67
s	Christ be the Lord of all our days				256									
s	Father, let us dedicate			257										
s	For thy/your mercy and thy/your grace			258	140					612			189	
s	God is our strength from days of old				171							220		
s	God is working his purpose out		495	191	172	189	769	573		303	444	451	221	189
s	Great God, we sing that mighty / your guiding hand						356	63	552	613				
s	Great is thy/your faithfulness			260	186	200	66	96	553		453	39	249	200
s	Here on the threshold of a new beginning										506	280		
s	How good is the God we adore / This, this is the God			450	217	244	277	542	338		464	41	293	244
s	Lead us, heavenly Father, lead us	224	393	595	293	400	68	543	597	90	496	640	379	400
s	Light a candle for thanksgiving											396		
s	Lord of our growing years			259					514			536		
s	Lord of the changing year			261								303		
s	Lord, for the years			328	310	428		603	535		51	602	409	428
s	Make me a channel of your peace			S19	328	456	776	629	634		519	691	437	456
s	New every morning is the love	2	238	270	349	480	636	536		47	6		467	480
s	O Christ the same, through all our story's pages		258	263									477	

continued on next page

s		AMS	NEH	HTC	HON	MP	H&P	R&S	BPW	CH3	CP	SG	ONC	MPC
s	O God of Bethel / O God of Jacob	216	416	35	364		442	71	599	72	536	241	491	907
s	O God, whom neither time nor space									82				
s	O/Our God, our help in ages past	99	417	37	366	498	358	705	389	611	537	542	494	498
s	Through all the changing scenes of life	209	467	46	516	702	73	685	544		604	654	686	702
s	Through the darkness of the ages										538			
s	When morning gilds the skies	146	473	223	551	756	276	292	73	370	619	74	739	756

See also The Naming and Circumcision of Jesus, page 229

Years A, B, C
The Second Sunday of Christmas

Jeremiah **31**: 7-14; Psalm **147**: 12-20; Ephesians **1**: 3-14; John **1**: [1-9] 10-18
or Ecclesiasticus **24**: 1-12; (Canticle) Wisdom **10**: 15-21; Ephesians **1**: 3-14;
John **1**: [1-9] 10-18

s		AMS	NEH	HTC	HON	MP	H&P	R&S	BPW	CH3	CP	SG	ONC	MPC
s	A great and mighty wonder	43	21	49	2		90		140	192	41		4	
s	A song was heard at Christmas			75										
s	Angel-voices ever singing	163	336	307	33	34	484	405	1	455	377	27	37	34
s	Before the world began							180				318		
s	Child in the manger			51	75	71		150	158	180			93	71
s	Fill your hearts with joy and gladness			30	147			40				80	172	147
s	Go tell it on the mountain			165	179	135	164	571					243	179
s	Had he not loved us			57										
s	Holy child, how still you lie			60		236								236
s	How brightly shines/beams the morning star		27					182		202	88		291	
s	Infant holy, infant lowly			86	251	342		149	167	186			320	342
s	Jesus, hope of every nation			58								336		
s	Lord, who left the highest heaven			97										
s	Love came down at Christmas			62	320	451	105	614	171	194			427	451
s	O little one sweet, O little one mild		31		376		111						507	

continued on next page

		AMS	NEH	HTC	HON	MP	H&P	R&S	BPW	CH3	CP	SG	ONC	MPC
s	Once in royal David's city	46	34	67	403	539	114	167	172	193	66	359	521	539
s	See him lying on a bed of straw			91	440	589	118	151	174		68	361	589	589
s	See, amid the winter's snow / in yonder manger low			90	439		117	157	173	179	67	360	588	
s	Son of the Lord most high	420					152	202	210	219				
s	The first Nowell		36	93	477	644	119		178	173			641	644
s	The great God of heaven		37								70			
s	The growing limbs of God the Son / The heavenly child	50	45											
s	Thou didst leave thy throne	250	465		513	697	154	192	179		601		683	697
s	To us a child of royal birth	45		64										
s	What child is this?		40		542	749		170			74		729	749
s	Who can measure heaven and earth			27										
s	Who would think that what was needed				558			178			78		750	
o	God is working his purpose out		495	191	172	189	769	573		303	444	451	221	189
es	Hidden Christ, alive for ever										530			
e	Oh, the mercy of God										195			
ge	Praise be to Christ in whom we see			220										
g	Hark! the herald angels sing	35	26	59	199	211	106	159	165	169	53	352	266	211
g	You laid aside your majesty				795									795

Years A, B, C
The Epiphany

Isaiah **60**: 1-6; Psalm **72**: [1-9] 10-15; Ephesians **3**: 1-12; Matthew **2**: 1-12

		AMS	NEH	HTC	HON	MP	H&P	R&S	BPW	CH3	CP	SG	ONC	MPC
s	Angel-voices ever singing	163	336	307	33	34	484	405	1	455	377	27	37	34
s	As with gladness	51	47	99	41	39	121	184	189	200	83	343	49	
s	Behold the great Creator makes	44	23	50	58			171		197	46		62	
s	Bethlehem, of noblest / Earth has many	48	48		113		122			199	85		152	

continued on next page

		AMS	NEH	HTC	HON	MP	H&P	R&S	BPW	CH3	CP	SG	ONC	MPC
s	Brightest and best of the sons of the morning	47	49	338	71	65	123	183	190	201	84	346	85	65
s	Child of the stable's secret birth		43	53			124				47			
s	Cloth for the cradle				86								107	
s	In the bleak midwinter	42	28	600	248	337	107	162	166	178	55	353	326	337
s	Jesus, good above all other	378	387	96	269		732	528		111	487		350	
s	Let earth and heaven combine						109	190						
s	Lord, when the wise men came from far							186						
s	Lord, who left the highest heaven			97										
s	Shepherds came, their praises / Angel voices, richly	180		74				156	192					
s	Songs of thankfulness and praise	53	56	98	451			191			90	376	609	
s	The first Nowell		36	93	477	644	119		178	173			641	644
s	What child is this?		40		542	749		170			74		729	749
s	Why, Herod, so unpitying / impious Herod / How vain		46					189		209				
s	Wise men, seeking Jesus						128	185		222				
s	Wise men, they came to look for wisdom			100								369		
l	Let all mortal flesh keep silence	256	295	61	295		266	454	441	577	309	472	381	
l	O worship / Worship the Lord in the beauty of holiness	49	52	344	394	529	505	187	22	40	89	204	552	529
o	Arise to greet the Lord of light											40		
o	Be thou my vision / Lord be my vision	343	339	545	56	51	378	489	521	87	386	669	70	51
o	City of God, Jerusalem			187										
o	The race that long / The people that in darkness	52	57	71	491		89	129		168	38		656	
o	Who would think that what was needed				558						78		750	
p	A king on high is reigning PR72													
p	Hail to the Lord's anointed	142	55	190	193	204	125	127	142	317	87		259	204
g	Faithful vigil ended	453	44	55	118	125					360	157		
g	From the eastern mountains	327	50								86			
g	Hail, thou source of every blessing		51											
g	Holy child, how still you lie			60		236								236
g	When our God came to earth				552								740	
g	Wise men of old came seeking, searching										368			

Year A
The Baptism of Christ (The First Sunday of Epiphany)

Isaiah **42**: 1-9; Psalm **29**; Acts **10**: 34-43; Matthew **3**: 13-17

		AMS	NEH	HTC	HON	MP	H&P	R&S	BPW	CH3	CP	SG	ONC	MPC
s	O worship / Worship the Lord in the beauty of holiness	49	52	344	394	529	505	187	22	40	89	204	552	529
l	Now is eternal life	402	114		351		203	432			152		470	
o	Be thou my vision / Lord be my vision	343	339	545	56	51	378	489	521	87	386	669	70	51
o	The Kingdom of God is justice and joy			333		651	139	200	321		591	184	646	651
o	The race that long / The people that in darkness	52	57	71	491		89	129		168	38		656	
o	With joy we meditate the grace	530				774	235	206	275		624			774
p	Let all in heaven and earth PR29													
p	The God of heaven thunders										315			
a	All hail the power of Jesus' name	140	332	587/ 203	13	13	252		29	382	163	24	16	13
a	I believe in Jesus				224	264						333	301	264
a	We believe in God the Father									363	286			
e	A man there lived in Galilee	334			3								28	
e	Awake, awake, fling off the night	342			49				404		334		57	
e	I believe in Jesus				224	264						333	301	264
e	The Church's one foundation	170	484	501	473	640	515	566	393	420	585	581	636	640
e	We have a gospel to proclaim	431	486	519	532	728	465		585		612		716	728
g	Christ, when for us you were baptized	442					129		405		92			
g	Crown him with many crowns	147	352	174	103	109	255	262	37	298	166	321	137	109
g	I bind unto myself today		159	5	225		695	36		402	203		302	
g	Name of all majesty			218		481					525	324	465	481
g	O love, how deep, how broad, how high	119	425		383		229	283	207	223	118		516	
g	On Jordan's bank the Baptist's cry	27	12	601	401	538	84	134	147	208	34	339	527	538
g	Songs of thankfulness and praise	53	56	98	451			191			90	376	609	
g	Spirit of God, unseen as the wind								295			233		
g	The sinless one to Jordan came		58											
g	To the Name of our / that brings salvation	121	470	222	523		80	291		373	610	72	698	
g	When Jesus came to Jordan	526					132				93			
g	Why, Herod, so unpitying / impious Herod / How vain		46					189		209				

28

Year B
The Baptism of Christ (The First Sunday of Epiphany)

Genesis **1**: 1-5; Psalm **29**; Acts **19**: 1-7; Mark **1**: 4-11

		AMS	NEH	HTC	HON	MP	H&P	R&S	BPW	CH3	CP	SG	ONC	MPC
s	Hail to the Lord's anointed	142	55	190	193	204	125	127	142	317	87		259	204
s	O worship / Worship the Lord in the beauty of holiness	49	52	344	394	529	505	187	22	40	89	204	552	529
l	God, that madest earth and heaven	12	245		178		641				15		232	
l	Now is eternal life	402	114		351		203	432			152		470	
og	Give to our God immortal praise	460		31	155	171	22	94	47		434	83	203	171
og	Spirit divine, attend/inspire our prayers			240		614	327	303		107	195			614
og	Thanks/Praise to God whose word	423	439	255			483	319	106		584	229		
o	Be thou my vision / Lord be my vision	343	339	545	56	51	378	489	521	87	386	669	70	51
o	God who created light										288			
o	Morning has broken		237	265	337	467	635	45	132		260		450	467
o	The race that long / The people that in darkness	52	57	71	491		89	129		168	38		656	
o	Thou/God whose almighty / Father your mighty word	180	466	506	514	699	29	38	591	494	267	684	597	699
p	Let all in heaven and earth PR29													
e	Awake, awake, fling off the night	342			49			404			334		57	
e	Breathe on me, Breath of God	157	342	226	69	67	280	295	282	103	174	554	84	67
e	Christ on whom the Spirit rested			228										
e	Come, gracious Spirit, heavenly dove	153	347							116	176		116	
e	O Breath of life, come sweeping / O Breath of love, come breathe			237	356	488	777	302	293	339			476	488
g	Christ, when for us you were baptized	442					129		405		92			
g	Christians, lift up your hearts … Praise for the Spirit	444		229							399		95	
g	Crown him with many crowns	147	352	174	103	109	255	262	37	298	166	321	137	109
g	How sweet the name of Jesus sounds	122	374	211	220	251	257	277	339	376	467	42	297	251
g	I bind unto myself today		159	5	225			695	36		402	203		302

continued on next page

		AMS	NEH	HTC	HON	MP	H&P	R&S	BPW	CH3	CP	SG	ONC	MPC
g	Name of all majesty			218		481					525	324	465	481
g	O love, how deep, how broad, how high	119	425		383		229	283	207	223	118		516	
g	On Jordan's bank the Baptist's cry	27	12	601	401	538	84	134	147	208	34	339	527	538
g	Songs of thankfulness and praise	53	56	98	451			191			90	376	609	
g	Spirit of the living God, fall afresh on me		S23	454	612	295	308	298					615	613
g	The sinless one to Jordan came		58											
g	To the Name of our / that brings salvation	121	470	222	523		80	291		373	610	72	698	
g	Why, Herod, so unpitying / impious Herod / How vain		46					189		209				

Year C
The Baptism of Christ (The First Sunday of Epiphany)

Isaiah **43**: 1-7; Psalm **29**; Acts **8**: 14-17; Luke **3**: 15-17, 21-22

		AMS	NEH	HTC	HON	MP	H&P	R&S	BPW	CH3	CP	SG	ONC	MPC
s	Crown him with many crowns	147	352	174	103	109	255	262	37	298	166	321	137	109
s	Hail to the Lord's anointed	142	55	190	193	204	125	127	142	317	87		259	204
s	O worship / Worship the Lord in the beauty of holiness	49	52	344	394	529	505	187	22	40	89	204	552	529
l	Christ, when for us you were baptized	442					129		405		92			
l	Now is eternal life	402	114		351		203	432			152		470	
o	Amazing grace			28	27	31	215	92	550		375	26	29	
o	How firm a foundation			430	216	243		589	380				292	243
o	The race that long / The people that in darkness	52	57	71	491		89	129		168	38		656	
p	Let all in heaven and earth PR29													
e	Awake, awake, fling off the night	342			49			404			334		57	
e	Be thou my vision / Lord be my vision	343	339	545	56	51	378	489	521	87	386	669	70	51
e	O Breath of life, come sweeping / O Breath of love, come breathe			237	356	488	777	302	293	339			476	488

continued on next page

		AMS	NEH	HTC	HON	MP	H&P	R&S	BPW	CH3	CP	SG	ONC	MPC
e	Spirit of the living God, fall afresh on me			S23	454	612	295	308	298				615	613
g	Christians, lift up your hearts … Praise for the Spirit	444		229							399		95	
g	Come, gracious Spirit, heavenly dove	153	347							116	176		116	
g	I bind unto myself today		159	5	225		695	36		402	203		302	
g	Like the murmur of the dove's song	185	17											
g	My song is love unknown	63	86	136	346	478	173	207	204	224	112	384	463	478
g	Name of all majesty			218		481					525	324	465	481
g	O love, how deep, how broad, how high	119	425		383		229	283	207	223	118		516	
g	On Jordan's bank the Baptist's cry	27	12	601	401	538	84	134	147	208	34	339	527	538
g	Spirit divine, attend/inspire our prayers			240		614	327	303		107	195			614
g	The sinless one to Jordan came		58											
g	To the Name of our / that brings salvation	121	470	222	523		80	291		373	610	72	698	
g	When Jesus came to Jordan	526					132				93			

Year A
The Second Sunday of Epiphany

14 → 20 JAN

Isaiah **49**: 1-7; Psalm **40**: 1-11; 1 Corinthians **1**: 1-9; John **1**: 29-42

		AMS	NEH	HTC	HON	MP	H&P	R&S	BPW	CH3	CP	SG	ONC	MPC
s	Hail to the Lord's anointed	142	55	190	193	204	125	127	142	317	87		259	204
s	Jesus, hope of every nation			58								336		
s	Jesus, the name high over all			213		385	264					323		385
s	Songs of thankfulness and praise	53	56	98	451			191			90	376	609	
s	The race that long / The people that in darkness	52	57	71	491		89	129		168	38		656	
o	God is our strength and refuge			527		188			308		443	650	219	188
o	God is working his purpose out		495	191	172	189	769	573		303	444	451	221	189
o	Like a river glorious			463		421								421
o	Safe in the shadow of the Lord			445		583						516		583

continued on next page

31

		AMS	NEH	HTC	HON	MP	H&P	R&S	BPW	CH3	CP	SG	ONC	MPC
o	Ye/You servants of God, your Master proclaim	149	476	520	565	784	278	293	76	372	627	75	784	756
p	Almighty God, my Redeemer										102			
p	I waited, I waited on the Lord										243			
e	God of gods, we sound his praises			340				46				504		
e	God of grace and God of glory	367		324	174	192	712	344	572	88	448	574	225	192
e	Great is thy/your faithfulness			260	186	200	66	96	553		453	39	249	200
g	Behold the Lamb of God										190			
g	Christ on whom the Spirit rested			228										
g	Christ, when for us you were baptized	442				129		405			92			
g	Come, let us join our cheerful songs	144	349	206	94	93	810	382	6		401	33	120	93
g	Crown him with many crowns	147	352	174	103	109	255	262	37	298	166	321	137	109
g	Glory, glory in the highest					174								174
g	Jesus calls us: o'er/in the tumult	312	200	104	266	359	141	355		211	233	668	347	359
g	Just as I am, without one plea	246	294	440	287	396	697	364	346	79	308	507	374	396
g	The sinless one to Jordan came		58											
g	There is a Redeemer				500	673						396	658	673
g	When Jesus came to Jordan	526					132				93			

Year B
The Second Sunday of Epiphany

1 Samuel **3**: 1-10 [11-20]; Psalm **139**: 1-6, 13-18; Revelation **5**: 1-10;
John **1**: 43-51

		AMS	NEH	HTC	HON	MP	H&P	R&S	BPW	CH3	CP	SG	ONC	MPC
s	Come and see the shining hope			188		86			271		110	86		
s	Hail to the Lord's anointed	142	55	190	193	204	125	127	142	317	87		259	204
s	Songs of thankfulness and praise	53	56	98	451			191			90	376	609	
s	The race that long / The people that in darkness	52	57	71	491		89	129		168	38		656	
l	Forth in thy/your name, O Lord	239	235	306	143	159	381	521	526	463	430	623	188	159
o	Be still and know that I am God, and there							347				18	66	

continued on next page

		AMS	NEH	HTC	HON	MP	H&P	R&S	BPW	CH3	CP	SG	ONC	MPC
o	Be still and know that I am God				52	48		347	280			18&24 2	66	
o	Hushed was the evening hymn					253	523	526		123				253
o	I, the Lord of sea and sky			235							470	633	332	857
o	Lord, speak to me, that I may speak			510		444	553	613	611	485	512			444
o	Speak, Lord, in the stillness			253		608			105					608
o	When heaven's voice was still: SS71													
p	Lord all-knowing, you have found me										683			
p	Lord, you have searched and known my ways						71	70	564					
p	My Lord, you called my name										203			
p	O God you search me										514			
p	There is no moment of my life					679	246		1498			185		
e	All heaven declares				14	14						420		14
e	Alleluia! sing to Jesus	262	271	170	26	207	592		270		278	458	12	207
e	Behold the glories of the Lamb PR 486													
e	Bright the vision that delighted / Round the Lord	96	343	578	70		445	665	71	353	392	29	86	
e	Come see the Lord in his breathtaking splendour										433			
e	Come, let us join our cheerful songs	144	349	206	94	93	810	382	6		401	33	120	93
e	Hail thou/our once-despisèd/rejected Jesus			175	192	203	222		273		168		258	203
e	Let us sing the God of glory										305			
e	Lion of Judah: SHF 330													1021
e	Lord, enthroned in heavenly splendour	263	296	416	309	431	616			583	311	52	408	
e	O worship the King all glorious above	101	433	24	393	528	28	47	63	35	546	90	551	528
e	There is a Redeemer				500	673						396	658	673
g	I cannot tell why/how he whom angels worship			194	226	266	238	265	381		54	437	303	266
g	Jesus calls us: o'er/in the tumult	312	200	104	266	359	141	355		211	233	668	347	359
g	Just as I am, without one plea	246	294	440	287	396	697	364	346	79	308	507	374	396
g	Will you come and follow me?				560			558	363		622	634	752	
g	You are the King of glory				570	790		271	74				762	790

The Second Sunday of Epiphany

Isaiah **62**: 1-5; Psalm **36**: 5-10; 1 Corinthians **12**: 1-11; John **2**: 1-11

		AMS	NEH	HTC	HON	MP	H&P	R&S	BPW	CH3	CP	SG	ONC	MPC
s	Hail to the Lord's anointed	142	55	190	193	204	125	127	142	317	87		259	204
s	The race that long / The people that in darkness	52	57	71	491		89	129		168	38		656	
o	Heaven shall not wait				207								272	
o	The Church's one foundation	170	484	501	473	640	515	566	393	420	585	581	636	640
p	Immortal, invisible, God only wise	199	377	21	242	327	9	67	383	32	474	44	314	327
e	Christ from whom all blessings flow			491			764	561						
e	Come down, O Love Divine	156	137	231	90	89	281	294	283	115	170	663	114	89
e	Filled with the Spirit's power	359		233	131		314				425	593	170	
e	Gracious Spirit, Holy Ghost / Holy Spirit, gracious Guest	154	367	474	184	198	301	310	288	438	182	556	245	198
e	Holy Spirit, come, confirm us	471	140		214		288	298	289		183		288	
e	Jesus is Lord! creation's voice proclaims it			S17	270	367	260	268	384		170		352	367
e	Men and women, let us walk										588			
e	O thou/Lord who came[st]	233	431	552/596	392	525	745	433	355	110	191	560	541	525
e	Of all the Spirit's gifts to me	503					320							
e	Spirit of holiness, wisdom and faithfulness			246		611					576	449		611
e	Take my life, and let it be	249		554	464	624	705	371	358	462	581	678	625	624
e	The Spirit came, as promised			244					297			450		
gl	God in the planning and purpose of life										698	213		
g	Jesus, come! for we invite you			109										
g	Jesus, Lord, we pray	475		302			365							
g	Lord Jesus Christ, invited guest and Saviour			297										
g	Songs of thankfulness and praise	53	56	98	451			191			90	376	609	
g	Why, Herod, so unpitying / impious Herod / How vain		46					189		209				

Year A
The Third Sunday of Epiphany

21→27 JAN

Isaiah **9**: 1-4; Psalm **27**: 1, 4-9; 1 Corinthians **1**: 10-18; Matthew **4**: 12-23

		AMS	NEH	HTC	HON	MP	H&P	R&S	BPW	CH3	CP	SG	ONC	MPC
s	As the bridegroom/bride is	340					30	517						
s	From many grains				149								196	
s	Hail to the Lord's anointed	142	55	190	193	204	125	127	142	317	87		259	204
s	Songs of thankfulness and praise	53	56	98	451			191			90	376	609	
l	Forth in the peace of Christ we go	458	361	542	142			602	607	589	429	594	187	
o	Christ, whose glory fills the skies	4	234	266	82	79	457	380		114	2	170	105	79
o	O God beyond all praising			36	363							53	489	
o	The light of Christ					652								652
o	The race that long / The people that in darkness	52	57	71	491		89	129		168	38		656	
p	Christ is the world's true light	346	494	323	78		456	601	618	505	396	432	100	
p	Nothing can trouble				347								659	
es	Christ is the King! O friends rejoice	345	345	492				571	475	474	165	31		
es	Father, Lord of all creation	356			122				620		418		163	
es	God is love, and where true love is / Here in Christ we gather	465	513				757	473			441			
es	I come with joy to meet my Lord	473		408	227		610	447	437		365	469	304	
es	Jesus, Lord, we look to thee	380	481				759	564			489			
es	Where love and loving-kindness dwell	528												
e	Christ from whom all blessings flow			491			764	561						
e	Father make us one				137									
e	Lord we come to ask your healing				319								422	
e	O thou who at thy eucharist / O Christ at your first eucharist	265	302	420	391		779			492	318		540	476
e	When I survey the wondrous cross	67	95	147	549	755	180	217	233	254	127	680	738	755
g	'The Kingdom is upon you!'	512									590			
g	Christ brings the kingdom where barrenness blooms										430			
g	Dear Lord and Father of mankind	115	353	356	106	111	673	492	84	76	411	497	144	111
g	I want to walk with Jesus Christ			S16		302		367						302

continued on next page

35

		AMS	NEH	HTC	HON	MP	H&P	R&S	BPW	CH3	CP	SG	ONC	MPC
g	Jesus calls us: o'er/in the tumult	312	200	104	266	359	141	355		211	233	668	347	359
g	Jesus who walked beside the lake: SS81													
g	Jesus, hope of every nation			58								336		
g	The Kingdom of God is justice and joy			333		651	139	200	321		591	184	646	651
g	Thy kingdom come! on bended knee	178	500		520					323	608		690	
g	Will you come and follow me				560			558	363		622	634	752	

Year B
The Third Sunday of Epiphany

Genesis **14**: 17-20; Psalm **128**; Revelation **19**: 6-10; John **2**: 1-11

		AMS	NEH	HTC	HON	MP	H&P	R&S	BPW	CH3	CP	SG	ONC	MPC
s	From many grains				149								196	
s	Hail to the Lord's anointed	142	55	190	193	204	125	127	142	317	87		259	204
l	Forth in the peace of Christ we go	458	361	542	142			602	607	589	429	594	187	
l	O thou who at thy eucharist / O Christ at your first eucharist	265	302	420	391		779			492	318		540	476
l	The race that long / The people that in darkness	52	57	71	491		89	129		168	38		656	
o	Behold the eternal King and Priest			397										
o	I will call upon the Lord					306								306
es	Christ is the King! O friends rejoice	345	345	492				571	475	474	165	31		
es	Father, Lord of all creation	356			122				620		418		163	
es	God is love, and where true love is / Here in Christ we gather	465	513				757	473			441			
es	I come with joy to meet my Lord	473		408	227		610	447	437		365	469	304	
es	Jesus, Lord, we look to thee	380	481				759	564			489			
es	Where love and loving-kindness dwell	528												
e	Alleluia, for the Lord our God					205								205

continued on next page

		AMS	NEH	HTC	HON	MP	H&P	R&S	BPW	CH3	CP	SG	ONC	MPC
e	Deck thyself/yourself, my soul, with gladness	257	280	400	108		606	446		567	295		146	
e	Glory, love, and praise, and honour	461	287		160		35				436		207	
e	Here, Lord, we take the broken bread			404			604	448	440				278	
e	Here, O my Lord, I see thee/you	274		406		230	608		436	573	304	468	279	230
e	Lift high the cross	72		508	303	417	170	422	575	550	499	601	394	417
e	Rejoice! the Lord is King	139	443	180	432	575	243	657	317	296	563	440	580	575
e	The Lord is King! lift up thy/your voice	107		183	485	656	58	76	322	36	592	98	650	656
gl	God in the planning and purpose of life										698	213		
g	Jesus, come! for we invite you			109										
g	Jesus, Lord, we pray	475		302			365							
g	Life for the poor was hard and tough											858		
g	Lord Jesus Christ, invited guest and Saviour			297										
g	One shall tell another				406	541							526	541
g	Songs of thankfulness and praise	53	56	98	451			191			90	376	609	
g	We come as guests invited			602		723								723

Year C
The Third Sunday of Epiphany

Nehemiah **8**: 1-3, 5-6, 8-10; Psalm **19**; 1 Corinthians **12**: 12-31a; Luke **4**: 14-21

		AMS	NEH	HTC	HON	MP	H&P	R&S	BPW	CH3	CP	SG	ONC	MPC
s	From many grains				149								196	
s	Songs of thankfulness and praise	53	56	98	451			191			90	376	609	
s	The race that long / The people that in darkness	52	57	71	491		89	129		168	38		656	
l	Forth in the peace of Christ we go	458	361	542	142			602	607	589	429	594	187	
og	Thanks/Praise to God whose word	423	439	255			483	319	106		584	229		
o	Father of mercies, in thy/your word	167		247				99				224		
o	God has spoken — by his prophets			248			64	100				225		831

continued on next page

		AMS	NEH	HTC	HON	MP	H&P	R&S	BPW	CH3	CP	SG	ONC	MPC
o	God, who has caused to be written thy word	467					472							
o	How sure the Scriptures are			249								227		
o	Lord, be thy word my rule / Lord, make your word	232		250										
o	Lord, I have made thy word my choice	490					475	316			504			
o	Lord, thy word abideth / Lord, your word shall guide us	166	407	251	318	446	476	317	102	130	515		420	446
p	God's glory fills the heaven with hymnsPR29B													
p	The heavens declare thy/your glory, Lord	168		254			481	320			264	230		
p	The stars declare his glory										314			
es	Christ is the King! O friends rejoice	345	345	492				571	475	474	165	31		
es	Father, Lord of all creation	356			122				620		418		163	
es	God is love, and where true love is / Here in Christ we gather	465	513				757	473			441			
es	I come with joy to meet my Lord	473		408	227		610	447	437		365	469	304	
es	Jesus, Lord, we look to thee	380	481				759	564			489			
es	Where love and loving-kindness dwell	528												
e	Brother, sister, let me serve you				73			474	473		393	619	88	
e	Christ from whom all blessings flow		491				764	561						
e	Living God your word has called us											404		
e	Lord of the Church, we pray for our renewing			499		442			486			577		442
e	Men and women let us walk										588			
g	Christ brings the kingdom where barrenness blooms										430			
g	Come to be our hope, Lord Jesus										273			
g	Cry 'freedom' in the name of God				104								138	
g	God has chosen me										612	830		
g	God of glory, we exalt				191									191
g	God's Spirit is deep in my heart				180		315	576	574					

continued on next page

		AMS	NEH	HTC	HON	MP	H&P	R&S	BPW	CH3	CP	SG	ONC	MPC
g	Hark the glad sound! The Saviour comes	30	6	193	198	210	82	137	143	160	27	435	265	210
g	Jesus, the name high over all			213		385	264					323		385
g	Like the murmur of the dove's song	185	17											
g	Make way, make way, for Christ the King				329	457		141					438	457
g	Now is the time, the time of God's favour										341			
g	O for a thousand tongues to sing	125	415	219	362	496	744	285	59	371	534	55	485	495
g	O thou who at thy eucharist / O Christ at your first eucharist	265	302	420	391		779			492	318		540	476
g	The Kingdom of God is justice and joy			333			651	139	200	321	591	184	646	651
g	Will you come and follow me				560			558	363		622	634	752	

Year A

28→3 FEB

The Fourth Sunday of Epiphany

1 Kings **17**: 8-16; Psalm **36**: 5-10; 1 Corinthians **1**: 18-31; John **2**: 1-11

2ND?

Year C.

		AMS	NEH	HTC	HON	MP	H&P	R&S	BPW	CH3	CP	SG	ONC	MPC
s	Christ is our corner-stone	161		564	77						395		98	
s	Hail to the Lord's anointed	142	55	190	193	204	125	127	142	317	87		259	204
s	The race that long / The people that in darkness	52	57	71	491		89	129		168	38		656	
o	O Lord my God, when I in awesome wonder [How great thou art]				380	506		117	62		262	56	511	506
p	Immortal, invisible, God only wise	199	377	21	242	327	9	67	383	32	474	44	314	327
e	Be thou my vision / Lord be my vision	343	339	545	56	51	378	489	521	87	386	669	70	51
e	Come, wounded healer											130		
e	Disposer supreme and judge of the earth	298	216		110						214		149	
e	Firmly I believe and truly	118	360	429	133					400	426	287	174	

continued on next page

		AMS	NEH	HTC	HON	MP	H&P	R&S	BPW	CH3	CP	SG	ONC	MPC
e	Glorious things of thee/you are spoken	172	362	494	158	173	817	560	480	421	435	35	205	173
e	In the Cross of Christ I glory		379		249	338	167	224	344	259	480		327	338
e	Lift high the cross	72		508	303	417	170	422	575	550	499	601	394	417
e	Nature with open volume stands	497	87				174	219			113			
e	We rest on thee / We trust in you			446		735						510		735
e	We sing the praise of him who died	138	94	146	536	738	182	229	231	258	125	390	723	738
e	When I survey the wondrous cross	67	95	147	549	755	180	217	233	254	127	680	738	755
gl	God in the planning and purpose of life										698	213		
g	Jesus, come! for we invite you			109										
g	Jesus, Lord, we pray	475		302			365							
g	Lord Jesus Christ, invited guest and Saviour			297										
g	Songs of thankfulness and praise	53	56	98	451			191			90	376	609	
g	We come as guests invited			602		723								723
g	Why, Herod, so unpitying / impious Herod / How vain		46					189		209				

Year B
The Fourth Sunday of Epiphany

Deuteronomy **18**: 15-20; Psalm **111**; Revelation **12**: 1-5a; Mark **1**: 21-28

		AMS	NEH	HTC	HON	MP	H&P	R&S	BPW	CH3	CP	SG	ONC	MPC
s	Christ is our corner-stone	161		564	77						395		98	
s	Hail to the Lord's anointed	142	55	190	193	204	125	127	142	317	87		259	204
s	Songs of thankfulness and praise	53	56	98	451			191			90	376	609	
s	The race that long / The people that in darkness	52	57	71	491		89	129		168	38		656	
o	Father of heaven, whose love profound	97	358	359	124		519			77	421	144		827
o	How sweet the name of Jesus sounds	122	374	211	220	251	257	277	339	376	467	42	297	251
o	Judge eternal, throned in splendour		490	329	285	395	409	626	627	519	356	600	372	395

continued on next page

		AMS	NEH	HTC	HON	MP	H&P	R&S	BPW	CH3	CP	SG	ONC	MPC
e	Thy/Your kingdom come, O God	177	499	334	519		783	638	644	322	607	269	691	949
g	'The Kingdom is upon you!'	512									590			
g	Firmly I believe and truly	118	360	429	133					400	426	287	174	
g	God you meet us in our weakness							475					237	
g	Jesus Christ is waiting				268				534			624	349	
g	Jesus, the name high over all			213		385	264					323		385
g	Join all the glorious names			214		392	78	280	557	304	493	46		392
g	King of glory, King of peace	194	391	603	288	397	499	97	53	364	494	178	375	
g	O for a thousand tongues to sing	125	415	219	362	496	744	285	59	371	534	55	485	495
g	Silence! Frenzied, unclean spiritBL106													
g	Son of God, eternal Saviour	132	498	102				605	639	454	573			
g	There is a Redeemer				500	673						396	658	673
g	Thine arm, O Lord, in days of old	285	324		502		397			214		671		

Year C
The Fourth Sunday of Epiphany

Ezekiel **43**:27 — **44**:4; Psalm **48**; 1 Corinthians **13**: 1-13; Luke **2**: 22-40

		AMS	NEH	HTC	HON	MP	H&P	R&S	BPW	CH3	CP	SG	ONC	MPC
s	Christ is our corner-stone	161		564	77						395		98	
s	Glorious things of thee/you are spoken	172	362	494	158	173	817	560	480	421	435	35	205	173
s	Songs of thankfulness and praise	53	56	98	451			191			90	376	609	
s	The race that long / The people that in darkness	52	57	71	491		89	129		168	38		656	
o	Jerusalem the golden	184	381	573	259			662	312	537	482		340	
o	We see the Lord				736									736
p	City of God, Jerusalem			187										
e	A/The new commandment I give			S26	4	1		745	470					1
e	Christ is the King! O friends rejoice	345	345	492				571	475	474	165	31		
e	Come, praise the name of Jesus			538					331					
e	Gracious Spirit, Holy Ghost / Holy Spirit, gracious Guest	154	367	474	184	198	301	310	288	438	182	556	245	198

continued on next page

		AMS	NEH	HTC	HON	MP	H&P	R&S	BPW	CH3	CP	SG	ONC	MPC
e	Help us to help each other / Jesus, united by thy grace	374		540	208		773	500			461		275	
e	Jesus Christ gives life and gladness										452			
e	Love divine, all loves excelling	131	408	217	321	449	267	663	559	437	516	179	428	449
e	O perfect love	280	320		387	517	370		509		343		533	517
e	Should I rehearse with human voice PR576													
e	Though gifts of knowledge and of tongues							307						
e	Where true love is found with charity											742		
g	Fairest Lord Jesus			209				273	334	375		199		823
g	Faithful vigil ended	453	44	55	118	125					360		157	
g	Hail to the Lord who comes	314	157				126				94			
g	Hail to the Lord's anointed	142	55	190	193	204	125	127	142	317	87		259	204
g	Jesus, hope of every nation		58									336		
g	Lord, now let your servant			611										
g	New Light has dawned										375			
g	Thanks be to God for his saints										64			
g	This child, secretly comes in the night				690							371		690
g	You give, Lord, the sign to your servant											764		

See Third Sunday of Epiphany for hymns on Christian Unity

Years A, B, C
Presentation of Christ in the Temple (Candlemas)
Malachi **3**: 1-5; Psalm **24**: [1-6] 7-10; Hebrews **2**: 14-18; Luke **2**: 22-40

		AMS	NEH	HTC	HON	MP	H&P	R&S	BPW	CH3	CP	SG	ONC	MPC
s	Christ, whose glory fills the skies	4	234	266	82	79	457	380		114	2	170	105	79
s	Earth was waiting, spent and restless			54					141					
s	Fairest Lord Jesus			209				273	334	375		199		823
s	Love divine, all loves excelling	131	408	217	321	449	267	663	559	437	516	179	428	449
s	Virgin-born, we bow before thee	311	187		527						244		701	
s	When candles are lighted on Candlemas-Day									80				
l	Angels from the realms of glory	39		77	34	35	92	163	155	182	44	344	36	
o	Make way, make way, for Christ the King				329	457		141					438	457
o	Purify my heart / Refiner's fire				428							163	574	921
o	Restore, O Lord, the honour of your name				434	579			324			274	582	579
p	Lift up your heads, ye/you mighty gates	483	8				240				12	30		
p	This earth belongs to God											99		
e	Hail thou/our once-despisèd/rejected Jesus			175	192	203	222		273		168		258	203
e	Join all the glorious names			214		392	78	280	557	304	493	46		392
e	Lead us, heavenly Father, lead us	224	393	595	293	400	68	543	597	90	496	640	379	400
e	Praise to the Holiest in the height	117	439	140	426	563	231	103	562	238	557	58	572	563
e	What a friend we have in Jesus			373	541	746	559	413	603			646	727	746
e	Where high the heavenly temple stands	130		184				259		295	75			
e	With joy we meditate the grace	530				774	235	206	275		624			774
g	Come, thou/O long-expected Jesus	31	3	52	98	102	81	138	139	320	24	335	128	102
g	Faithful vigil ended	453	44	55	118	125					360		157	
g	Hail to the Lord who comes	314	157				126				94			
g	Jesus, hope of every nation			58								336		
g	Lord, now let your servant			611										
g	New Light has dawned										375			
g	Thanks be to God for his saints										64			
g	You give, Lord, the sign to your servant											764		

Year A
CLC: Ordinary Time: Proper 1
RCL: Fifth Sunday after the Epiphany

Isaiah **58**: 1-9a[b-12]; Psalm **112**: 1-9 [10]; 1 Corinthians **2**: 1-12 [13-16]; Matthew **5**: 13-20

		AMS	NEH	HTC	HON	MP	H&P	R&S	BPW	CH3	CP	SG	ONC	MPC
s	Here on the threshold of a new beginning										506	280		
o	Almighty Father, who for us thy Son didst give	338					401	621			374			
o	Come faithful pilgrims all											115		
o	Eternal Ruler of the ceaseless round	353	355		115			623	477	514	181		154	
o	God of freedom, God of justice							625	623		447		224	
o	Judge eternal, throned in splendour		490	329	285	395	409	626	627	519	356	600	372	395
o	O Christ the Lord, O Christ the King		496				406	630						
o	O day of God, draw near/nigh In beauty	405						632	635	511	33			
o	Praise and thanksgiving, Father, we offer	415					350	48			272		558	
o	The Church of Christ in every age						804	636	613					
o	This we can do for justice and for peace							639						
o	Thy/Your kingdom come, O God	177	499	334	519		783	638	644	322	607	269	691	949
o	We pray for peace						413	641			613			4
o	We utter our cry: that peace may prevail							642						
o	What shall we bring											730		
e	Can we/man by searching find out God	438					76	80			201	496		
e	Glory be to Jesus	66	83	126	159						108	146	206	
e	Nature with open volume stands	497	87				174	219			113			
e	We sing the praise of him who died	138	94	146	536	738	182	229	231	258	125	390	723	738
gl	Here in this place the new light is streaming										4			
g	Blest are the pure in heart	238	341	110	63	58	724		588	113	391	372	77	58
g	Dearest Jesus, we are here / Look upon us, blessed Lord	269			107						129	294		

continued on next page

		AMS	NEH	HTC	HON	MP	H&P	R&S	BPW	CH3	CP	SG	ONC	MPC
g	Father of mercies, in thy/your word	167		247					99			224		
g	Lord Jesus, once you spoke	392		112					598					
g	Lord, I have made thy word my choice	490					475	316			504			
g	Lord, speak to me, that I may speak			510		444	553	613	611	485	512			444
g	O changeless Christ, for ever new			108					206			374		
g	O Lord, you are the life of the world							510						
g	The Kingdom of God is justice and joy			333		651	139	200	321			591	184	646	651
g	When Jesus walked upon this earth			317										

Year B
CLC: Ordinary Time: Proper 1
RCL: Fifth Sunday after the Epiphany

Isaiah **40**: 21-31; Psalm **147**: 1-11, 20c; 1 Corinthians **9**: 16-23; Mark **1**: 29-39

		AMS	NEH	HTC	HON	MP	H&P	R&S	BPW	CH3	CP	SG	ONC	MPC
og	God is love: let heaven adore him	365	364		170	187	36	95	374		442		217	187
o	Awake our souls, away our fears	436					663	488			382	59		
o	Do you not know? This is our God										297			
o	Hast thou not known						446	61						
o	O comfort my people											481		
o	We will run and not grow weary										552			
p	Fill your hearts with joy and gladness			30	130				40			80	172	147
p	Praise ye the Lord! 'Tis good to raise						338	50						338
p	Praise ye the Lord; for it is good									136				
p	We have a dream											715		
e	Go forth and tell			505	164	178	770	574	570		437	596	238	178
e	Lord, if at thy command						771							
e	Lord, speak to me, that I may speak			510		444	553	613	611	485	512			444
e	O Spirit of the living God			513			322	577	579	496	190	605		
e	Send out/forth the gospel			517		593			584					593
e	Shout it in the street						782							
e	Speak forth thy/your word, O Father								581	468				

continued on next page

45

		AMS	NEH	HTC	HON	MP	H&P	R&S	BPW	CH3	CP	SG	ONC	MPC
e	Tell all the world of Jesus			521					582			608		
e	Thou/Lord, you have given thyself/yourself for our healing				698				576					
e	We have a gospel to proclaim	431	486	519	532	728	465		585		612		716	728
e	We've a story to tell to the nations				744				586					
g	A stranger once did bless the earth	335						198						
g	At even[ing], ere/when the sun was/had set	9	243	315	43	43	142	644	616	52	12	487	50	
g	From the town's dusty clamour: SS84													
g	Heal me, hands of Jesus			319								488		
g	Jesus' hands were kind hands						393	197		228				
g	Lord Christ, who on thy heart didst bear	388			308		394						407	
g	O Christ the healer, we have come						395				346	489		395
g	O God, by whose almighty plan	406					396	651			204			
g	O God, whose will is life and good	408												
g	Thine arm, O Lord, in days of old	285	324		502		397			214		671		
g	Thou to whom the sick and dying		325											
g	When Jesus walked upon this earth			317										
g	With loving hands			106								187		
g	Your will for us and others, Lord						398							

Year C
CLC: Ordinary Time: Proper 1
RCL: Fifth Sunday after the Epiphany

Isaiah 6: 1-8 [9-13]; Psalm 138; 1 Corinthians 15: 1-11; Luke 5: 1-11

		AMS	NEH	HTC	HON	MP	H&P	R&S	BPW	CH3	CP	SG	ONC	MPC
ol	Forth in the peace of Christ we go	458	361	542	142			602	607	589	429	594	187	
o	'How shall they hear?', who have not heard					250						598		250
o	Be still for the presence /Spirit of the Lord			53		50			5		383	67	50	

continued on next page

		AMS	NEH	HTC	HON	MP	H&P	R&S	BPW	CH3	CP	SG	ONC	MPC
o	Bright the vision that delighted / Round the Lord	96	343	578	70		445	665	71	353	392	29	86	
o	Eternal Light! Eternal Light!			454			458	83	85	357	414	527		
o	God of gods, we sound his praises			340					46			504		
o	God of love and truth and beauty	368					403					5		
o	God, we praise you! God, we bless you!			341							450	38		
o	God, your glory we have seen in your Son						459	746		469				
o	Holy, holy, holy, Lord God almighty	95	146	7/594	212	237	594	34	51	352	202	290	286	237
o	How shall they hear the word of God			507		250						599		250
o	How shall they hear who have not heard					250						598		250
o	I the Lord of sea and sky				235						470	633	332	857
o	Immortal, invisible, God only wise	199	377	21	242	327	9	67	383	32	474	44	314	327
o	Inspired by love and anger				252								325	
o	Let all mortal flesh keep silence	256	295	61	295		266	454	441	577	309	472	381	
o	My God, how wonderful thou art / you are	102	410	369	343	468	51	408		356	523	202	457	468
o	Saviour from sin, I wait to prove						747							
o	Spirit of truth, essential God						480	313						
o	Stand up, and bless the Lord	201	452	351	456	615	513	391		39	577	63	616	615
o	We praise, we worship thee/you, O God						443	755	490			258		
p	I'll praise you, Lord, with heart content and joyful PR138													
e	And can it be			588	30	33	216	136	328	409	376	168	32	
e	As man and woman we were made						364	466	506					
e	Christ is the world's Redeemer						219	272		301				
e	Come, let us with our Lord arise	449	254	375			575	383			142			
e	Come, thou everlasting Spirit						298	315						
e	The Saviour died, but rose again						233	597		293				
e	The strife is o'er/past	78	119	163	495	670	214	250	261	266	159	416	667	670
e	These are the facts			162		687						284		687
e	We sing the praise of him who died	138	94	146	536	738	182	229	231	258	125	390	723	738

continued on next page

		AMS	NEH	HTC	HON	MP	H&P	R&S	BPW	CH3	CP	SG	ONC	MPC
gl	Forth in thy/your name, O Lord	239	235	306	143	159	381	521	526	463	430	623	188	159
g	Fisherman, come and fish for men							196						
g	Hear us, O Lord, from heaven						346							
g	Will you come and follow me							558	363			622	634	752
g	Wise men, seeking Jesus						128	185		222				

Year A
CLC: Proper 2
RCL: Sixth Sunday after the Epiphany, Proper 1

Deuteronomy 30: 15-20 or Ecclesiasticus 15: 15-20; Psalm 119: 1-8; 1 Corinthians 3: 1-9; Matthew 5: 21-37

		AMS	NEH	HTC	HON	MP	H&P	R&S	BPW	CH3	CP	SG	ONC	MPC
ol	Fill thou/now my/our life	200		541	129	146	792	406	569	457	424	665	171	146
ol	Lord, as I wake I turn to you	485	236	267			634	534				561		
o	Come, let us to the Lord our God						33	81		69	402			
o	Freedom and life are ours			544					528			171		
o	In full and glad surrender			557	245	330							322	330
o	Lord Jesus, let these eyes of mine			549										
o	My God, accept my heart this day	279	318	551	341		701			429	338	559	455	
o	O happy day that fixed my choice			442	369	499	702	359	539				498	499
o	Take my life, and let it be	249		554	464	624	705	371	358	462	581	678	625	624
o	Thy/Your way, not mine			555	521								692	950
p	Teach me, O Lord, the perfect way									127				
el	O thou who at thy eucharist / O Christ at your first eucharist	265	302	420	391		779			492	318		540	476
e	Bless and keep us, Lord, in your love united							471					73	
e	Christ from whom all blessings flow			491			764	561						
e	Christ is the world's light	440		321			455	600	34		213	591	99	
e	Christ's Church shall glory in his power			522										
e	Come build the church											111		
e	God our Father, bless your people			496										
e	God, you meet us in our weakness							475					237	
e	Jesus, where'er thy people meet / Lord Jesus, when your people	162	390	371	282		549	476			492	16	367	

continued on next page

		AMS	NEH	HTC	HON	MP	H&P	R&S	BPW	CH3	CP	SG	ONC	MPC
e	Jesus, with thy Church abide									490				
e	Lord Christ, the Father's mighty Son	386						568						
e	Lord of our life, and God of our salvation		404	529	315	441				491			417	441
e	Lord of the Church, we pray for our renewing			499		442			486			577		442
e	O Jesus Christ, grow thou in me / within me grow						742	508	540					
e	Risen Lord, whose name we cherish			500										
e	We are your people	519						483						
g	Forgive our sins as we forgive	362	66	111	141		134	84	83		428	145	180	
g	I come with joy to meet my Lord	473		408	227		610	447	437		365	469	304	
g	Lord, speak to me, that I may speak			510		444	553	613	611	485	512			444
g	The Kingdom of God is justice and joy			333		651	139	200	321		591	184	646	651

Year B
CLC: Proper 2
RCL: Sixth Sunday after the Epiphany, Proper 1

2 Kings 5: 1-14; Psalm 30; 1 Corinthians 9: 24-27; Mark 1: 40-45

		AMS	NEH	HTC	HON	MP	H&P	R&S	BPW	CH3	CP	SG	ONC	MPC
o	I greet thee, who my sure Redeemer art						391	501		86				
o	O Christ the healer, we have come						395				346	489		395
o	We cannot measure how you heal							653			348	490	712	
p	Where there once was only hurt										140			
e	Awake, my soul, stretch every nerve							487						
e	Christ's Church shall glory in his power			522										
e	Fight the good fight	220	359	526	128	143	710	496	524	442	423	635	169	143
e	O Lord my / Thee will I love, my strength, my tower			485			40			678				
e	Thee will I love, my God and King			485			40			678				

continued on next page

		AMS	NEH	HTC	HON	MP	H&P	R&S	BPW	CH3	CP	SG	ONC	MPC
g	A man there lived in Galilee	334			3							28		
g	Christ's is the world in which we move				83							252	101	
g	Father of mercy, God of consolation		323					645						
g	From thee/you all skill and science flow	286		310			389			525	345			
g	He/they want/lack not friends	183	371				495	481			459			
g	Heal me, hands of Jesus			319								488		
g	Inspired by love and anger				252								325	
g	Jesus, lover of my soul	123	383	438	261	372	528	332	345	78	96	201	343	372
g	Lord Christ, who on thy heart didst bear	388			308		394						407	
g	Love inspired the anger: SS90													
g	O God, by whose almighty plan	406					396	651			204			
g	The crippled hands reached out: SS95													
g	Thine arm, O Lord, in days of old	285	324		502		397			214		671		
g	We give God thanks for those who knew			318										
g	With loving hands at work among the suffering			106								187		
g	Your will for us and others, Lord						398							

Year C
CLC: Proper 2
RCL: Sixth Sunday after the Epiphany, Proper 1

Jeremiah 17: 5-10; Psalm 1; 1 Corinthians 15: 12-20; Luke 6: 17-26

		AMS	NEH	HTC	HON	MP	H&P	R&S	BPW	CH3	CP	SG	ONC	MPC
o	All my hope on God is founded	336	333	451	15	16	63	586	327	405	368	525	19	16
o	Christ is the world's Redeemer						219	272		301				
o	I hunger and I thirst			409			730	449			306	470		
o	Lord of the Church, we pray for our renewing			499		442			486			577		442
o	Open, Lord, my inward ear						540							

continued on next page

		AMS	NEH	HTC	HON	MP	H&P	R&S	BPW	CH3	CP	SG	ONC	MPC
p	Happy are they who walk in God's wise way							669						
p	Happy the people who refuse PR1													
e	Come build the church											111		
e	Hail the day that sees him rise	87	130	176	191	202	197	252	272		167	434	255	202
e	If Christ had not been raised from death										407			
e	Now lives the Lamb of God			159					255			413		
e	This joyful Eastertide		121	165	509		213	248	258	271	161		680	
e	Ye/You choirs of new Jerusalem	73	124	168	563		823				162	419	754	·
g	Christ is the world's light	440		321			455	600	34		213	591	99	
g	Heal us, Immanuel! Hear our prayer						390	335						
g	How blest the poor who love the Lord								197					
g	Jesus, thy far-extended fame						148							
g	Lord Jesus, once you spoke to men	392		112					598					
g	O changeless Christ, for ever new			108					206			374		
g	O Christ the healer, we have come						395				346	489		395
g	When Jesus walked upon this earth			317										
g	You gave us, Lord, by word and deed								89					

Year A
CLC: Proper 3
RCL: Seventh Sunday after the Epiphany, Proper 2

Leviticus **19**: 1-2, 9-18; Psalm **119**: 33-40; 1 Corinthians **3**: 10-11, 16-23; Matthew **5**: 38-48

		AMS	NEH	HTC	HON	MP	H&P	R&S	BPW	CH3	CP	SG	ONC	MPC
l	Strengthen for service, Lord, the hands	421	306	423	460		626	461	453	588	323	473	619	
o	Creator of the earth and skies	351		320			419	82			410	296		
o	Father of all, whose laws have stood			539					335			664		
o	For the fruits of his/all creation	457		286	138	153	342	42	123		254	299	185	153
o	God's glory fills the universe							275				283		
o	Here, Lord, we come to you			327										
o	Holy, holy, holy, Lord God almighty	95	146	7/594	212	237	594	34	51	352	202	290	286	237
o	Judge eternal, throned in splendour		490	329	285	395	409	626	627	519	356	600	372	395
o	O Christ the Lord, O Christ the King		496				406	630						
o	O day of God, draw near/nigh In beauty	405						632	635	511	33			
o	One holy apostolic Church			514										
o	Remember, Lord, the world you made			332										
o	The Church of Christ in every age						804	636	613					
o	The Kingdom of God is justice and joy			333		651	139	200	321		591	184	646	651
o	This we can do for justice and for peace							639						
o	Thy/Your kingdom come, O God	177	499	334	519		783	638	644	322	607	269	691	949
o	When Christ was lifted from the earth	525		335				655				142		
p	Teach me, O Lord, the perfect way									127				
e	Christ is made the sure foundation / Blessed city, heavenly Salem	283/ 332	204-5	559	76	73	485	559	474	10	208	572	97	73
e	Christ is our corner-stone	161		564	77						395		98	
e	Come down, O Love Divine	156	137	231	90	89	281	294	283	115	170	663	114	89

continued on next page

52

		AMS	NEH	HTC	HON	MP	H&P	R&S	BPW	CH3	CP	SG	ONC	MPC
e	Come, thou/O fount of every blessing			337			517	360			406			
e	How firm a foundation			430	216	243		589	380				292	243
e	My God, accept my heart this day	279	318	551	341		701			429	338	559	455	
e	The Church's one foundation	170	484	501	473	640	515	566	393	420	585	581	636	640
e	The Lord is King! lift up thy/your voice	107		183	485	656	58	76	322	36	592	98	650	656
g	A stranger once did bless the earth	335						198						
g	At even[ing], ere/when the sun was/had set	9	243	315	43	43	142	644	616	52	12	487	50	
g	Beloved, let us love			468				610					64	
g	From the town's dusty clamour: SS84													
g	God is here! As we his people	464		560			653				301			
g	Heal me, hands of Jesus			319								488		
g	I am trusting thee/you, Lord Jesus			433	233	258			340	685			300	258
g	Jesus' hands were kind hands						393	197		228				
g	Look and learn from the birds of the air										521			
g	Lord Christ, who on thy heart didst bear	388			308		394						407	
g	Love is the only law											430		
g	Love of the Father	159	409		323					335				
g	O Christ the healer, we have come						395				346	489		395
g	O God, by whose almighty plan	406					396	651			204			
g	O God, whose will is life and good	408												
g	O Lord, all the world belongs to you				378			90					509	
g	Thine arm, O Lord, in days of old	285	324		502		397			214		671		
g	Thou to whom the sick and dying		325											
g	We are your people	519						483						
g	When Jesus walked upon this earth			317										
g	Where love and loving-kindness dwell	528												
g	Your will for us and others, Lord						398							

Year B
CLC: Proper 3
RCL: Seventh Sunday after the Epiphany, Proper 2

Isaiah **43**: 18-25; Psalm **41**; 2 Corinthians **1**: 18-22; Mark **2**: 1-12

		AMS	NEH	HTC	HON	MP	H&P	R&S	BPW	CH3	CP	SG	ONC	MPC
o	Let the mountains dance and sing											857		
o	How good is the God we adore / This, this is the God			450	217	244	277	542	338		464	41	293	244
o	Through the night of doubt and sorrow	211	468	466	517		441		546	423	605	544	687	948
o	To Abraham and Sarah							553						
o	Will you come and follow me?				560			558	363		622	634	752	
p	Lord, you have weaned my heart from pride PR131													
e	A debtor to mercy alone			449										
e	A mighty mystery we set forth								403					
g	Come, O thou all-victorious Lord / O come, our all-victorious			441			418							
g	Four friends brought to Capernaum: SS94													
g	Open, Lord, my inward ear						540							
g	The love of God comes close							107				186		

See also hymns for CLC Year B Proper 1, page 45

Year C
CLC: Proper 3
RCL: Seventh Sunday after the Epiphany, Proper 2

Genesis **45**: 3-11, 15; Psalm **37**: 1-11, 39-40; 1 Corinthians **15**: 35-38, 42-50; Luke **6**: 27-38

		AMS	NEH	HTC	HON	MP	H&P	R&S	BPW	CH3	CP	SG	ONC	MPC
o	Glory, love, and praise, and honour	461	287		160		35				436		207	
o	Great God, we sing that mighty / your guiding hand						356	63	552	613				
o	Praise and thanksgiving be to our creator	506												

continued on next page

		AMS	NEH	HTC	HON	MP	H&P	R&S	BPW	CH3	CP	SG	ONC	MPC
o	Put thou thy trust / Commit thou all thy griefs	223			429		672	550		669	562		576	
p	Lord, may our hearts within us burn PR41													
e	Father in heaven, grant to your children			2			3		38			200		
e	God has promised many things										503			
e	In Adam we have all been one	474					420							
e	Low in the grave he lay			158	326	453	202		256			411	435	453
e	Now lives the Lamb of God			159					255			413		
e	Praise to the Holiest in the height	117	439	140	426	563	231	103	562	238	557	58	572	563
e	Seed, secret sown in the earth: SS26													
e	Spirit of God within me			243			294	304	296		196	677	612	
e	The Lord made man, the Scriptures tell			143										
e	What Adam's disobedience cost	524					430							
g	Brother, sister, let me serve you				73			474	473		393	619	88	
g	Forgive our sins as we forgive	362	66	111	141		134	84	83		428	145	180	
g	God! when human bonds are broken							652						
g	God, you have / who hast given us power	469					345				256			
g	Help us to help each other / Jesus, united by thy grace	374		540	208		773	500			461		275	
g	Lord, save thy world; in bitter need	397					425							
g	Lord/Great God, your love has called us here	489		480			500	339	442		133		246	
g	O matchless beauty of our God							101						
g	Peace with the Father, peace with Christ his Son							616						
g	Take this moment, sign and space								360					
g	The great Creator of the worlds	511									588			
g	The love of God is broad							108						940

Years A, B, C
CLC only: Second Sunday before Lent

Year A: Genesis **1**:1 — **2**:3; Psalm **136**: all or 1-9, 23-26; Romans **8**: 18-25;
(Matthew **6**: 25-34 DO NOT WORRY)
Year B: Proverbs **8**: 1, 22-31; Psalm **104**: 24-35; Colossians **1**: 15-20; John
1: 1-14
Year C: Genesis **2**: 4b-9, 15-25; Psalm **65**; Revelation 4; Luke **8**: 22-25

		AMS	NEH	HTC	HON	MP	H&P	R&S	BPW	CH3	CP	SG	ONC	MPC
s	All creatures of our God and King	105	263	13	9	7	329	39	28	30	250	23	6	7
s	Bless the Lord, creation sings			604										
s	Carpenter, carpenter, make me a tree								118					
s	Come and see the shining hope			188		86			271		110	86		
s	Come, let us praise the Lord					92			119					92
s	Creating God, your fingers trace							56						
s	Creation sings a new song						332							
s	Dance and sing all the earth			105									139	
s	God in his love for us lent us this planet						343	85				300		832
s	God is a name my soul adores						24	31			255			
s	God who spoke in the beginning	468						60						
s	How wonderful this world of thine						336			152				
s	I sing the almighty power of God				293	334	43							293
s	Let us, with a gladsome mind / Let us gladly with one mind	204	397	23	302	415	27		56	33	498	312	392	415
s	Lord God almighty												878	
s	Lord of beauty, thine the splendour	106	265		314					120	258		415	
s	Lord of the boundless curves of space	493	405				335	44			210			
s	Lord of the changing year			261								303		
s	Lord, bring the day to pass						347	87			257			
s	Now praise the protector of heaven			19										
s	O God, the joy of heaven above									149				

continued on next page

		AMS	NEH	HTC	HON	MP	H&P	R&S	BPW	CH3	CP	SG	ONC	MPC
s	O Lord of every shining constellation	411		314					130	141	263		512	
s	O praise him! O praise him! O praise him!						503	46						
s	Praise ye the Lord! 'Tis good to raise						338	50						338
s	The Lord of heaven confess									135				
s	The spacious firmament	103	267		493		339			143	265		665	
s	The works of the Lord are created in wisdom			26							266			
s	With wonder, Lord we see your works	531					353				269	316		
oe	Creation sings! Each plant and tree										295			
op	Let us sing the God of glory										305			
op	Waterfall and ocean										630			
o	God who created light										288			
o	Listen ! Wisdom cries aloud PR669													
o	O God, we bear the imprint of your face										250			
o	Thou/God whose almighty / Father your mighty word	180	466	506	514	699	29	38	591	494	267	684	597	699
p	Every heart its tribute pays PR65													
p	Give to our God immortal praise	460		31	155	171	22	94	47		434	83	203	171
p	Praise, O praise our God and King	288			423		359				273		566	
e	Behold the Lord												807	
e	O Firstborn of the Unseen Lord										326			
e	Praise be to Christ, in whom we see			220										
e	The universe was waiting											669		
e	The victory of our God is won										68			
g3	Before the world began							180				31		
g	Look and learn from the birds of the air										521			
g	O changeless Christ, for ever new			108						206		374		
g	Seek ye first the kingdom of God				442	590	138	512	357				590	590
g	Word of God come down on earth									625				

Year A
RCL only: Eighth Sunday after Epiphany, Proper 3

Isaiah **49**: 8-16a; Psalm **131**; 1 Corinthians **4**: 1-5; Matthew **6**: 24-34

		AMS	NEH	HTC	HON	MP	H&P	R&S	BPW	CH3	CP	SG	ONC	MPC
oi	Let the mountains dance and sing											857		
o	Be thou my vision / Lord be my vision	343	339	545	56	51	378	489	521	87	386	669	70	51
o	Faithful Shepherd, feed me		282	29	117							498	156	
o	Hark, my soul, it is the Lord / Christian, do you hear the Lord	244		472	197	209	521	348		676	264		457	209
o	Here from all nations, all tongues, and all peoples			571					309		462	455		
o	Hills of the north, rejoice	470	7		209		237		311		29		282	
o	Immortal, invisible, God only wise	199	377	21	242	327	9	67	383	32	474	44	314	327
o	O Lord of heaven and earth and sea	287	422	287			337		387	145	540	306		
o	O Lord, I would delight in thee							593				510		
o	O what shall I do my Saviour to praise						569							
o	Sometimes a light surprises	108					571	595			572			
p	Lord, you have weaned my heart from pride PR131													
e	Almighty Father, who for us thy Son didst give	338					401	621			374			
e	Come, thou/O long-expected Jesus	31	3	52	98	102	81	138	139	320	24	335	128	102
e	Hark what a sound, and too divine for hearing						236	660		314	28			
e	Lo, he / Jesus comes with clouds descending	28	9	196	307	424	241	656	185	316	31	438	405	424
e	O thou, my Judge and King									666				
e	The Lord will come and not be slow	29	15		489		245	128		321	37		655	
e	Thou Judge of quick and dead						247							
e	Ye/You servants of the Lord	150	18	598	566		248			319	40		757	
g	All my hope on God is founded	336	333	451	15	16	63	586	327	405	368	525	19	16
g	In heavenly love abiding			458	246	331	678	590	555	681	478		323	331
g	Mine eyes have seen the glory				336		242			318			449	
g	Put thou thy trust / Commit thou all thy griefs	223			429		672	550		669	562		576	
g	Seek ye first the Kingdom of God				442	590	138	512	357				590	590
g	We plough the fields and scatter	290	262	292	534	732	352	124	135	620	275	311	719	732

Hosea **2**: 14-20; Psalm **103**: 1-13, 22; 2 Corinthians **3**: 1-6; Mark **2**: 13-22

		AMS	NEH	HTC	HON	MP	H&P	R&S	BPW	CH3	CP	SG	ONC	MPC
o	Church of God, elect and glorious			504					406			592		
o	O Christ the great foundation			502										
o	The Church's one foundation	170	484	501	473	640	515	566	393	420	585	581	636	640
p	Bless the Lord, my soul				61	76						105		76
p	O bless the Lord, my soul, his saving								129					
p	O bless the Lord, my soul, let all			34										
p	O Lord of every shining constellation	411		314					130	141	263		512	
p	O thou my soul, bless God the Lord							715		351				
p	Praise to the Lord, the Almighty	207	440	40	427	564	16	74	68	9	558	59	573	564
p	Praise, my soul, the King of heaven	192	436	38	422	560	13	104	65	360	555		565	560
p	When all thy/your mercies	109	472	39	544	751	573	109		150	617	73	732	751
e	Help us, O Lord, to learn	373	370	493			474				460	226		
e	O Spirit of the living God			513			322	577	579	496	190	605		
gl	Here, O my Lord, I see thee/you	274		406		230	608		436	573	304	468	279	230
g	And can it be			588	30	33	216	136	328	409	376	168	32	
g	At the name of Jesus	148	338	172	46	41	74	261	370	300	380	317	54	
g	He gave his life in selfless love			405		214			435			467		214
g	Here, Lord, we take the broken bread			404			604	448	440				278	
g	Jesus calls us: o'er/in the tumult	312	200	104	266	359	141	355		211	233	668	347	359
g	Jesus came — the heavens adoring			195										
g	Jesus who walked beside the lake: SS81													
g	Jesus, whose all-redeeming love	383								215				
g	O Lord of the kingdom where losing is winning								316					
g	Shout for joy, loud and long			348										
g	The great love of God						45	105		415				
g	The Kingdom of God is justice and joy			333		651	139	200	321		591	184	646	651

Year C
RCL only: Eighth Sunday after Epiphany, Proper 3

Sirach **27**: 4-7 or Isaiah **55**: 10-13; Psalm **92**: 1-4, 12-15; 1 Corinthians **15**: 51-58; Luke **6**: 39-49

		AMS	NEH	HTC	HON	MP	H&P	R&S	BPW	CH3	CP	SG	ONC	MPC
o2	Lord, thy word abideth / Lord, your word shall guide us	166	407	251	318	446	476	317	102	130	515		420	446
o2	You shall go out with joy				571	796		415					766	796
p	For the music of creation									36				
p	Make music to the Lord most high PR92													
p	Sweet is the work, my God, my King			377		620	514				580	97		620
p	To render thanks unto the Lord									29				
e	Abide with me	13	331	425	6	4	665	336	515	695	10	495	2	4
e	Christ above all glory seated						189				164			
e	Christ the Lord is risen today / Love's redeeming work is done / All creation	83	113	150	324	76	193	232	246	275	150	412	433	76
e	Come, let us worship Christ			S10		96								96
e	For this purpose					155			372					155
e	God, that madest earth and heaven	12	245		178		641				15		232	
e	Great God, what do I see and hear			189										
e	In Christ shall all be made alive			459								533		
e	Jesus lives! Thy/Your terrors now	82	112	156	272	373	198	239	253	605	148	409	354	373
e	Let saints on earth / Come let us join our friends above	182	396	574	297	409	812	472		543	222	578	384	409
e	Name of all majesty			218		481					525	324	465	481
e	Now is eternal life	402	114		351		203	432			152		470	
e	Rejoice! the Lord is King	139	443	180	432	575	243	657	317	296	563	440	580	575
e	Ride on Jesus, all-victorious						272							
e	Sing we the King who is coming to reign					602	244		318					602
e	Sing we the song of those who stand						821	666						
e	The strife is o'er/past	78	119	163	495	670	214	250	261	266	159	416	667	670
e	These are the facts			162		687						284		687
e	Thine/Yours be/is the glory	428	120	167	503	689	212	247	260	279	160	417	672	689
e	When the Lord in glory comes			201		758								758
g	My hope is built on nothing less			462		473				411		537		473
g	O changeless Christ, for ever new			108				206				374		
g	Risen Lord, whose name we cherish			500										
g	Rock of ages	135	445	593	437	582	273	365	545	83	565	150	584	582

Deuteronomy **11**: 18-21, 26-28; Psalm **31**: 1-5, 19-24;
Romans **1**: 16-17, **3**: 22b-28 (29-31); Matthew **7**: 21-29

		AMS	NEH	HTC	HON	MP	H&P	R&S	BPW	CH3	CP	SG	ONC	MPC
o	God of the morning, at whose voice								9					
o	O happy day that fixed my choice			442	369	499	702	359	539				498	499
o	Take my life, and let it be	249		554	464	624	705	371	358	462	581	678	625	624
o	Who is on the Lord's side?					769	722		615	479				769
pg	Rock of ages	135	445	593	437	582	273	365	545	83	565	150	584	582
p	Lord, we believe when we call										244			
e	Amazing grace			28	27	31	215	92	550		375	26	29	
e	And can it be			588	30	33	216	136	328	409	376	168	32	
e	Approach, my soul, the mercy-seat									667				
e	Father, whose everlasting love						520				107			
e	Great is the gospel of our glorious God PR178													
e	Have faith in God, my heart	372		431	201		675	499	336		458		268	
e	I'm not ashamed to own/name my Lord			448	240	323	677	428	343	591		532	316	323
e	In an age of twisted values											317		
e	Jesus, our Lord and King							429						
e	Just as I am, without one plea	246	294	440	287	396	697	364	346	79	308	507	374	396
e	Out of the depths I cry to thee							429	331					
e	Souls of men / Restless souls / There's a wideness	251	461	443	501	607, 683	230	353	573	218	598	188	662	607
e	Thy ceaseless, unexhausted love						48	106					688	
g	All my hope on God is founded	336	333	451	15	16	63	586	327	405	368	525	19	16
g	Christ, our King before creation			428			75							
g	Come, O thou / O come, our all-victorious Lord			441			418							
g	Firmly I believe and truly	118	360	429	133					400	426	287	174	
g	Glorious things of thee/you are spoken	172	362	494	158	173	817	560	480	421	435	35	205	173
g	How firm a foundation			430	216	243		589	380				292	243
g	Jesus, lover of my soul	123	383	438	261	372	528	332	345	78	96	201	343	372
g	Lord, dismiss us with thy blessing						652				638	503		
g	My hope is built on nothing less			462		473				411		537		473
g	We come unto our fathers'/faithful God					724	453	484	488	14				724

Year B
RCL only: Ninth Sunday after the Epiphany, Proper 4

Deuteronomy **5**: 12-15; Psalm **81**: 1-10; 2 Corinthians **4**: 5-12;
Mark **2**:23 — **3**:6

		AMS	NEH	HTC	HON	MP	H&P	R&S	BPW	CH3	CP	SG	ONC	MPC
og	Father of all, whose laws have stood			539					335			664		
el	Author of life divine	258	274	395	48		596	440		587	281		56	
e	All praise to thee/Christ, for thou / our Lord and King divine	337	335	204	18		253	750		297	372		22	
e	Before the heaven and earth			612										
e	Christ, whose glory fills the skies	4	234	266	82	79	457	380		114	2	170	105	79
e	Come, Holy Ghost, our hearts inspire (Wesley)	448	348		91		469	312	97	122	177		117	
e	Eternal light, shine in my heart			339							415			
e	Lord of all being, throned afar		403			439	11	69		34	506			439
e	O Jesus, King most wonderful	120	386	484			269	356	353	378	539			
e	Out of darkness let light shine			447										
e	The Son of God proclaim	427		415			627	458	455		328			
g	Come, let us with our Lord arise	449	254	375			575	383			142			
g	First of the week and finest day			376								2		
g	Jesus, stand among us in thy/your risen power			364	280	380	530	388	88	11			362	
g	Let the Lord's people, heart and voice uniting	479												
g	Most glorious Lord of life, that on this day		255							44	151		452	
g	On this day, the first of days		256			402							530	
g	Sweet is the work, my God, my King			377		620	514				580	97		620
g	The first day of the week	424					576							
g	Thine arm, O Lord, in days of old	285	324		502		397				214		671	
g	This is the day of light	21		380							46			
g	This is the day the Lord hath/has made	22	257	379			577	376			9	70	677	
g	This is the day, this is the day			S28	508	691	578	377	21				676	691

RCL only: Ninth Sunday after the Epiphany, Proper 4

1 Kings **8**: 22-23, 41-43; Psalm **96**: 1-9; Galatians **1**: 1-12; Luke **7**: 1-10

		AMS	NEH	HTC	HON	MP	H&P	R&S	BPW	CH3	CP	SG	ONC	MPC
o	Christ is made the sure foundation / Blessed city, heavenly Salem	283/ 332	204-5	559	76	73	485	559	474	10	208	572	97	73
o	God of light and life's creation			561										
o	O God, in whom we live and move							409						
o	Saviour, and can it be						541						587	
o	Send out/forth the gospel			517		593			584					593
o	That mighty, resurrected Word						658							
o	The heaven of heavens / Where the appointed		312					78						
p	Let all the world in every corner sing	202	394	342	296	404	10	114	54	361	497	47	382	404
p	New songs of celebration render	498		343	350		491	709			527	87	468	
p	O sing a new song to the Lord									22				
p	O sing a new song										89			
p	Sing a new song of glory and salvation										94			
e	Go forth and tell			505	164	178	770	574	570		437	596	238	178
e	Lord, thy Church on earth is seeking						774	579				604		
e	May the grace of Christ our Saviour	181		370	333		762		110	634	520	579	446	
e	Revive thy work / Revive your church			515		578	780							578
e	The Church of Christ in every age						804	636	613					
e	We have a gospel to proclaim	431	486	519	532	728	465		585		612		716	728
g	I am not worthy, holy Lord			407						570				
g	Lord Christ, who on thy heart didst bear	388			308		394						407	
g	Lord of all power, I give you my will / Lord of creation, to you be all praise	395		547		440	699	532		428	508			
g	Lord/Great God, your love has called us here	489		480			500	339	442		133		246	
g	O for a heart to praise my God	230	74	483	361	495	536	514	538	85	533	149	484	495
g	We cannot measure how you heal							653			348	490	712	

Years A, B, C
CLC: The Sunday next before Lent
RCL: Last Sunday after the Epiphany (Transfiguration Sunday)

Year A: Exodus **24**: 12-18; Psalm **2** or **99**; 2 Peter **1**: 16-21; Matthew **17**: 1-9
Year B: 2 Kings **2**: 1-12; Psalm **50**: 1-6; 2 Corinthians **4**: 3-6; Mark **9**: 2-9
Year C: Exodus **34**: 29-35; Psalm **99**; 2 Corinthians **3**:12 — **4**:2; Luke **9**: 28-36 [37-43]

		AMS	NEH	HTC	HON	MP	H&P	R&S	BPW	CH3	CP	SG	ONC	MPC
sl	Thee we adore	254	308		497			459		584	329		640	
s	Christ is the world's true light	346	494	323	78		456	601	618	505	396	432	100	
s	Christ upon the mountain peak	441	177	115			155		195					
s	Christ, whose glory fills the skies	4	234	266	82	79	457	380		114	2	170	105	79
s	Come, praise the name of Jesus		538					331						
s	Eternal Light! Eternal Light!		454				458	83	85	357	414	527		
s	How/It's/'Tis good, Lord, to be here	318	178				156		201		248			
s	Jesus, these eyes have never seen	245	389					592		674	491		365	
s	Lord Jesus, once you spoke to men	392		112					598					
s	O raise your eyes	502									544			
s	O splendour of God's glory						461	537			7			
s	O vision blest / O wondrous type		176					204		217				
s	Once on a mountain top						157							
s	Our Saviour Christ once knelt in prayer			116										
s	Stay, Master, stay upon this heavenly hill						158							
s	The brightness of God's glory			221										
s	When Jesus led his chosen three			117										
p	God the Lord, the king almighty PR50													
p	Why are the nations conspiring										270			
g	Transfigured Christ, none comprehends PR393													

Years A, B, C
Ash Wednesday

Joel **2**: 1-2, 12-17 or Isaiah **58**: 1-12; Psalm **51**: 1-17; 2 Corinthians **5**:20b —
6:10;
Matthew **6**: 1-6, 16-21 or John **8**: 1-11

		AMS	NEH	HTC	HON	MP	H&P	R&S	BPW	CH3	CP	SG	ONC	MPC
s	Approach, my soul, the mercy-seat									667				
s	Begone, unbelief						667							
s	Christian, dost thou see them	55	65											
s	Come, let us to the Lord our God						33	81		69	402			
s	Dear Lord and Father of mankind	115	353	356	106	111	673	492	84	76	411	497	144	111
s	Father of heaven, whose love profound	97	358	359	124		519			77	421	144		827
s	Forgive our sins as we forgive	362	66	111	141		134	84	83		428	145	180	
s	Forty days and forty nights	56	67	103	145	160	130		218	210	95	381	190	160
s	How can we sing with joy to God			362					86			147		
s	I am trusting thee/you Lord Jesus			433	223	258			340	685			300	258
s	Into a desert place: SS23													
s	Into our world from God: SS78													
s	Lord Jesus, think on/of me	129	70	316	312		533	363		80	97		412	
s	Lord we know that we have failed you													
s	Now let us all with one accord										148			
s	O for a heart to praise my God	230	74	483	361	495	536	514	538	85	533	149	484	495
s	O Jesus, I have promised	235	420	531	372	501	704	509	352	434	538	676	503	501
s	O love, how deep, how broad, how high	119	425		383		229	283	207	223	118		516	
s	Who would true valour / He who would valiant / Who honours courage	212	372	537 +590	205	224	688	557	362	443	621	639	281	224
l	Awake, my soul, and with the sun	1	232	264	50		632	378		42	1	618	58	804
l	Great Shepherd of thy/your people, hear	164		363			490	387			454	238	250	
l	Lord, as I wake I turn to you	485	236	267			634	534				561		
l	Now is the healing time decreed		59											

continued on next page

		AMS	NEH	HTC	HON	MP	H&P	R&S	BPW	CH3	CP	SG	ONC	MPC
o	Judge eternal, throned in splendour		490	329	285	395	409	626	627	519	356	600	372	395
o	O Lord, the clouds are gathering				509							255		509
p	Create in us clean hearts, O God										682			
p	God, be merciful to me										153			
p	Have mercy on us, O Lord											269		
p	Jesus, lover of my soul	123	383	438	261	372	528	332	345	78	96	201	343	372
p	Lord of our life, and God of our salvation		404	529	315	441				491			417	441
p	My Lord, what love is this						476					194	462	476
p	Rock of ages	135	445	593	437	582	273	365	545	83	565	150	584	582
p	Show mercy to us, loving Father										164			
e	Be thou my vision / Lord be my vision	343	339	545	56	51	378	489	521	87	386	669	70	51
e	Christian, seek not yet repose			355										
e	Fight the good fight	220	359	526	128	143	710	496	524	442	423	635	169	143
e	Now is the time, the time of God's favour										341			
e	Soldiers of Christ, arise	219	449	533	449	604	719	370	580	441	571	643	606	604
e	Stand up, stand up for Jesus	221	453	535	457	617	721			481	578	644	617	617
g	Prayer is the soul's sincere/supreme desire		442	372		567	557				561			567
g	Teach us how grave a thing it is										151			
g	What shall I do my God to love									615				

Year A
The First Sunday of Lent

Genesis **2**: 15-17, **3**: 1-7; Psalm **32**; Romans **5**: 12-19; Matthew **4**: 1-11

		AMS	NEH	HTC	HON	MP	H&P	R&S	BPW	CH3	CP	SG	ONC	MPC
s	'Lift up your hearts!' We lift them	241	398	366	304		405			440	500		395	
s	Awake our souls, away our fears	436					663	488			382		59	
s	Be thou / O Lord, my/our guardian	217	64	374	55	385		68			385		68	
s	Christian, dost thou see them	55	65											
s	Father of heaven, whose love profound	97	358	359	124		519			77	421	144		827
s	Father, hear the prayer we offer	113	357	360	120	132	436	495	523		416	237	161	132
s	He lives in us, the Christ of God			457				554				173		
s	Jesus, grant me this I pray	136	382		260						110		342	
s	O Jesus, I have promised	235	420	531	372	501	704	509	352	434	538	676	503	501
s	O love, how deep, how broad, how high	119	425		383		229	283	207	223	118		516	

continued on next page

		AMS	NEH	HTC	HON	MP	H&P	R&S	BPW	CH3	CP	SG	ONC	MPC
s	What a friend we have in Jesus			373	541	746	559	413	603			646	727	746
s	Where high the heavenly temple stands	130		184				259		295	75			
s	With joy we meditate the grace	530				774	235	206	275		624			774
l	At even[ing], ere/when the sun was/had set	9	243	315	43	43	142	644	616	52	12	487	50	
o	All hail the power of Jesus' name	140	332	587 /203	13	13	252		29	382	163	24	16	13
o	Born of Adam, torn from Eden PR685													
o	From the apple in the garden										528			
o	From the sinews of the earth: SS4													
o	O lift us up, strong Son of God						427	337						
o	Praise to the Holiest in the height	117	439	140	426	563	231	103	562	238	557	58	572	563
o	The Lord made man, the Scriptures tell			143										
o	Walking in a garden	518	123					334					705	
o	What Adam's disobedience cost	524					430							
p	Happy are those, beyond all measure blessed										172			
p	Restore, O Lord, the honour of your name				434	579			324			274	582	579
e	How can I be free from sin										518		846	
g	A safe stronghold/fortress/refuge	114		523		2	661	585	375	406/7				2
g	Be thou my vision/Lord be my vision	343	339	545	56	51	378	489	521	87	386	669	70	51
g	Christ our Redeemer knew temptation's power										373			
g	Father of all, whose laws have stood			539					335			664		
g	Forty days and forty nights	56	67	103	145	160	130		218	210	95	381	190	160
g	Into a desert place: SS23													
g	Jesus went away into the desert											852		
g	Lead us, heavenly Father, lead us	224	393	595	293	400	68	543	597	90	496	640	379	400
g	Lord, the light of your love is shining [Shine, Jesus, shine]				317	445			347		513	614	419	445
g	Lord, who throughout these forty days						131							
g	My dear Redeemer and my Lord							205	205					
g	Name of all majesty			218		481					525	324	465	481
g	Now let us all with one accord										148			
g	O happy band of pilgrims	208	418	530	368								497	
g	Seek ye first the Kingdom of God				442	590	138	512	357				590	590
g	Shepherd divine, our wants relieve	228					558				566			

Year B
The First Sunday of Lent

Genesis 9: 8-17; Psalm 25: 1-10; 1 Peter 3: 18-22; Mark 1: 9-15

		AMS	NEH	HTC	HON	MP	H&P	R&S	BPW	CH3	CP	SG	ONC	MPC
s	As pants the hart	226	337		38		416	689			379		44	
s	Be thou / O Lord, my/our guardian	217	64	374	55	385		68			385		68	
s	Christian, dost thou see them	55	65											
s	Forty days and forty nights	56	67	103	145	160	130		218	210	95	381	190	160
s	How firm a foundation			430	216	243		589	380				292	243
s	Lord Jesus, think on/of me	129	70	316	312		533	363		80	97		412	
s	O for a closer walk with God	231	414	368	360	494		551		663	532		483	494
s	O love, how deep, how broad, how high	119	425		383		229	283	207	223	118		516	
s	Shepherd divine, our wants relieve	228					558				566			
o	Creatures, once in safety held: SS5													
o	God almighty set a rainbow											804		
o	O love that will/wilt not let me go			486	384	515	685	511	541	677	542		517	515
o	The Kingdom of God is justice and joy		333		651	139	200	321			591	184	646	651
p	All my soul to God I raise PR25													
p	Blest are the pure in heart	238	341	110	63	58	724		588	113	391	372	77	58
p	Christian, seek not yet repose			355										
p	Lord of our life, and God of our salvation		404	529	315	441				491			417	441
p	Remember, remember your mercy, Lord										154			
p	Thy/Your way, not mine			555	521								692	950
p	To you, O Lord, I lift up my soul										545			
e	Christ is the world's Redeemer						219	272		301				
e	Jesus, lover of my soul	123	383	438	261	372	528	332	345	78	96	201	343	372
g	Be thou my vision/Lord be my vision	343	339	545	56	51	378	489	521	87	386	669	70	51
g	Christ who called disciples to him										620			
g	I bind unto myself / myself to God today / Christ be with me		159	5	225		695	36		402	203		302	
g	Into a desert place: SS23													
g	Jesus went away into the desert											852		
g	Lord, the light of your love is shining [Shine, Jesus, shine]				317	445			347		513	614	419	445
g	My dear Redeemer and my Lord						205	205						
g	Name of all majesty			218		481					525	324	465	481
g	On Jordan's bank the Baptist's cry	27	12	601	401	538	84	134	147	208	34	339	527	538
g	Songs of thankfulness and praise	53	56	98	451			191			90	376	609	
g	Spirit divine, attend/inspire our prayers			240		614	327	303		107	195			614
g	The sinless one to Jordan came		58											
g	When he was baptized in Jordan								234					
g	When Jesus came to Jordan	526					132				93			

Year C
The First Sunday of Lent

Deuteronomy **26**: 1-11; Psalm **91**: 1-2, 9-16; Romans **10**: 8b-13; Luke **4**: 1-13

		AMS	NEH	HTC	HON	MP	H&P	R&S	BPW	CH3	CP	SG	ONC	MPC
s	Awake our souls, away our fears	436					663	488			382		59	
s	Christian, dost thou see them	55	65											
s	Father of heaven, whose love profound	97	358	359	124		519			77	421	144		827
s	He lives in us, the Christ of God			457					554			173		
s	Lord, in this thy mercy's day		69											
s	Now let us all with one accord										148			
s	O Jesus, I have promised	235	420	531	372	501	704	509	352	434	538	676	503	501
s	Still near me, O my Saviour			464										
s	What a friend we have in Jesus			373	541	746	559	413	603			646	727	746
o	My father was a wandering Aramean: SS54													
p	I bind unto myself / myself to God today / Christ be with me		159	5	225		695	36		402	203		302	
p	Jesus, lover of my soul	123	383	438	261	372	528	332	345	78	96	201	343	372
p	Safe in the shadow of the Lord			445		583						516		583
e	He is Lord, he is Lord			S7	204	220	256	264	378				274	220
e	I'm not ashamed to own/name my Lord			448	240	323	677	428	343	591		532	316	323
e	Jesus is Lord! creation's voice proclaims it			S17	270	367	260	268	384		170		352	367
e	Jesus, the very thought of thee/you is sweet	120	291, 385	478	264	386	265	509	352	377	486	471, 534	368	
e	Jesus, thou/the joy of loving hearts	255	292	413		383	258	389	439	571		369	383	
e	Lord of the Church			499		442			486			577		442
e	Name of all majesty			218		481					525	324	465	481
e	O Jesus, King most wonderful	120	386	484			269	356	353	378	539			
e	O Spirit of the living God			513			322	577	579	496	190	605		
e	Saviour, again to thy/your dear name	15	250	281	438	584	643	640		649	20		587	584
e	Spirit of faith, come down						325							
e	What shall our greeting be						806					584		
g	Be thou /Lord be my vision	343	339	545	56	51	378	489	521	87	386	669	70	51
g	Christ our Redeemer knew temptation's power										373			
g	Forty days and forty nights	56	67	103	145	160	130		218	210	95	381	190	160
g	Into a desert place: SS23													
g	Jesus went away into the desert											852		
g	Lead us, heavenly Father, lead us	224	393	595	293	400	68	543	597	90	496	640	379	400
g	Lord, the light of your love is shining [Shine, Jesus, shine]				317	445			347		513	614	419	445
g	My dear Redeemer and my Lord							205	205					
g	Name of all majesty			218		481					525	324	465	481
g	O happy band of pilgrims	208	418	530	368								497	
g	Seek ye first the Kingdom of God				442	590	138	512	357				590	590

Year A
The Second Sunday of Lent

Genesis **12**: 1-4a; Psalm **121**; Romans **4**: 1-5, 13-17; John **3**: 1-17

		AMS	NEH	HTC	HON	MP	H&P	R&S	BPW	CH3	CP	SG	ONC	MPC
s	Oft in danger, oft in woe / Christian soldiers, onward go	210	434	524	396	533	715				547		487	533
s	Thy/Your hand, O God, has guided	171	485	536	518	705	784	567	398	424	606	649	689	705
o	Deep in the shadows of the past						447							
o	Fill thou/now my/our life	200		541	129	146	792	406	569	457	424	665	171	146
o	The God of Abraham praise	331	148	9	478	645	452	121	131	358	586	66	642	645
o	Thy/Your way, not mine			555	521								692	950
o	To Abraham and Sarah							553						
p	I lift my eyes to the quiet hills				281			64	595			515	312	281
p	I to the hills will lift mine eyes						496	726	126	139	471			
p	Unto the hills around			48										
e	Father of Jesus Christ, my Lord						693	351						
g	Blessed assurance			62	59		668		329		390		74	59
g	Born by the Holy Spirit's breath			225		61	279		281			446		
g	Born of the water			382										
g	Christ for the world we sing	344					789	599		500	394			
g	Give to our God immortal praise	460		31	155	171	22	94	47		434	83	203	171
g	God of love, you freely give us											226		
g	Immortal Love, for ever full	133	378	105	243	328	392	267	198	306	475	176	315	328
g	Name of all majesty			218		481					525	324	465	481
g	O lift us up, strong Son of God						427	337						
g	O praise ye the Lord / Sing praise to the Lord	203	427	354	388	518		49	70		543	96	534	518
g	Spirit divine, attend/inspire our prayers			240		614	327	303		107	195			614
g	Spirit of God within me			243			294	304	296		196	677	612	
g	To God be the glory			584	522	708	463	289	566	374	609	71	695	708
g	Under the cloak of evening: SS67													
g	We give immortal praise	520		11			18	37	72		206	331	713	
g	We know that Christ is raised and dies no more			389				426						
g	When Christ was lifted from the earth	525		335			655						142	
g	With loving hands at work among the suffering			106								187		

Year B
The Second Sunday of Lent

Genesis **17**: 1-7, 15-16; Psalm **22**: 23-31; Romans **4**: 13-25; Mark **8**: 31-38

		AMS	NEH	HTC	HON	MP	H&P	R&S	BPW	CH3	CP	SG	ONC	MPC
s	Art thou weary: AHB 467													
s	Christ's Church shall glory in his power			522										
s	Jesus, grant me this I pray	136	382		260						110		342	
s	Jesus, Lord of life and glory		68											
s	Lord Christ, when first thou cam'st to men	387						270		255				
s	My God, how wonderful thou art / you are	102	410	369	343	468	51	408		356	523	202	457	468
s	My spirit longs for thee	57	299					333			99			
s	This day God gives me	516						79			205			
o	From the apple in the garden										528			
o	The God of Abraham praise	331	148	9	478	645	452	121	131	358	586	66	642	645
o	To Abraham and Sarah							553						
p	I, the Lord of sea and sky				235						470	633	332	857
p	O Lord my God, O Lord my God										491			
p	The Lord is King! lift up thy/your voice	107		183	485	656	58	76	322	36	592	98	650	656
p	Why, God, have you forsaken me PR22													
p	Ye/You servants of God, your Master proclaim	149	476	520	565	784	278	293	76	372	627	75	784	756
e	Father of Jesus Christ, my Lord							693	351					
e	Jesus, if still the same thou art							529						
g	At the name of Jesus	148	338	172	46	41	74	261	370	300	380	317	54	
g	I'm not ashamed to own/name my Lord			448	240	323	677	428	343	591		532	316	323
g	It was easy up to Caesarea Philippi: SS27													
g	Light of the minds that know him		400	477				529			501	626	397	
g	Lord Christ, we praise your sacrifice	487		132			532	611				627		
g	New every morning is the love	2	238	270	349	480	636	536		47	6		467	480
g	Take up thy/your cross	237	76	114	465					430	582	645	626	935
g	Take up your cross, he says											627		
g	When things began to happen			69										
g	Will you come and follow me?				560			558	363		622	634	752	

Year C
The Second Sunday of Lent

Genesis **15**: 1-12, 17-18; Psalm **27**; Philippians **3**:17 — **4**:1;
Luke **13**: 31-35 or [RCL] **9**: 28-36

		AMS	NEH	HTC	HON	MP	H&P	R&S	BPW	CH3	CP	SG	ONC	MPC
s	All my hope on God is founded	336	333	451	15	16	63	586	327	405	368	525	19	16
s	All ye who seek a comfort / for sure relief	64	63		22						101		26	
s	Come, O thou traveller unknown	243	350			434					407			
s	In the Cross of Christ I glory		379		249	338	167	224	344	259	480		327	338
s	Maker of Earth, to thee alone		71											
s	My faith looks up to thee		72		339	469	683			81	522		453	469
s	My Lord, you wore no royal crown			118								628		
s	Now is the healing time decreed		59											
s	Souls of men / Restless souls / There's a wideness	251	461	443	501	607, 683	230	353	573	218	598	188	662	607
l	O Christ who art the light and day		61							652			478	
l	O kind creator, bow thine ear		60											
o	A safe stronghold/fortress/refuge	114		523		2	661	585	375	406/7				2
o	Christ is the world's true light	346	494	323	78		456	601	618	505	396	432	100	
o	Creatures, once in safety held: SS5													
o	Lord, be thy word my rule / Lord, make your word	232		250										
o	The God of Abraham praise	331	148	9	478	645	452	121	131	358	586	66	642	645
o	Timeless love! we sing the story		47		707	60						100		707
o	To Abraham and Sarah						553							
p	O God beyond all praising		36	363								53	489	
p	Safe in the hands of God who made me										653			
p	The Lord is my light, my light and my salvation										660			
e	Church of God, elect and glorious			504					406			592		
e	Fight the good fight	220	359	526	128	143	710	496	524	442	423	635	169	143
e	Light's abode, celestial Salem	185	401		305						502		398	
e	Lord of the Cross of shame			548		443						558		443
e	Thou Judge of quick and dead					247								
g	All who love and serve your city WOV562													

Year A
The Third Sunday of Lent

Exodus **17**: 1-7; Psalm **95**; Romans **5**: 1-11; John **4**: 5-42

		AMS	NEH	HTC	HON	MP	H&P	R&S	BPW	CH3	CP	SG	ONC	MPC
I	A Virgin most pure, as the prophets do tell						93							
I	Jesus, where'er thy people meet / Lord Jesus, when your people	162	390	371	282		549	476			492	16	367	
og	I have no bucket						340							
o	At the dawning of creation							424					52	
o	Father, hear the prayer we offer	113	357	360	120	132	436	495	523		416	237	161	132
o	From the apple in the garden										528			
o	Guide me, O thou/my great Redeemer/Jehovah	214	368	528	188	201	437	345	593	89	455	638	252	201
o	I hunger and I thirst			409			730	449			306	470		
p	Come with all joy to sing to God			16										
p	Come worship God who is worthy			18				36						
p	How sure the Scriptures are			249								227		
p	Let all the world in every corner sing	202	394	342	296	404	10	114	54	361	497	47	382	404
p	Let us sing to the God of salvation								15			86		
P	O worship / Worship the Lord in the beauty of holiness	49	52	344	394	529	505	187	22	40	89	204	552	529
e	Come down, O Love Divine	156	137	231	90	89	281	294	283	115	170	663	114	89
e	God of all human history											223		
e	Here is love, vast as the ocean										174		987	
e	I bless the Christ of God			435								175		
e	Jesus my Lord, my God, my all		384	476							483			
e	Let us rejoice, God's gift to us is peace											389		
e	My God, I love thee/you; not because	65	73	479	344		171	357		379	524		458	
e	Not what these hands / I bless the Christ of God			435		487				410		175		
e	The Kingdom of God is justice and joy			333		651	139	200	321		591	184	646	651
e	To God be the glory			584	522	708	463	289	566	374	609	71	695	708

continued on next page

		AMS	NEH	HTC	HON	MP	H&P	R&S	BPW	CH3	CP	SG	ONC	MPC
g	As water to the thirsty			470							252	553		803
g	Broken promises: SS11													
g	Come, thou/O fount of every blessing			337			517	360			406			
g	Glorious things of thee/you are spoken	172	362	494	158	173	817	560	480	421	435	35	205	173
g	God is here! As we his people	464		560			653				301			
g	Holy Spirit, Truth divine			235			289	301	292	106	184		289	
g	How sweet the name of Jesus sounds	122	374	211	220	251	257	277	339	376	467	42	297	251
g	I cannot tell why/how he whom angels worship			194	226	266	238	265	381		54	437	303	266
g	I heard the voice of Jesus say	247	376		231	275	136	349		212	469		310	275
g	Jesus our hope, our heart's desire	86		178							169			
g	Jesus, lover of my soul	123	383	438	261	372	528	332	345	78	96	201	343	372
g	Jesus, the broken bread											363		
g	Jesus, the very thought of thee/you is sweet	120	291, 385	478	264	386	265	509	352	377	486	471, 534	368	
g	Jesus, thou/the joy of loving hearts	255	292	413	265	383	258	389	439	571	486	471		
g	Lord of the Church, we pray for our renewing			499		442			486			577		442
g	Rock of ages	135	445	593	437	582	273	365	545	83	565	150	584	582
g	There was a woman: SS83													
g	Woman in the night: SS76													

Year B
The Third Sunday of Lent
Exodus **20**: 1-17; Psalm **19**; 1 Corinthians **1**: 18-25; John **2**: 13-22

		AMS	NEH	HTC	HON	MP	H&P	R&S	BPW	CH3	CP	SG	ONC	MPC
o	Father of all, whose laws have stood			539					335			664		
o	Lord, I have made thy word my choice	490					475	316			504			
o	Sweet is the work, my God, my King			377		620	514				580	97		620
p	Creator of the earth and skies	351		320			419	82			410	296		
p	Father of mercies, in thy/your word	167		247					99			224		

continued on next page

		AMS	NEH	HTC	HON	MP	H&P	R&S	BPW	CH3	CP	SG	ONC	MPC
p	From all that/who dwell/live beneath	98		580	146		489	723		362	431	82	192	
p	God be in my head	236	328	543	166		694	498	592	433	439	666	211	
p	I know that my Redeemer lives, what joy			169	232	278	196	278	251			406	311	278
p	Jesus, Lord of life and glory		68											
p	Lord, thy word abideth / Lord, your word	166	407	251	318	446	476	317	102	130	515		420	446
p	O for a heart to praise my God	230	74	483	361	495	536	514	538	85	533	149	484	495
p	O for a thousand tongues to sing	125	415	219	362	496	744	285	59	371	534	55	485	495
p	Powerful in making us wise to salvation			252			479					228		
p	Tell all the world of Jesus			521				582				608		
p	The heavens declare thy/your glory, Lord	168		254			481	320			264	230		
p	The spacious firmament	103	267		493		339			143	265		665	
p	The stars declare his glory										314			
e	All my hope on God is founded	336	333	451	15	16	63	586	327	405	368	525	19	16
e	Be thou my vision / Lord be my vision	343	339	545	56	51	378	489	521	87	386	669	70	51
e	Come, wounded healer											130		
e	Here hangs a man discarded							225					276	
e	Nature with open volume stands	497	87				174	219			113			
e	Rejoice, O people, in the mounting years						657							
e	We sing the praise of him who died	138	94	146	536	738	182	229	231	258	125	390	723	738
g	Come to us, creative Spirit			308			377					621		
g	God our Father and Creator			562										
g	His Father's house is where the Son must be LUTR 88													
g	I greet thee, who my sure Redeemer art						391	501		86				
g	Love inspired the anger: SS90													
g	O thou/Lord who came[st]	233	431	552/ 596	392	525	745	433	355	110	191	560	541	525

Isaiah **55**: 1-9; Psalm **63**: 1-8; 1 Corinthians **10**: 1-13; Luke **13**: 1-9

		AMS	NEH	HTC	HON	MP	H&P	R&S	BPW	CH3	CP	SG	ONC	MPC
I	Bread of the world in mercy broken	270	277	396	68		599	443	428	574	285	465	83	
I	Draw nigh and take / Draw near and take		281	401							296			
I	Faithful Shepherd, feed me		282	29	117							498	156	
I	I am not worthy, holy Lord			407						570				
I	O bread to pilgrims given / O food of men wayfaring		300				620	456	317					
I	O for a closer walk with God	231	414	368	360	494		551		663	532		483	494
I	O God, unseen yet ever near	272		421	367							496		
o	All who are thirsty, come to the Lord										546			
o	Father of mercies, in thy/your word	167		247					99			224		
o	Great God of wonders! All thy ways					197	38				452			197
o	Hear our cry, O hear our cry										253			
o	Leader of faithful souls and guide						819							
o	Our hunger cries from plenty, Lord							341			551			
p	As water to the thirsty			470							252	553		803
p	God is my great desire PR63													
p	Jesus, priceless treasure			461	262		259				484	535	344	
p	Jesus, thou/the joy of loving hearts	255	292	413	265	383	258	389	439	571	486	471		
e	Blessed Jesu, Mary's Son		275											
e	Bread of heaven, on thee we feed	271	276	398	67			442			284	464	82	
e	Christ is the heavenly food	439									288	14		
e	For all the saints	305	197	567	134	148	814	658	478	534	232	636	177	148
e	Glorious things of thee/you are spoken	172	362	494	158	173	817	560	480	421	435	35	205	173
e	Guide me, O thou/my great Redeemer/Jehovah	214	368	528	188	201	437	345	593	89	455	638	252	201
e	How sweet the name of Jesus sounds	122	374	211	220	251	257	277	339	376	467	42	297	251

continued on next page

		AMS	NEH	HTC	HON	MP	H&P	R&S	BPW	CH3	CP	SG	ONC	MPC
e	I come with joy to meet my Lord	473		408	227		610	447	437		365	469	304	
e	I hunger and I thirst			409			730	449			306	470		
e	Jesus, the very thought of thee/you is sweet	120	291, 385	478	264	386	265	509	352	377	486	471, 534	368	
e	Lord, enthroned in heavenly splendour	263	296	416	309	431	616			583	311	52	408	
e	O bless the Lord, my soul, let all			34										
e	Rock of ages	135	445	593	437	582	273	365	545	83	565	150	584	582
e	Through the night of doubt and sorrow	211	468	466	517	.	441		546	423	605	544	687	948
g	Come, O thou all-victorious Lord / O come, our all-victorious			441			418							
g	Come, we that love the Lord						487	384	525					

Year A
The Fourth Sunday of Lent

1 Samuel **16**: 1-13; Psalm **23**; Ephesians **5**: 8-14; John **9**: 1-41

		AMS	NEH	HTC	HON	MP	H&P	R&S	BPW	CH3	CP	SG	ONC	MPC
s	Ah, holy Jesus, how hast thou offended		62	123	8		164	215	215	251	100		5	
o	Lord, you have searched and known my ways						71	70	564					
p	Because the Lord is my shepherd										513			
p	Faithful Shepherd, feed me		282	29	117							498	156	
p	I will sing the wondrous story			212	237	315	223		382	381		43	337	315
p	My Father, for another night	3		269	340						5		454	
p	My God, and/now is thy table spread	259		418	342						313	474	456	
p	My Shepherd will supply my need CP50													
p	The God of love my shepherd is	110	77		479		43	677			587		643	649
p	The King of love my shepherd is	126	457	44	484	649	69	552	394	388	589	205	649	649
p	The Lord my pasture shall prepare	111	458								593		653	
p	The Lord's my shepherd, I'll not want	426	459	591/ 45	490	660	70	679	395	387	594	207	654	660
p	When circumstances make my life										540			

continued on next page

		AMS	NEH	HTC	HON	MP	H&P	R&S	BPW	CH3	CP	SG	ONC	MPC
e	Awake, awake, fling off the night	342			49				404		334		57	
e	Awake, my soul, and with the sun	1	232	264	50		632	378		42	1	618	58	804
e	The Spirit lives to set us free				494	664							666	664
e	Wake, O wake / Sleepers, wake	32	16	199	529		249	132		315	39		703	
g	Amazing grace			28	27	31	215	92	550		375	26	29	
g	Christ is the world's light	440		321			455	600	34		213	591	99	
g	Christ is the world's true light	346	494	323	78		456	601	618	505	396	432	100	
g	Christ, whose glory fills the skies	4	234	266	82	79	457	380		114	2	170	105	79
g	Come, Holy Ghost, our souls inspire	93	138	589	92	90	283	751		342	178	555	118	90
g	Come, light of the world										21			
g	Father of mercies, in thy/your word	167		247					99			224		
g	He gave his life in selfless love			405		214			435			467		214
g	His eyes will guide my footsteps			301								505		
g	I heard the voice of Jesus say	247	376		231	275	136	349		212	469		310	275
g	I saw the grass: SS91													
g	I'll praise my Maker while I've breath			20		320	439	734	127		473	84		320
g	In heavenly love abiding			458	246	331	678	590	555	681	478		323	331
g	Just as I am, without one plea	246	294	440	287	396	697	364	346	79	308	507	374	396
g	Lord, I was blind			437		433	423	358	558					433
g	O Jesus, King most wonderful	120	386	484			269	356	353	378	539			
g	One thing I know, that Christ has healed me PR694													
g	Thou/God whose almighty / Father your mighty word	180	466	506	514	699	29	38	591	494	267	684	597	699
g	To God be the glory			584	522	708	463	289	566	374	609	71	695	708

See also Mothering Sunday, page 81

Year B
The Fourth Sunday of Lent

Numbers **21**: 4-9; Psalm **107**: 1-3, 17-22; Ephesians **2**: 1-10; John **3**: 14-21

		AMS	NEH	HTC	HON	MP	H&P	R&S	BPW	CH3	CP	SG	ONC	MPC
o	Bread of heaven, on thee we feed	271	276	398	67			442			284	464	82	
p	Give to our God immortal praise	460		31	155	171	22	94	47		434	83	203	171
a	When Christ was lifted/Dear Christ uplifted	525	335				655				453	142		
e	All hail the power of Jesus' name	140	332	587/203	13	13	252		29	382	163	24	16	13
e	Amazing grace			28	27	31	215	92	550		375	26	29	
e	Come, thou/O fount of every blessing			337			517	360			406			
e	Great God, whose mercy has found us												834	
e	Jesus my Lord, my God, my all		384	476							483			
e	Jesus! the name high over all			213		385	264					323		385
e	Lord, I was blind			437		433	423	358	558					433
e	Lord/Great God, your love has called us here	489		480			500	339	442		133		246	
e	Not what these hands / I bless the Christ of God			435		487				410		175		
e	Rock of ages	135	445	593	437	582	273	365	545	83	565	150	584	582
e	Souls of men / Restless souls / There's a wideness	251	461	443	501	607, 683	230	353	573	218	598	188	662	607
e	Tell all the world of Jesus			521					582			608		
g	And can it be			588	30	33	216	136	328	409	376	168	32	
g	Downtrodden Christ			125										
g	Eternal Light! Eternal Light!			454			458	83	85	357	414	527		
g	It is a thing most wonderful	70	84	131	255	346	224	503	219	385	109	557	333	346
g	Lift high the cross	72		508	303	417	170	422	575	550	499	601	394	417
g	Man of sorrows			130	330	458	228		350	380		383	439	458
g	Name of all majesty			218		481					525	324	465	481
g	O God of truth, whose living word	222												
g	O lift us up, strong Son of God						427	337						
g	Sing, my tongue, the glorious battle / Here proclaim the glorious	59	78	142	446		177	228	226	256	256	121	387	602
g	To God be the glory			584	522	708	463	289	566	374	609	71	695	708
g	We give immortal praise	520		11			18	37	72		206	331	713	
g	When all the world to life is waking		240											
g	When Christ was lifted from the earth	525		335			655						142	
g	With loving hands at work among the suffering			106								187		

See also Mothering Sunday, page 81

Year C
The Fourth Sunday of Lent

Joshua **5**: 9-12; Psalm **32**; 2 Corinthians **5**: 16-21; Luke **15**: 1-3, 11b-32

		AMS	NEH	HTC	HON	MP	H&P	R&S	BPW	CH3	CP	SG	ONC	MPC
s	All for Jesus!		272	469	10		251		332		277	661	13	
s	Forgive our sins as we forgive	362	66	111	141		134	84	83		428	145	180	
s	Lord we know that we have failed you													
l	On this day, the first of days		256		402							530		
o	O bread to pilgrims given / O food of men wayfaring		300				620	456	317					
o	We come unto our fathers'/faithful God				724		453	484	488	14				724
p	Happy are those, beyond all measure blessed										172			
p	How firm a foundation			430	216	243		589	380				292	243
p	None other Lamb						271							
e	He gave his life in selfless love			405		214			435			467		214
e	Holy Spirit, come, confirm us	471	140		214		288	298	289		183		288	
e	In Christ there is no east or west	376	480	322	244	329	758	647	482	425	477	575	319	329
e	Lord/Great God, your love has called us here	489		480			500	339	442		133		246	
e	Love divine, all loves excelling	131	408	217	321	449	267	663	559	437	516	179	428	449
e	No weight of gold or silver			138								181		
e	O Spirit of the living God			513			322	577	579	496	190	605		
e	O what shall I do my Saviour to praise						569							
e	One there is above all others					542	149		560					542
e	Sing for God's glory											598		
e	Stupendous height of heavenly love						462							
e	The Church's one foundation	170	484	501	473	640	515	566	393	420	585	581	636	640
g	Amazing grace			28	27	31	215	92	550		375	26	29	
g	Father we have sinned against you										158			
g	Give me joy in my heart / oil in my lamp	459		S11	153	167	492	523	530		433		201	167
g	God makes his rain to fall: SS96													
g	Hail thou/our once-despisèd/rejected Jesus			175	192	203	222		273		168		258	203
g	I cannot tell why/how he whom angels worship			194	226	266	238	265	381		54	437	303	266
g	I will sing the wondrous story			212	237	315	223		382	381		43	337	315
g	Jesus came — the heavens adoring			195										
g	Just as I am, without one plea	246	294	440	287	396	697	364	346	79	308	507	374	396
g	Lord I come to you										689		880	

continued on next page

		AMS	NEH	HTC	HON	MP	H&P	R&S	BPW	CH3	CP	SG	ONC	MPC
g	Lord of all power, I give you my will / Lord of creation, to you be all praise	395		547		440	699	532		428	508			
g	Lord, I was blind			437		433	423	358	558					433
g	O where, O where's my silver piece: SS97													
g	The Kingdom of God is justice and joy			333		651	139	200	321		591	184	646	651

See also Mothering Sunday, below

Years A, B, C
Mothering Sunday

Exodus **2**: 1-10 or 1 Samuel **1**: 20-28; Psalm **34**: 11-20 or Psalm **127**: 1-4;
2 Corinthians **1**: 3-7 or Colossians **3**: 12-17; Luke **2**: 33-35 or John **19**: 25-27

		AMS	NEH	HTC	HON	MP	H&P	R&S	BPW	CH3	CP	SG	ONC	MPC
g	Jesus' hands were kind hands						393	197		228				
s	All things bright and beautiful	116	264	283	21	23	330		116	154	251	294	25	23
s	Children of the heavenly King	213	344	566	63									
s	Come and praise the Lord our King			S8										
s	Come down, O Love Divine	156	137	231	90	89	281	294	283	115	170	663	114	89
s	Father on high, to whom we pray			296					499					
s	Father, I place into your hands				121	133		518					162	133
s	For the beauty of the earth	104	285	298	137	152	333	41	121	367	253	298	184	152
s	From east to west, from shore to shore		20				99	172		189			193	
s	Glorious things of thee/you are spoken	172	362	494	158	173	817	560	480	421	435	35	205	173
s	God is our strength and refuge			527		188			308		443	650	219	188
s	Great God, we praise the mighty love			299										
s	Happy are they, they that/who love God	176	369	473	195		711			408	456		262	
s	Happy the home that welcomes you			300			366							

continued on next page

		AMS	NEH	HTC	HON	MP	H&P	R&S	BPW	CH3	CP	SG	ONC	MPC
s	He's got the whole world in his hands				206	225							819	225
s	Jerusalem the golden	184	381	573	259			662	312	537	482		340	
s	Jesus, good above all other	378	387	96	269		732	528		111	487		350	
s	Life is great! So sing about it	482											393	
s	Lord of all hopefulness	394	239	101	313		552	531	517	92	507	509	413	882
s	Lord of our growing years			259					514			536		
s	Lord of the home, your only Son	494					367		500		510			
s	Now thank we all our God	205	413	33	354	486	566	72	128	368	530	54	474	486
s	O Lord of heaven and earth and sea	287	422	287			337		387	145	540	306		
s	Once in royal David's city	46	34	67	403	539	114	167	172	193	66	359	521	539
s	Son of God, eternal Saviour	132	498	102				605	639	454	573			
l	God, we praise you! God, we bless you!			341							450	38		
l	I come with joy to meet my Lord	473		408	227		610	447	437		365	469	304	
o	Tell out, my soul, the greatness of the Lord	422	186	42	467	631	86	740	391	164	362	62	631	631
p	Lift up your heads, ye/you mighty gates	483	8				240			12	30			
p	O God in heaven, whose loving plan	407					369				535			
p	Our Father, by whose name	505					371			522				
p	Unless the Lord constructs the house PR127													
e	In an age of twisted values											317		
e	When, in our music, God is glorified				550		388	414			618		737	
g	Lord, who left the highest heaven			97										
g	What have we to show our Saviour										391			

See also the Fourth Sunday of Lent, pages 81

Year A
The Fifth Sunday of Lent (Passiontide begins)
Ezekiel **37**: 1-14; Psalm **130**; Romans **8**: 6-11; John **11**: 1-45

		AMS	NEH	HTC	HON	MP	H&P	R&S	BPW	CH3	CP	SG	ONC	MPC
s	Great Son of God, you once on Calvary's cross				187								251	
o	Breathe on me, Breath of God	157	342	226	69	67	280	295	282	103	174	554	84	67
o	Come, let us with our Lord arise	449	254	375			575	383			142			
o	Father of Jesus Christ, my Lord						693	351						
o	Here within this house of prayer			563										
o	O Breath of life, come sweeping / O Breath of love, come breathe			237	356	488	777	302	293	339			476	488
o	O Spirit of the living God			513			322	577	579	496	190	605		
o	O Trinity, O Trinity			6								291		
o	Revive thy work / Revive your church			515		578	780							578
o	Spirit of God most high			242										
o	This is the day of light	21		380						46				
p	Out of our failure to create						88					549		
p	Souls of men / Restless souls / There's a wideness	251	461	443	501	607, 683	230	353	573	218	598	188	662	607
a	When Christ was lifted/Dear Christ uplifted	525	335				655				453	142		
e	Come down, O Love Divine	156	137	231	90	89	281	294	283	115	170	663	114	89
e	Father of heaven, whose love profound	97	358	359	124		519			77	421	144		827
e	First of the week and finest day			376								2		
e	Holy Spirit, come, confirm us	471	140		214		288	298	289		183		288	
e	O for a thousand tongues to sing	125	415	219	362	496	744	285	59	371	534	55	485	495
e	Spirit of God within me			243			294	304	296		196	677	612	
g	Eternal light, shine in my heart			339							415			
g	God our Father and Creator			562										
g	God who created light										288			
g	Hark, my soul, it is the Lord / Christian, do you hear the Lord	244		472	197	209	521	348		676	264		457	209
g	I lay there in my bed AFJ14													
g	In Christ shall all be made alive			459								533		
g	It is a thing most wonderful	70	84	131	255	346	224	503	219	385	109	557	333	346
g	Jesus the Lord said/says, I am the Bread					384	137	199	202					384
g	Jesus, the name high over all			213		385	264					323		385
g	Jesus, thy/your blood and righteousness			460			225				111	177		
g	Light of the minds that know him		400	477				529			501	626	397	
g	Lord, I was blind			437		433	423	358	558					433
g	Poor Lazarus is sick: SS29													
g	Thou art / You are the way	128	464	113	512	695	234	554		121	600		682	695
g	Up from the earth, and surging like a wave										418			
g	We give immortal praise	520		11			18	37	72		206	331	713	

83

Year B
The Fifth Sunday of Lent (Passiontide begins)

Jeremiah **31**: 31-34; Psalm **51**: 1-12 or Psalm **119**: 9-16; Hebrews **5**: 5-10;
John **12**: 20-33

		AMS	NEH	HTC	HON	MP	H&P	R&S	BPW	CH3	CP	SG	ONC	MPC
s	Great Son of God, you once on Calvary's cross				187								251	
s	Meekness and majesty				335	465			58			395	448	465
s	The royal banners forward go / As royal banners are unfurled	58	79		492		179	216	228	257	122		663	
o	Creatures, once in safety held: SS5													
o	Help us, O Lord, to learn	373	370	493			474				460	226		
o	Jesus, lover of my soul	123	383	438	261	372	528	332	345	78	96	201	343	372
o	My hope is built on nothing less		462		473				411		537		473	
p	Christian, seek not yet repose			355										
p	Create in us clean hearts, O God										682			
p	God be merciful to me										153			
p	My Lord, what love is this				345	476						194	462	476
p	O for a heart to praise my God	230	74	483	361	495	536	514	538	85	533	149	484	495
p	O God, be gracious to me in thy/your love							695		64				
p	How can the way of youth be pure PR119													
a	When Christ was lifted/Dear Christ uplifted	525	335				655				453	142		
e	A debtor to mercy alone			449										
e	It is a thing most wonderful	70	84	131	255	346	224	503	219	385	109	557	333	346
e	Join all the glorious names			214		392	78	280	557	304	493	46		392
e	Lead us, heavenly Father, lead us	224	393	595	293	400	68	543	597	90	496	640	379	400
e	The Lord ascendeth up on high		135				210			287	173			
e	Where high the heavenly temple stands	130		184			259			295	75			
e	With loving hands at work among the suffering			106								187		
g	As we break the bread			393				439				460	48	
g	God's glory fills the universe							275				283		
g	Great God, we praise the mighty love			299										
g	Lift high the cross	72		508	303	417	170	422	575	550	499	601	394	417
g	Man of sorrows			130	330	458	228		350	380		383	439	458

continued on next page

		AMS	NEH	HTC	HON	MP	H&P	R&S	BPW	CH3	CP	SG	ONC	MPC
g	Now the green blade rises/riseth	501	115		355		204	243	257	278	153	414	475	
g	O Jesus, I have promised	235	420	531	372	501	704	509	352	434	538	676	503	501
g	O lift us up, strong Son of God						427	337						
g	O my Saviour, lifted	248			386	516							519	516
g	Seed, secret sown in the earth: SS26													
g	Sing, my tongue, the glorious battle / Here proclaim the glorious	59	78	142	446		177	228	226	256	256	121	387	602
g	When Christ was lifted from the earth	525		335				655					142	
g	With joy we meditate the grace	530				774	235	206	275		624			774

Year C
The Fifth Sunday of Lent (Passiontide begins)

Isaiah **43**: 16-21; Psalm **126**; Philippians **3**: 4b-14; John **12**: 1-8

		AMS	NEH	HTC	HON	MP	H&P	R&S	BPW	CH3	CP	SG	ONC	MPC
s	Great Son of God, you once on Calvary's cross				187								251	
s	Never further than thy cross							507						
o	Lord, for the years			328	310	428		603	535		51	602	409	428
o	When the King shall come again			200										
p	Forth in thy/your name, O Lord	239	235	306	143	159	381	521	526	463	430	623	188	159
p	Go forth and tell			505	164	178	770	574	570		437	596	238	178
p	I will sing, I will sing a song			S15		313		279						313
p	The Lord restored us - we were freed PR126													
p	To God be the glory			584	522	708	463	289	566	374	609	71	695	708
a	When Christ was lifted/Dear Christ uplifted	525	335				655				453	142		
e	All I once held dear										562	18		
e	All that I am, I lay before you										686		973	
e	And can it be			588	30	33	216	136	328	409	376	168	32	
e	Awake, my soul, stretch every nerve							487						
e	Beneath the cross of Jesus				59	55	165			684	105		65	55

continued on next page

e/g		AMS	NEH	HTC	HON	MP	H&P	R&S	BPW	CH3	CP	SG	ONC	MPC
e	Can we/man by searching find out God	438					76	80			201	496		
e	Fight the good fight	220	359	526	128	143	710	496	524	442	423	635	169	143
e	Here, O my Lord, I see thee/you	274		406		230	608		436	573	304	468	279	230
e	In Christ shall all be made alive			459								533		
e	Jesus, the name high over all			213		385	264					323		385
e	Jesus, the very thought of thee/you is sweet	120	291, 385	478	264	386	265	509	352	377	486	471, 534	368	
e	Jesus, thou/the joy of loving hearts	255	292	413	265	383	258	389	439	571	486	471		
e	Jesus, thy/your blood and righteousness			460			225				111	177		
e	My hope is built on nothing less			462		473				411		537		473
e	No more, my God, I boast						369							
e	O happy band of pilgrims	208	418	530	368							497		
e	One thing I know: STG 128													
e	Thou hidden source of calm repose						275				603			
e	To him we come			518		709			547			679		709
e	We sing the praise of him who died	138	94	146	536	738	182	229	231	258	125	390	723	738
e	When I survey the wondrous cross	67	95	147	549	755	180	217	233	254	127	680	738	755
g	How good a thing it is			497								585		
g	Said Judas to Mary: SS32													

Palm Sunday: Liturgy of the Palms

Year A: Matthew **21**: 1-11; Psalm **118**: 1-2, 19-29
Year B: Mark **11**: 1-11 or John **12**: 12-16; Psalm **118**: 1-2, 19-24
Year C: Luke **19**: 28-40; Psalm **118**: 1-2, 19-29

s/p		AMS	NEH	HTC	HON	MP	H&P	R&S	BPW	CH3	CP	SG	ONC	MPC
s	O thou who through this holy week		96											
p	All people that on earth do dwell	100	334	14	17	20	1	712	2	1	369	77	21	20
p	Christ is made the sure foundation / Blessed city, heavenly Salem	283/ 332	204-5	559	76	73	485	559	474	10	208	572	97	73
p	Christ is our corner-stone	161		564	77						395		98	
p	Come, let us with our Lord arise	449	254	375			575	383			142			

continued on next page

		AMS	NEH	HTC	HON	MP	H&P	R&S	BPW	CH3	CP	SG	ONC	MPC
p	Give thanks to God, for he is good PR118													
p	I will enter his gates				236	307		386	11				336	307
p	Lord, enthroned in heavenly splendour	263	296	416	309	431	616			583	311	52	408	
p	This earth belongs to God: CFW 584											99		
p	This is the day the Lord hath/has made	22	257	379			577	376			9	70	677	
p	This is the day, this is the day			S28	508	691	578	377	21				676	691
p	We are marching in the light of God						555	487				551	709	954
g	A stable lamp is lighted: PFT 1										42			
g	All glory, laud, and honour / All glory, praise	60	509	120	11	9	160	208	216	233	128	380	14	9
g	Children of Jerusalem				70	163				236				70
g	Give me joy in my heart / oil in my lamp	459		S11	153	167	492	523	530		433		201	167
g	Hail to the Lord's anointed	142	55	190	193	204	125	127	142	317	87		259	204
g	Hark the glad sound! The Saviour comes	30	6	193	198	210	82	137	143	160	27	435	265	210
g	Here comes Jesus: SS79													
g	Hosanna, hosanna, hosanna in the highest					242						119	290	242
g	Lift up your heads, ye/you mighty gates	483	8				240			12	30			
g	Listen to the shouts of praises								222					
g	Make way, make way, for Christ the King				329	457		141					438	457
g	My song is love unknown	63	86	136	346	478	173	207	204	224	112	384	463	478
g	Ride on, ride on in majesty	61	511	119	435	580	159	209	225	234	129	386	583	580
g	The glory of our King was seen						161	230						
g	Trotting, trotting through Jerusalem						162							
g	You are the King of glory				570	790		271	74				762	790

Year A
Palm Sunday: Liturgy of the Passion

Isaiah **50**: 4-9a; Psalm **31**: 9-16; Philippians **2**: 5-11; Matthew **26**:14 — **27**:66
or Matthew **27**: 11-54

Lists for the three years overlap only slightly; but many hymns are interchangeable as the Gospel is the only variable reading.
Distinctive features of the Gospels are taken into account.

		AMS	NEH	HTC	HON	MP	H&P	R&S	BPW	CH3	CP	SG	ONC	MPC
s	Great Son of God, you once on Calvary's cross				187								251	
s	I do not know the man				229								306	
s	Jesus, meek and lowly		85											
s	Light of the lonely pilgrim's heart		399											
s	Nature with open volume stands	497	87				174	219			113			
s	O love, how deep, how broad, how high	119	425		383		229	283	207	223	118		516	
s	O sing a song of Bethlehem	413						201		220	545		536	
s	O thou who through this holy week		96											
s	Son of God, eternal Saviour	132	498	102				605	639	454	573			
s	To Christ, the Prince of peace	127												
s	We sing the praise of him who died	138	94	146	536	738	182	229	231	258	125	390	723	738
s	With glorious clouds encompassed round						184				623			
o	He lives in us, the Christ of God			457					554			173		
o	O sacred head	68	90	139	389	520	176	220	223	253	120	385	535	520
o	See, Christ was wounded for our sake			137					229					
p	Give thanks to God, for he is good PR118													
p	In you, O Lord I find my refuge PR31													
e	And can it be			588	30	33	216	136	328	409	376	168	32	
e	At the name of Jesus	148	338	172	46	41	74	261	370	300	380	317	54	
e	Empty he came			127							622			
e	God's glory fills the universe							275			283			
e	He gave his life in selfless love			405		214			435		467			214
e	He has been given a name											838		
e	Meekness and majesty			335	465				58		395	448		465
e	Morning glory, starlit sky	496						99			259			
e	Name of all majesty			218		481					525	324	465	481

continued on next page

		AMS	NEH	HTC	HON	MP	H&P	R&S	BPW	CH3	CP	SG	ONC	MPC
e	The head that once was crowned with thorns	141	134	182	480	647	209	257	274	286	172	442		644
e	You have been given												971	
g	Great God, what do I see and hear			189										
g	Lord, teach us how to pray aright	227	406	367	316		551				98		418	
g	My Lord of light, who made the worlds			4										
g	Praise to the Holiest in the height	117	439	140	426	563	231	103	562	238	557	58	572	563
g	That night at table: SS36													
g	The hands of Christ			141										
g	This is the night, dear friends: SS37													
g	Thy/Your way, not mine			555	521								692	950
g	To mock your reign	517						221			124			

Year B
Palm Sunday: Liturgy of the Passion

Isaiah **50**: 4-9a; Psalm **31**: 9-16; Philippians **2**: 5-11; Mark **14**:1 — **15**:47 or Mark **15**: 1-39 [40-47]

Lists for the three years overlap only slightly; but many hymns are interchangeable as the Gospel is the only variable reading. Distinctive features of the Gospels are taken into account.

		AMS	NEH	HTC	HON	MP	H&P	R&S	BPW	CH3	CP	SG	ONC	MPC
s	A man there lived in Galilee	334			3								28	
s	All ye who seek a comfort / for sure relief	64	63		22						101		26	
s	Great Son of God, you once on Calvary's cross				187								251	
s	I am not skilled to understand			432		257	221			687				257
s	I do not know the man				229								306	
s	In the Cross of Christ I glory		379		249	338	167	224	344	259	480		327	338
s	Lord Christ, we praise your sacrifice	487		132			532	611				627		

continued on next page

		AMS	NEH	HTC	HON	MP	H&P	R&S	BPW	CH3	CP	SG	ONC	MPC
s	The royal banners forward go / As royal banners are unfurled	58	79		492		179	216	228	257	122		663	
l	Forth in thy/your name, O Lord	239	235	306	143	159	381	521	526	463	430	623	188	159
l	Glory in the highest		363	582							300	37		
l	The sun is sinking fast	14								50				
o	Christ triumphant, ever reigning			173	81	77			306		398	319	104	74
p	Give thanks to God, for he is good PR118													
e	All praise to thee/Christ, for thou / our Lord and King divine	337	335	204	18		253	750		297	372		22	
e	Before the heaven and earth			612										
e	God's glory fills the universe							275				283		
e	He has been given a name												838	
e	Meekness and majesty				335	465			58			395	448	465
e	You have been given												971	
g	Christ is the world's light	440		321			455	600	34		213	591	99	
g	Christian, seek not yet repose			355										
g	From heaven you came (The servant King)				148	162		522	529		432	632	195	16
g	God of unexampled grace						166							
g	Hail thou/our once-despisèd/rejected Jesus			175	192	203	222		273		168		258	203
g	Lord, in our lonely hours										641			
g	My heart and voice I raise						268							
g	My Lord, you wore no royal crown			118								628		
g	My song is love unknown	63	86	136	346	478	173	207	204	224	112	384	463	478
g	Now, my soul, thy voice upraising		88											
g	O crucified Redeemer	404					424	604						
g	Stand up, stand up for Jesus	221	453	535	457	617	721			481	578	644	617	617
g	The head that once was crowned with thorns	141	134	182	480	647	209	257	274	286	172	442		644
g	Thy/Your way, not mine			555	521								692	950
g	Won, the victor's crown			185										

Year C
Palm Sunday: Liturgy of the Passion

Isaiah **50**: 4-9a; Psalm **31**: 9-16; Philippians **2**: 5-11; Luke **22**:14 — **23**:56 or
Luke **23**: 1-49

Lists for the three years overlap only slightly; but many hymns are
interchangeable as the Gospel is the only variable reading.
Distinctive features of the Gospels are taken into account.

		AMS	NEH	HTC	HON	MP	H&P	R&S	BPW	CH3	CP	SG	ONC	MPC
s	Come, ye faithful / Alleluia, raise the anthem	145	351	205	99	103			269		409	25	131	103
s	Great Son of God, you once on Calvary's cross				187								251	
s	I do not know the man				229								306	
s	My Lord, what love is this				345	476						194	462	476
s	No weight of gold or silver			138								181		
s	O the bitter shame and sorrow			487		524	538							524
s	There is a fountain			144		671								671
s	Thou who wast rich / Lord, you were rich			63		700					72	356		700
s	To the Name of our / that brings salvation	121	470	222	523		80	291		373	610	72	698	
l	O Sacrifice of Calvary			424								478		
p	Give thanks to God, for he is good PR118													
e	God's glory fills the universe							275				283		
e	He has been given a name												838	
e	Meekness and majesty			335	465				58			395	448	465
e	What if the One who shapes the stars										364			
e	You have been given												971	
g	Alas! and did my Saviour bleed			124										
g	All hail the power of Jesus' name	140	332	587/ 203	13	13	252		29	382	163	24	16	13
g	Forgive our sins as we forgive	362	66	111	141		134	84	83		428	145	180	
g	Hail Redeemer, King divine			210										
g	How deep the Father's love for us										193		988	
g	I cannot tell why/how he whom angels worship			194	226	266	238	265	381		54	437	303	266
g	I will sing the wondrous story			212	237	315	223		382	381		43	337	315

continued on next page

		AMS	NEH	HTC	HON	MP	H&P	R&S	BPW	CH3	CP	SG	ONC	MPC
g	Look, ye/you saints, the sight is glorious			179		426	201			289	171			426
g	Lord Jesus Christ, you have come to us	391	297	417	311	435	617	373	444		505	670	411	435
g	Lord Jesus, are we one with thee: AHB 269													
g	Lord Jesus, for my sake you come			133				224						
g	Lord Jesus, think on/of me	129	70	316	312		533	363		80	97		412	
g	Lord, who left the highest heaven			97										
g	So dies this man, this carpenter: SS41													
g	The hands of Christ			141										
g	They borrowed a bed: SS77													
g	Thou didst leave thy throne	250	465		513	697	154	192	179		601		683	697
g	We have a gospel to proclaim	431	486	519	532	728	465		585		612		716	728
g	We were not there to see you come			121										
g	When my love to God/Christ grows weak						183	218						
g	When you prayed beneath the trees: WAM 98													

Years A, B, C
Maundy Thursday

Exodus **12**: 1-4 [5-10] 11-14; Psalm **116**: 1-2, 12-19; 1 Corinthians **11**: 23-26; John **13**: 1-17, 31b-35

		AMS	NEH	HTC	HON	MP	H&P	R&S	BPW	CH3	CP	SG	ONC	MPC
se	Gather around for the table is spread				152								199	
se	God of the Passover											228		
se	Jesus took a piece of bread				281								366	
se	See the holy table spread for our healing											592		
s	By gracious powers so wonderfully sheltered							486	117					
s	Go to dark Gethsemane									132				
s	Jesus in the olive grove						169							
s	Thy will be done											693		
s	When you prayed beneath the trees: WAM 98													
s	Where true love is present											743		

continued on next page

		AMS	NEH	HTC	HON	MP	H&P	R&S	BPW	CH3	CP	SG	ONC	MPC
ls	Blest by the sun, the olive tree		512								131			
e	According to thy gracious word		270						585		276			
e	As we gather at your table										461			
e	Before I take the body of the Lord										463			
e	Draw nigh and take / Draw near and take		281	401							296			
e	Father, it is right and fitting								433					
e	For the bread which you have broken	456		403								466		
e	He gave his life in selfless love			405	214				435			467		214
e	I come with joy to meet my Lord	473		408	227		610	447	437		365	469	304	
e	Jesus, we thus / Now Jesus we obey	477					614	450	446		307			
e	Let us break bread together	480			299	414	615	452	443				387	414
e	Lord Jesus Christ, you have come to us	391	297	417	311	435	617	373	444		505	670	411	435
e	My God, and/now is thy table spread	259		418	342						313	474	456	
e	Now/Sing my tongue / Of the glorious body	252	268		353		624	457	449	578	316		473	
e	O Lord, sustaining all who live										477			
e	The church is like a table						480							
e	The heavenly Word proceeding forth	253	269								326			
e	The life within the standing corn										481			
e	The Son of God proclaim	427		415			627	458	455		328			
e	We come as guests invited			602		723								723
e	We come to this your table, Lord									330				
e	Where true love is found with charity											742		
g	An upper room did our Lord prepare	434			29		594	438	429		130		38	
g	At the supper, Christ the Lord			394								462		
g	Jesus, in dark Gethsemane							213						
g	Kneels at the feet of his friends / Jesus, Jesus						145	648	606					
g	Lord/Great God, your love has called us here	489		480			500	339	442		133		246	
g	Love is his word			481	322				445			180	429	
g	Meekness and majesty				335	465			58			395	448	465
g	O thou who at thy eucharist / O Christ at your first eucharist	265	302	420	391		779			492	318		540	476
g	There's a spirit in the air	515		245			326	329	300			69	661	
g	This is my will				507								675	
g	This is the night, dear friends: SS37													

Years A, B, C
Good Friday

Isaiah **52**:13 — **53**:12; Psalm **22**; Hebrews **10**: 16-25
or Hebrews **4**: 14-16, **5**: 7-9; John **18**:1 — **19**:42

(See also Palm Sunday — Liturgy of the Passion Years A, B, C)

		AMS	NEH	HTC	HON	MP	H&P	R&S	BPW	CH3	CP	SG	ONC	MPC
s	Great Son of God, you once on Calvary's cross				187								251	
s	Here is love vast as the ocean										174		987	
s	I do not know the man				229								306	
s	I give you love											309		
s	My God, I love thee/you; not because	65	73	479	344		171	357		379	524		458	
s	Praise to the Holiest in the height	117	439	140	426	563	231	103	562	238	557	58	572	563
s	There is a green hill far away	137	92	148	499	674	178	223	230	241	123	388	657	674
s	When I survey the wondrous cross	67	95	147	549	755	180	217	233	254	127	680	738	755
o	Lord Christ, we praise your sacrifice	487		132			532	611				627		
o	Praise to Christ, the Lord incarnate										327			
o	See, Christ was wounded for our sake			137					229					
p	O Lord my God, O Lord my God										491			
p	Why, God, have you forsaken me PR22													
g	A purple robe			122								379	39	
g	Ah, holy Jesus, how hast thou offended		62	123	8		164	215	215	251	100		5	
g	Alas! and did my Saviour bleed			124										
g	Alone thou goest / you once went / now going forth, O Lord							212	217	242	102			
g	At the cross, her station keeping	69	97		44						246	104	51	
g	Before the cock crew twice							214						
g	Beneath the cross of Jesus				59	55	165				684	105	65	55
g	Downtrodden Christ			125										
g	Glory be to Jesus	66	83	126	159							108	146	206

continued on next page

		AMS	NEH	HTC	HON	MP	H&P	R&S	BPW	CH3	CP	SG	ONC	MPC
g	He stood before the court			129										
g	How deep the Father's love for us										193		988	
g	It is a thing most wonderful	70	84	131	255	346	224	503	219	385	109	557	333	346
g	It is finished! Blessed Jesus		99											
g	Lord, in our lonely hours										641			
g	Man of sorrows			130	330	458	228		350	380		383	439	458
g	Mary, blessed grieving mother				331								441	
g	My song is love unknown	63	86	136	346	478	173	207	204	224	112	384	463	478
g	O Christ, the master carpenter			135								673		
g	O come and mourn with me awhile	114								243	114			
g	O come and stand beneath the cross		98											
g	O dearest Lord, thy/your sacred head	71	89	134	359		172	222	351	252	116	674	482	
g	O love divine, what hast thou done						175				117			
g	O perfect life of love [Also AHB 175]									249				
g	O sacred head	68	90	139	389	520	176	220	223	253	120	385	535	520
g	Rock of ages	135	445	593	437	582	273	365	545	83	565	150	584	582
g	Sing, my tongue, the glorious battle / Here proclaim the glorious	59	78	142	446		177	228	226	256	256	121	387	602
g	Throned upon the awesome/aweful tree [Also AHB 177]									247				
g	We sing your mercies											139	1015	
g	What have we to show our Saviour											391		

Year A
Easter Day

Acts **10**: 34-43 or Jeremiah **31**: 1-6; Psalm **118**: 1-2, 14-24; Colossians **3**: 1-4
or Acts **10**: 34-43; John **20**: 1-18 or Matthew **28**: 1-10

		AMS	NEH	HTC	HON	MP	H&P	R&S	BPW	CH3	CP	SG	ONC	MPC
s	Christ is risen												812	
s	Christ is the one who calls												813	
s	From the very depths of darkness				151								198	
s	Hail thee festival day [Easter]		109										257	
s	Jesus Christ is risen today	77	110	155	267	357			252	264	147	408	348	357
s	Light's glittering morn	329		157								149		
s	Now is Christ risen from the dead												901	
s	Welcome, happy morning			166						272				
s	Ye/You choirs of new Jerusalem	73	124	168	563		823				162	419	754	
o	Come ye faithful, raise the strain / Spring has come	76	106	160	100		194	236	248	269	142			
o	This hallowed chosen morn		122											
p	O set ye open unto me									263				
p	This is the day the Lord hath/has made	22	257	379			577	376			9	70	677	
p	This is the day, this is the day			S28	508	691	578	377	21				676	691
a	Christ the Lord is risen again	79	105	153	80		192	233			141	400	103	
e	Away with gloom	437					187			292				
e	Lift up your hearts to things above						820							
e	Ye faithful souls who Jesus know						751							
g1	At break of day three women came: SS45													
g1	Early morning. 'Come, prepare him'	451												
g1	Good Joseph had a garden						195				280	146		
g1	Too early for the blackbird							249						
g	Comes Mary to the grave			152								401		
g	Exult, creation, round God's throne										403			
g	First of the week and finest day			376								2		
g	See how a light shines: SS46													
g	The day of resurrection	75	117	161	474		208	246			267	157	415	637
g	Thine/Yours be/is the glory	428	120	167	503	689	212	247	260	279	160	417	672	689

Acts **10**: 34-43 or Isaiah **25**: 6-9; Psalm **118**: 1-2, 14-24; 1 Corinthians **15**: 1-11
or Acts **10**: 34-43;
John **20**: 1-18 or Mark **16**: 1-8

		AMS	NEH	HTC	HON	MP	H&P	R&S	BPW	CH3	CP	SG	ONC	MPC
s	Christ is risen												812	
s	Christ is the one who calls												813	
s	Come ye faithful, raise the strain / Spring has come	76	106	160	100		194	236	248	269	142			
s	From the very depths of darkness				151								198	
s	Hail thee festival day [Easter]		109										257	
s	Light's glittering morn	329		157							149			
s	Now is Christ risen from the dead												901	
s	The day of resurrection	75	117	161	474		208	246		267	157	415	637	
s	Thine/Yours be/is the glory	428	120	167	503	689	212	247	260	279	160	417	672	689
s	Welcome, happy morning			166						272				
s	Ye/You choirs of new Jerusalem	73	124	168	563		823				162	419	754	
oa	The strife is o'er/past	78	119	163	495	670	214	250	261	266	159	416	667	670
a	Christ the Lord is risen again	79	105	153	80		192	233			141	400	103	
p	O set ye open unto me									263				
p	This is the day the Lord hath/has made	22	257	379			577	376			9	70	677	
p	This is the day, this is the day			S28	508	691	578	377	21				676	691
e	These are the facts			162		687						284		687
e	When Easter to the dark world came						200	251						
g1	Early morning. 'Come, prepare him'	451												
g1	Good Joseph had a garden						195			280	146			
g1	Too early for the blackbird							249						
g2	Jesus Christ is risen today	77	110	155	267	357			252	264	147	408	348	357
g	Comes Mary to the grave			152								401		
g	It fell upon a summer day				254					213			331	
g	Now the green blade rises/riseth	501	115		355		204	243	257	278	153	414	475	
g	See how a light shines: SS46													

Year C
Easter Day

Acts **10**: 34-43 or Isaiah **65**: 17-25; Psalm **118**: 1-2, 14-24;
1 Corinthians **15**: 19-26 or Acts **10**: 34-43;
John **20**: 1-18 or Luke **24**: 1-12

		AMS	NEH	HTC	HON	MP	H&P	R&S	BPW	CH3	CP	SG	ONC	MPC
s	Christ is risen												812	
s	Christ is the one who calls												813	
s	Come ye faithful, raise the strain / Spring has come	76	106	160	100		194	236	248	269	142			
s	From the very depths of darkness				151								198	
s	Hail thee festival day [Easter]		109										257	
s	Jesus Christ is risen today	77	110	155	267	357			252	264	147	408	348	357
s	Light's glittering morn	329		157							149			
s	Now is Christ risen from the dead												901	
s	The day of resurrection	75	117	161	474		208	246		267	157	415	637	
s	Thine/Yours be/is the glory	428	120	167	503	689	212	247	260	279	160	417	672	689
s	Welcome, happy morning			166						272				
o	Ye/You choirs of new Jerusalem	73	124	168	563		823				162	419	754	
a	Christ the Lord is risen again	79	105	153	80		192	233			141	400	103	
a	The strife is o'er/past	78	119	163	495	670	214	250	261	266	159	416	667	670
p	O set ye open unto me									263				
p	This is the day the Lord hath/has made	22	257	379			577	376			9	70	677	
p	This is the day, this is the day			S28	508	691	578	377	21				676	691
es	Paschal Feast! Upon the cross									155				
e	Christ is risen - hallelujah, hallelujah										423		812	
e	If Christ had not been raised from death										407			
e	Jesus lives! Thy/Your terrors now	82	112	156	272	373	198	239	253	605	148	409	354	373
e	Now is eternal life	402	114		351		203	432			152		470	
g1	Early morning. 'Come, prepare him'	451												
g1	Good Joseph had a garden						195			280	146			
g1	Too early for the blackbird							249						
g2	All ye that seek the Lord who died						188							
g2	Christ is alive! Let Christians sing						190	260	244		140	32	96	
g	At break of day three women came: SS45													
g	Comes Mary to the grave			152								401		
g	Exult, archangels bright										402			
g	See how a light shines: SS46													

Year A
The Second Sunday of Easter

Acts **2**: 14a, 22-32; Psalm **16**; 1 Peter **1**: 3-9; John **20**: 19-31

		AMS	NEH	HTC	HON	MP	H&P	R&S	BPW	CH3	CP	SG	ONC	MPC
s	At the Lamb's high feast we sing	81	104		45						138		53	
s	Christ the Lord is risen today / Love's redeeming work is done / All creation	83	113	150	324	76	193	232	246	275	150	412	433	76
s	Come ye faithful, raise the strain / Spring has come	76	106	160	100		194	236	248	269	142			
s	Easter glory fills the sky									276				
s	Good Christian men / Good Christians all, rejoice	85	107	154	181		191	238	250	183	145	404	240	
s	He is Lord, he is Lord			S7	204	220	256	264	378				274	220
s	The Lamb's high banquet we await		101											
s	This joyful Eastertide		121	165	509		213	248	258	271	161		680	
s	When fear and grief had barred the door								259					
a	The strife is o'er/past	78	119	163	495	670	214	250	261	266	159	416	667	670
a	Up from the earth										418			
p	Lord, when the storms of life arise												886	
p	Now is eternal life	402	114		351		203	432			152		470	
p	O Lord, you are the centre of my life										543			
e	Blest be the everlasting God						669	588		530	139			
e	Jesus, these eyes have never seen	245	389					592		674	491		365	
e	O Christ, the King of glory												905	
g	Blessed Thomas, doubt no longer		173											
g	Jesus, Lord, Redeemer						199	240		283				
g	Jesus, stand among us in thy/your risen power			364	280	380	530	388	88	11			362	
g	Jesus, stand among us				279	381		565					362	381
g	My daughters and my sons: SS48													
g	O Lord, we long to see your face	412											514	
g	O sons and daughters, let us sing	74	125				205	244		277	154			
g	Peace be with you										282			
g	Rushing wind that fills: SS51													
g	Spirit of God come dwell within me											611		
g	That Easter-tide with joy was bright	329iii									149iii			
g	The spirit lives to set us free				494	664							666	664
g	These things did Thomas: SS49													
g	When Easter to the dark world came						200	251						

For those who require an Old Testament reading on the Sundays in Eastertide, provision is made in the table on page 60 of *Calendar, Lectionary and Collects*

Year B
The Second Sunday of Easter

Acts **4**: 32-35; Psalm **133**; 1 John **1**:1 — **2**:2; John **20**: 19-31

		AMS	NEH	HTC	HON	MP	H&P	R&S	BPW	CH3	CP	SG	ONC	MPC
s	At the Lamb's high feast we sing	81	104		45						138		53	
s	Christ the Lord is risen today / Love's redeeming work is done / All creation	83	113	150	324	76	193	232	246	275	150	412	433	76
s	Come ye faithful, raise the strain / Spring has come	76	106	160	100		194	236	248	269	142			
s	Good Christian men / Good Christians all, rejoice	85	107	154	181		191	238	250	183	145	404	240	
s	The Lamb's high banquet we await		101											
s	This joyful Eastertide		121	165	509		213	248	258	271	161		680	
a	Help us to help each other / Jesus, united by thy grace	374		540	208		773	500			461		275	
a	Jesus, Lord, we look to thee	380	481				759	564			489			
a	The gifts we bring express our love										278			
p	How good a thing it is			497								585		
p	How good and how pleasant it is										587			
p	O Holy Spirit, Lord of grace	152	419		371		310				188		501	
el	Fill thou/now my/our life	200		541	129	146	792	406	569	457	424	665	171	146
e	Christ is the world's true light	346	494	323	78		456	601	618	505	396	432	100	
e	Eternal Light! Eternal Light!			454			458	83	85	357	414	527		
e	O sons and daughters, let us sing	74	125				205	244		277	154			
g	Blessed Thomas, doubt no longer		173											
g	Jesus, Lord, Redeemer						199	240		283				
g	Jesus, stand among us in thy/your risen power			364	280	380	530	388	88	11			362	
g	Jesus, stand among us				279	381		565					362	381
g	O Lord, we long to see your face	412											514	
g	Spirit of God come dwell within me											611		
g	That Easter-tide with joy was bright	329iii									149iii			
g	The spirit lives to set us free			494	664								666	664
g	These things did Thomas: SS49													
g	When Easter to the dark world came						200	251						
g	When fear and grief had barred the door								259					

For those who require an Old Testament reading on the Sundays in Eastertide, provision is made in the table on page 60 of *Calendar, Lectionary and Collects*

Year C
The Second Sunday of Easter

Acts **5**: 27-32; Psalm **118**: 14-29 or Psalm **150**; Revelation **1**: 4-8;
John **20**: 19-31

		AMS	NEH	HTC	HON	MP	H&P	R&S	BPW	CH3	CP	SG	ONC	MPC
s	At the Lamb's high feast we sing	81	104		45						138		53	
s	At the name of Jesus	148	338	172	46	41	74	261	370	300	380	317	54	
s	Come ye faithful, raise the strain / Spring has come	76	106	160	100		194	236	248	269	142			
s	Lord, enthroned in heavenly splendour	263	296	416	309	431	616			583	311	52	408	
s	The Lamb's high banquet we await		101											
s	This is the day the Lord hath/has made	22	257	379			577	376			9	70	677	
s	Thou Shepherd of Israel and mine						750							
s	We have a gospel to proclaim	431	486	519	532	728	465		585		612		716	728
p	Bring to the Lord a glad new song			336					30			78		
p	For the music of creation										36			
p	O set ye open unto me									263				
p2	O praise ye the Lord / Sing praise to the Lord	203	427	354	388	518		49	70		543	96	534	518
p2	Praise the Lord, his glories show			345			14	102		359				
p2	Praise to the Lord, the Almighty	207	440	40	427	564	16	74	68	9	558	59	573	564
gl	'Peace be with you all' we sing										480			
g	Blessed Thomas, doubt no longer		173											
g	Good Christian men / Good Christians all, rejoice	85	107	154	181		191	238	250	183	145	404	240	
g	Jesus, Lord, Redeemer						199	240		283				
g	Jesus, stand among us in thy/your risen power			364	280	380	530	388	88	11			362	
g	Jesus, stand among us				279	381		565					362	381
g	O Lord, we long to see your face	412											514	
g	O sons and daughters, let us sing	74	125				205	244		277	154			
g	Spirit of God come dwell within me											611		
g	That Easter-tide with joy was bright	329iii									149iii			
g	The spirit lives to set us free				494	664							666	664
g	These things did Thomas: SS49													
g	This joyful Eastertide		121	165	509		213	248	258	271	161		680	
g	When Easter to the dark world came						200	251						
g	When fear and grief had barred the door								259					

For those who require an Old Testament reading on the Sundays in Eastertide, provision is made in the table on page 60 of *Calendar, Lectionary and Collects*

Year A
The Third Sunday of Easter

Acts **2**: 14a, 36-41; Psalm **116**: 1-4, 12-19; 1 Peter **1**: 17-23; Luke **24**: 13-35

		AMS	NEH	HTC	HON	MP	H&P	R&S	BPW	CH3	CP	SG	ONC	MPC
s	Alleluia, alleluia, give thanks to the risen Lord			S3	24	30	250	234	31		136	398	8	30
s	Alleluia, alleluia, hearts to heaven	80	103	151	25						137		9	
s	Christ is alive! Let Christians sing						190	260	244		140	32	96	
s	Christ Jesus lay in death's strong bands							235		268				
s	I know that my Redeemer lives, what joy			169	232	278	196	278	251			406	311	278
s	Jesus lives! Thy/Your terrors now	82	112	156	272	373	198	239	253	605	148	409	354	373
s	Now the green blade rises/riseth	501	115		355		204	243	257	278	153	414	475	
s	The day of resurrection	75	117	161	474		208	246		267	157	415	637	
s	The Lord is risen indeed	84	118		488					265	158		652	
al	Baptized in water			381								492		
a	We have a gospel to proclaim	431	486	519	532	728	465		585		612		716	728
p	I'll of salvation take the cup							722		565				
p	What shall I render to my God						703							
e	Come, ye faithful / Alleluia, raise the anthem	145	351	205	99	103			269		409	25	131	103
e	Led like a lamb to the slaughter				294	402		241	254			424	380	402
g	Abide with me	13	331	425	6	4	665	336	515	695	10	495	2	4
g	Amidst us out Beloved stands CHH410													
g	Among us and before us				28								30	
g	As Jesus walked the Emmaus road										526			
g	As we walked home: SS47													
g	Be known to us in breaking bread			(410)			597	441			282			
g	Come, risen Lord, and deign to be our guest	349	279		96		605			572	293		126	
g	Hail thee festival day [Easter]		109										257	
g	Light of the minds that know him		400	477				529			501	397		
g	O thou who this mysterious bread						621							
g	The time was early evening: SS33													
g	|I do not know tomorrow's way										531			

Year B
The Third Sunday of Easter

Acts **3**: 12-19; Psalm **4;** 1 John **3**: 1-7; Luke **24**: 36b-48

		AMS	NEH	HTC	HON	MP	H&P	R&S	BPW	CH3	CP	SG	ONC	MPC
s	Alleluia, alleluia, give thanks to the risen Lord			S3	24	30	250	234	31		136	398	8	30
s	Alleluia, alleluia, hearts to heaven	80	103	151	25						137		9	
s	Christ is alive! Let Christians sing						190	260	244		140	32	96	
s	Christ Jesus lay in death's strong bands							235		268				
s	Come, let us to the Lord our God						33	81		69	402			
s	He is Lord, he is Lord			S7	204	220	256	264	378				274	220
s	I know that my Redeemer lives, what joy			169	232	278	196	278	251			406	311	278
s	Jesus lives! Thy/Your terrors now	82	112	156	272	373	198	239	253	605	148	409	354	373
s	Now is eternal life	402	114		351		203	432			152		470	
s	Now the green blade rises/riseth	501	115		355		204	243	257	278	153	414	475	
s	The day of resurrection	75	117	161	474		208	246		267	157	415	637	
s	The Lord is risen indeed	84	118		488					265	158		652	
a	To the Name of our / that brings salvation	121	470	222	523		80	291		373	610	72	698	
a	Up from the earth										418			
p	O hear my cry, my righteous God PR4													
e	Behold the amazing gift of love						666	587		396	389			
e	Led like a lamb to the slaughter				294	402		241	254			424	380	402
e	My Lord, what love is this				345	476						194	362	476
g	Among us and before us				28								30	
g	Come, ye faithful / Alleluia, raise the anthem	145	351	205	99	103			269		409	25	131	103
g	How deep the Father's love for us										193		988	
g	How sure the scriptures are			249								227		
g	O sons and daughters, let us sing	74	125				205	244		277	154			

Year C
The Third Sunday of Easter

Acts **9**: 1-6 [7-20]; Psalm **30**; Revelation **5**: 11-14; John **21**: 1-19

		AMS	NEH	HTC	HON	MP	H&P	R&S	BPW	CH3	CP	SG	ONC	MPC
s	Alleluia, alleluia, give thanks to the risen Lord			S3	24	30	250	234	31		136	398	8	30
s	Alleluia, alleluia, hearts to heaven	80	103	151	25						137		9	
s	Christ Jesus lay in death's strong bands							235		268				
s	Christ the Lord is risen today / Love's redeeming work is done / All creation	83	113	150	324	76	193	232	246	275	150	412	433	76
s	Come, ye faithful / Alleluia, raise the anthem	145	351	205	99	103			269		409	25	131	103
s	Easter glory fills the sky								276					
s	Hark, my soul, it is the Lord / Christian, do you hear the Lord	244		472	197	209	521	348		676	264		457	209
s	He is Lord, he is Lord			S7	204	220	256	264	378				274	220
s	I know that my Redeemer lives, what joy			169	232	278	196	278	251			406	311	278
s	Now the green blade rises/riseth	501	115		355		204	243	257	278	153	414	475	
s	The day of resurrection	75	117	161	474		208	246		267	157	415	637	
s	The Lord is risen indeed	84	118		488					265	158		652	
ap	All shall be well			149					243			397		
ap	Where there once was only hurt										140			
a	God moves in a mysterious way	112	365		173	193	65	59	122	147	445		222	193
a	Lord of glory, in our darkness										603			
a	We sing the glorious conquest	313	155								237			
p	Through all the changing scenes of life	209	467	46	516	702	73	685	544		604	654	686	702
e	Awake and sing the song							379						
e	Behold the glories of the Lamb PR486													
e	Come, let us join our cheerful songs	144	349	206	94	93	810	382	6		401	33	120	93
e	From all that/who dwell/live beneath	98		580	146		489	723		362	431	82	192	
e	Hail thou/our once-despisèd/rejected Jesus			175	192	203	222		273		168		258	203
e	Heavenly hosts in ceaseless worship			570								40		
e	I believe in Jesus					224	264					333	301	264
e	Ye/You servants of God, your Master proclaim	149	476	520	565	784	278	293	76	372	627	75	784	756
g	Among us and before us				28							30		
g	James and Andrew, Peter and John				257							338		
g	Long before the world is waking LEH p107													
g	We shall see him in the morning										539			

Year A
The Fourth Sunday of Easter

Acts **2**: 42-47; Psalm **23**; 1 Peter **2**: 19-25; John **10**: 1-10

		AMS	NEH	HTC	HON	MP	H&P	R&S	BPW	CH3	CP	SG	ONC	MPC
s	What Adam's disobedience cost	524					430							
ael	Now let us from this table rise	403		419	352		619	463	451		315	475	472	
a	Body broken for our good FF p79													
a	Jesus, where'er thy people meet / Lord Jesus, when your people	162	390	371	282		549	476			492	16	367	
pg	Faithful Shepherd, feed me		282	29	117							498	156	
pg	The God of love my shepherd is	110	77		479		43	677			587		643	649
pg	The King of love my shepherd is	126	457	44	484	649	69	552	394	388	589	205	649	649
pg	The Lord's my shepherd, I'll not want	426	459	591/45	490	660	70	679	395	387	594	207	654	660
e	As we gather at your table										461			
e	In heavenly love abiding			458	246	331	678	590	555	681	478		323	331
e	Lord your voice in Eden's garden											426		
e	Shepherd divine, our wants relieve	228					558				566			
g	Jesus the Lord said/says, I am the Bread					384	137	199	202					384
g	Loving Shepherd of thy/your sheep	134		305	325					93	517		424	
g	Souls of men / Restless souls / There's a wideness	251	461	443	501	607, 683	230	353	573	218	598	188	662	607
g	Thou Shepherd of Israel and mine						750							

For seasonal hymns see those marked s in the lists for the First, Second and Third Sundays of Easter

Year B
The Fourth Sunday of Easter

Acts **4**: 5-12; Psalm **23**; 1 John **3**: 16-24; John **10**: 11-18

		AMS	NEH	HTC	HON	MP	H&P	R&S	BPW	CH3	CP	SG	ONC	MPC
s	What Adam's disobedience cost	524					430							
a	Christ is made the sure foundation/ Blessed city, heavenly Salem	283	205	559	73		485	559	474	10	207-8	572	97	73
a	Christ is our corner-stone	161		564	77						395		98	
a	Jesus! the name high over all			213		385	264					323		385
p	The God of love my shepherd is	110	77		479		43	677			587		643	649
p	The Lord my shepherd rules my life			45										
e	Almighty Father, who for us thy Son didst give	338					401	621			374			
e	I come with joy to meet my Lord	473		408	227		610	447	437		365	469	304	
g	Good Christian men / Good Christians all, rejoice	85	107	154	181		191	238	250	183	145	404	240	
g	How sweet the name of Jesus sounds	122	374	211	220	251	257	277	339	376	467	42	297	251
g	Priest and victim, Jesus dies										328			
g	Sing we the song of those who stand						821	666						

For seasonal hymns see those marked s in the lists for the First, Second and Third Sundays of Easter

Year C
The Fourth Sunday of Easter

Acts **9**: 36-43; Psalm **23**; Revelation **7**: 9-17; John **10**: 22-30

		AMS	NEH	HTC	HON	MP	H&P	R&S	BPW	CH3	CP	SG	ONC	MPC
s	Jesus, good above all other	378	387	96	269		732	528		111	487		350	
s	Now is eternal life	402	114		351		203	432			152		470	
s	What Adam's disobedience cost	524					430							
a	All you have given calls us, Lord, to praise you FF p.76													
a	God is the giver of all things that are FF p.88													
a	How privileged we are FF p.88													
p	Faithful Shepherd, feed me		282	29	117							498	156	
p	The God of love my shepherd is	110	77		479		43	677			587		643	649
p	The King of love my shepherd is	126	457	44	484	649	69	552	394	388	589	205	649	649
p	The Lord's my shepherd, I'll not want	426	459	591/45	490	660	70	679	395	387	594	207	654	660
e	How bright these glorious spirits shine	306	227	572						533	221			
e	There is a louder shout to come										444			
e	Who are these, like stars appearing	323	231		555						229		746	
g	Christ who knows all his sheep	347						470		672				
g	Loving Shepherd of thy/your sheep	134		305	325					93	517		424	
g	Thine/Yours for ever	234	463	556	504						599		673	992

For seasonal hymns see those marked s in the lists for the First, Second and Third Sundays of Easter

Year A
The Fifth Sunday of Easter

Acts **7**: 55-60; Psalm **31**: 1-5, 15-16; 1 Peter **2**: 2-10; John **14**: 1-14

		AMS	NEH	HTC	HON	MP	H&P	R&S	BPW	CH3	CP	SG	ONC	MPC
s	A brighter dawn is breaking		102		1						135		3	
s	Creatures, once in safety held: SS5													
a	Forgive our sins as we forgive	362	66	111	141		134	84	83		428	145	180	
a	Head of thy Church triumphant						818							
a	Stephen, first of Christian martyrs		201											
p	Put thou thy trust / Commit thou all thy griefs	223			429		672	550		669	562		576	
el	Forth in the peace of Christ	458	361	542	142			602	607	589	429	594	187	
e	Christ is made the sure foundation / Blessed city, heavenly Salem	283/ 332	204-5	559	76	73	485	559	474	10	208	572	97	73
e	Christ is our corner-stone	161		564	77						395		98	
e	Church of God elect and glorious			504					406			592		
e	See where our great High Priest						622							
e	The Church's one foundation	170	484	501	473	640	515	566	393	420	585	581	636	640
e	We are not our own							484					510	
e	Ye that know the Lord is gracious	175	477								628			
g	Christ the way of life possess me				78						397			78
g	Come, my way, my truth, my life						254	352			405		123	
g	How sweet the name of Jesus sounds	122	374	211	220	251	257	277	339	376	467	42	297	251
g	Let us rejoice											389		
g	Thou art / You are the way	128	464	113	512	695	234	554		121	600		682	695

For seasonal hymns see those marked s in the lists for the First, Second and Third Sundays of Easter

Year B
The Fifth Sunday of Easter

Acts **8**: 26-40; Psalm **22**: 25-31; 1 John **4**: 7-21; John **15**: 1-8

		AMS	NEH	HTC	HON	MP	H&P	R&S	BPW	CH3	CP	SG	ONC	MPC
sg	Bless and keep us God											73		
s	Come, let us to the Lord our God						33	81		69	402			
s	Creatures, once in safety held: SS5													
s	Lord, teach us how to pray aright	227	406	367	316		551				98		418	
s	Where true love is present											743		
al	Baptized in water			381								492		
a	Glory to God, the source of all our mission										595			
a	O love, how deep, how broad, how high	119	425		383		229	283	207	223	118		516	
pa	Ye/you servants of God your master proclaim	149	476	520	565	784	278	293	76	372	627	75	756	784
pe	My lips shall praise you										130		896	
p	Christ the Lord is risen today / Love's redeeming work is done / All creation	83	113	150	324	76	193	232	246	275	150	412	433	76
e	Beloved let us love			468			610						64	
e	Come wounded healer											130		
e	Love divine, all loves excelling	131	408	217	321	449	267	663	559	437	516	179	428	449
e	Love is his word, love is his way			481	322				445	180	429			
e	Now the green blade rises/riseth	501	115		355		204	243	257	278	153	414	475	
e	Thank you for the cross					632						198		632
e	Where true love is found with charity											742		
g	Bread of heaven, on thee we feed	271	276	398	67			442			284	464	82	
g	Come dearest Lord, descend and dwell							381	284	673	291		113	
g	Come, we that love the Lord						487	384	525					
g	Let love be real											383		

For seasonal hymns see those marked s in the lists for the First, Second and Third Sundays of Easter

Year C
The Fifth Sunday of Easter

Acts **11**: 1-18; Psalm **148**; Revelation **21**: 1-6; John **13**: 31-35

		AMS	NEH	HTC	HON	MP	H&P	R&S	BPW	CH3	CP	SG	ONC	MPC
s	Come, let us to the Lord our God						33	81		69	402			
s	Lord, teach us how to pray aright	227	406	367	316		551				98		418	
a	All hail the power of Jesus' name	140	332	587/ 203	13	13	252		29	382	163	24	16	13
a	In Christ there is no east or west	376	480	322	244	329	758	647	482	425	477	575	319	329
a	Jesus shall reign where'er the sun	143	388	516	277	379	239	269	313	413	490	45	359	379
a	When Christ was lifted/Dear Christ uplifted	525	335				655				453	142		
pa	By every nation race and tongue			579								30		
p	Praise the Lord! ye/you/let heaven(s), adore him	195	437	583	425		15	116	67	37	556	92	570	920
p	The Lord of heaven confess									135				
e	A city radiant as a bride									364				
e	Come, we that love the Lord						487	384	525					
e	Creating God, we bring our song of praise											134		
e	Lord God, by whom all change is wrought						39	68						
e	Now from the heavens descending									341	439			
e	O holy City, seen of/by John	409						628		509				
e	O what their joy / What of those sabbaths	186	432					659		535	225		550	
e	Songs of praise the angels sang	196	451	350			512	667		38	574		608	
e	There's a place where the streets shine										457		1011	
g	Christ from whom all blessings flow			491			764	561						
g	Come down, O Love Divine	156	137	231	90	89	281	294	283	115	170	663	114	89
g	Let love be real											383		
g	The great love of God						45	105		415				
g	This is my one command											675		

For seasonal hymns see those marked s in the lists for the First, Second and Third Sundays of Easter

Year A
The Sixth Sunday of Easter

Acts **17**: 22-31; Psalm **66**: 8-20; 1 Peter **3**: 13-22; John **14**: 15-21

		AMS	NEH	HTC	HON	MP	H&P	R&S	BPW	CH3	CP	SG	ONC	MPC
s	Creatures, once in safety held: SS5													
s	God moves in a mysterious way	112	365		173	193	65	59	122	147	445		222	193
o	Spirit of God within me			243			294	304	296			196	677	612	
a	Lord you need no house			546					349					
a	Lord of beauty, thine the splendour	106	265		314					120	258		415	
a	O Lord of heaven and earth and sea	287	422	287			337		387	145		540	306	
p	Jesus, my Truth, my Way						734							
p	O God of Bethel / O God of Jacob	216	416	35	364		442	71	599	72	536	241	491	907
p	Shout with joy to God, all nations PR66													
p	Sing to the Lord new songs of worship											603		
e	Come ye faithful, raise the strain / Spring has come	76	106	160	100		194	236	248	269	142			
e	God of wilderness and jungle: SS3													
e	Lord, thy Church on earth is seeking						774	579				604		
e	Lord, you give the great commission						580							
g	Beloved, let us love			468				610					64	
g	Come down, O Love Divine	156	137	231	90	89	281	294	283	115	170	663	114	89
g	Come light of the world										21			
g	Come, thou everlasting Spirit						298	315						
g	Gift of Christ from God our Father										447			
g	Our blest/great Redeemer	151		241	410	548	312	330		336	193	448	543	548
g	The spirit lives to set us free				494	664							666	664

See also hymns for Rogationtide, page 232

Year B
The Sixth Sunday of Easter

Acts **10**: 44-48; Psalm **98**; 1 John **5**: 1-6; John **15**: 9-17

		AMS	NEH	HTC	HON	MP	H&P	R&S	BPW	CH3	CP	SG	ONC	MPC
s	Bless and keep us God											73		
s	God makes his rain to fall: SS96													
s	Spread, O spread, thou mighty word		482											
s	Thy ceaseless, unexhausted love						48	106					688	
al	Baptized in water			381								492		
a	Holy Spirit, come, confirm us	471	140		214		288	298	289		183		288	
p	New songs of celebration render	498		343	350		491	709			527	87	468	
p	Sing to the Lord new songs of worship											603		
e	Rock of ages	135	445	593	437	582	273	365	545	83	565	150	584	582
e	Spirit of faith, come down						325							
g	Be still and know that I am God										242			
g	Beloved, let us love			468				610					64	
g	Come down, O Love Divine	156	137	231	90	89	281	294	283	115	170	663	114	89
g	Gift of Christ from God our Father										447			
g	Here is love vast as the ocean										174		987	
g	Lord/Great God, your love has called us here	489		480			500	339	442		133		246	
g	The Son of God proclaim	427		415			627	458	455		328			

See also hymns for Rogationtide, page 232

Year C
The Sixth Sunday of Easter

Acts **16**: 9-15; Psalm **67**; Revelation **21**:10, 22—**22**:5;
John **14**: 23-29 or John **5**: 1-9

		AMS	NEH	HTC	HON	MP	H&P	R&S	BPW	CH3	CP	SG	ONC	MPC
s	Breathe on me, Breath of God	157	342	226	69	67	280	295	282	103	174	554	84	67
s	God as Fire, send your Spirit: SS52													
a	Glory to God, the source of all our mission										595			
a	The Spirit led by day LUTR120													
p	God of mercy, God of grace	179	366	293	175			575	48	497	449		227	
e	A city radiant as a bride									364				
e	City of God, how broad and far	173	346		85		809			422	400		106	
e	Jesus calls us: o'er/in the tumult	312	200	104	266	359	141	355		211	233	668	347	359
e	Light's abode, celestial Salem	185	401		305						502		398	
e	Now from the heavens descending									341	439			
e	O holy City, seen of/by John	409						628		509				
e	The stream of life is flowing here: SS13													
e	There is a redeemer				500	673						396	658	673
g2	Have faith in God, my heart	372		431	201		675	499	336		458		268	
g2	O for a thousand tongues to sing	125	415	219	362	496	744	285	59	371	534	55	485	495
gl	Bless and keep us, God											73		
gl	If we only seek peace											307		
g	A charge to keep I have						785							
g	Come, light of the world										21			
g	Dear Lord and Father of mankind	115	353	356	106	111	673	492	84	76	411	497	144	111
g	Gift of Christ from God our Father										447			
g	Grant us your peace: SS14													
g	Peace, perfect peace, in this dark world of sin			467	413	555			561		553		554	555
g	Peace, perfect peace, is the gift			414				594	112				555	
g	Put peace into each other's hands							635	637			479	575	

See also hymns for Rogationtide, page 232

Years A, B, C
Ascension Day

Acts **1**: 1-11; Daniel **7**: 9-14; Psalm **47** or **93**;
Ephesians **1**: 15-23 or Acts **1**: 1-11; Luke **24**: 44-53

		AMS	NEH	HTC	HON	MP	H&P	R&S	BPW	CH3	CP	SG	ONC	MPC
s	All hail the power of Jesus' name	140	332	587/ 203	13	13	252		29	382	163	24	16	13
s	Alleluia! sing to Jesus	262	271	170	26	207	592		270		278	458	12	207
s	Be still for the presence / Spirit of the Lord				53	50			5		383	7	67	
s	Christ triumphant, ever reigning			173	81	77			306		398	319	104	74
s	Come, let us join our cheerful songs	144	349	206	94	93	810	382	6		401	33	120	93
s	Crown him with many crowns	147	352	174	103	109	255	262	37	298	166	321	137	109
s	Eternal Monarch, King most high		128											
s	God is gone up on high							253						
s	Hail the day that sees him rise	87	130	176	191	202	197	252	272		167	434	255	202
s	Head of the Church, our risen Lord						547	562						
s	Heaven's throne ascending												840	
s	Jesus invites his saints						612	434	438					
s	Join all the glorious names			214		392	78	280	557	304	493	46		392
s	Lord of the worlds above	165									511			
s	Rejoice! the Lord is King	139	443	180	432	575	243	657	317	296	563	440	580	575
s	See the Conqueror mounts in triumph	88	132	181	441								591	
s	The golden gates are lifted up							256						
s	The head that once was crowned with thorns	141	134	182	480	647	209	257	274	286	172	442		644
s	The Lord ascendeth up on high		135				210			287	173			
s	The Lord Jehovah reigns						59							
s	We have a gospel to proclaim	431	486	519	532	728	465		585		612		716	728
s	We turn to Christ alone												956	
p	Clap your hands, all you nations										79			
p	The Lord is King! Lift up your voice	107		183	485	656	58	76	322	36	592	98	650	656
ao	Immortal, invisible, God only wise	199	377	21	242	327	9	677	383	32	474	44	314	327
ap	Ascended Christ, who gained										429			
e	Come see the Lord in his breathtaking splendour										433			
g	God of wilderness and jungle: SS3													
g	Handed over to be orphaned: SS50													

Year A
The Seventh Sunday of Easter (Sunday after Ascension Day)

Acts **1**: 6-14; Psalm **68**: 1-10, 32-35; 1 Peter **4**: 12-14, **5**: 6-11; John **17**: 1-11

		AMS	NEH	HTC	HON	MP	H&P	R&S	BPW	CH3	CP	SG	ONC	MPC
s	Heaven's throne ascending												840	
s	Who is he in yonder stall					767				221	77			767
ls	All hail the power of Jesus' name	140	332	587/203	13	13	252		29	382	163	24	16	13
ls	Alleluia! sing to Jesus	262	271	170	26	207	592		270		278	458	12	207
ls	Christ triumphant, ever reigning			173	81	77			306		398	319	104	74
ls	Come, let us join our cheerful songs	144	349	206	94	93	810	382	6		401	33	120	93
ls	Crown him with many crowns	147	352	174	103	109	255	262	37	298	166	321	137	109
ls	Eternal Monarch, King most high		128											
ls	Jesus shall reign where'er the sun	143	388	516	277	379	239	269	313	413	490	45	359	379
ls	Lord, enthroned in heavenly splendour	263	296	416	309	431	616			583	311	52	408	
ls	Rejoice! the Lord is King	139	443	180	432	575	243	657	317	296	563	440	580	575
ls	The golden gates are lifted up							256						
ls	The Lord ascendeth up on high		135				210			287	173			
o	Breathe on me, Breath of God	157	342	226	69	67	280	295	282	103	174	554	84	67
o	O for a heart to praise my God	230	74	483	361	495	536	514	538	85	533	149	484	495
a	Hail the day that sees him rise	87	130	176	191	202	197	252	272		167	434	255	202
a	O Spirit of the living God			513			322	577	579	496	190	605		
a	Rejoice, the Lord of life ascends										441			
p	Let God arise! His enemies, be gone PR68													
p	See the Conqueror mounts in triumph	88	132	181	441								591	
e	The head that once was crowned with thorns	141	134	182	480	647	209	257	274	286	172	442		644
g	Christ is the King! O friends rejoice	345	345	492				571	475	474	165	31		
g	Let love be real											383		
g	Lord Christ, the Father's mighty Son	386					568							
g	O thou who at thy eucharist / O Christ at your first eucharist	265	302	420	391		779			492	318		540	476

115

Year B
The Seventh Sunday of Easter (Sunday after Ascension Day)

Acts **1**: 15-17, 21-26; Psalm **1**; 1 John **5**: 9-13; John **17**: 6-19

		AMS	NEH	HTC	HON	MP	H&P	R&S	BPW	CH3	CP	SG	ONC	MPC
sl	All hail the power of Jesus' name	140	332	587/ 203	13	13	252		29	382	163	24	16	13
s	Heaven's throne ascending												840	
ls	Alleluia! sing to Jesus	262	271	170	26	207	592		270		278	458	12	207
ls	Christ triumphant, ever reigning			173	81	77			306		398	319	104	74
ls	Come, let us join our cheerful songs	144	349	206	94	93	810	382	6		401	33	120	93
ls	Crown him with many crowns	147	352	174	103	109	255	262	37	298	166	321	137	109
ls	Hail the day that sees him rise	87	130	176	191	202	197	252	272		167	434	255	202
ls	Lord, enthroned in heavenly splendour	263	296	416	309	431	616			583	311	52	408	
ls	Rejoice! the Lord is King	139	443	180	432	575	243	657	317	296	563	440	580	575
ls	See the Conqueror mounts in triumph	88	132	181	441								591	
ls	The golden gates are lifted up							256						
ls	The head that once was crowned with thorns	141	134	182	480	647	209	257	274	286	172	442		644
ls	The Lord ascendeth up on high		135				210			287	173			
o	'How shall they hear?', who have not heard					250						598		250
o	Breathe on me, Breath of God	157	342	226	69	67	280	295	282	103	174	554	84	67
o	O for a heart to praise my God	230	74	483	361	495	536	514	538	85	533	149	484	495
a	The eternal gifts of Christ the King	297	213		476					540			639	
a	The Saviour, when to heaven he rose						211							
a	To know God's mind and do his will LUTR112													
p	Happy are they who walk in God's wise way							669						
g	Let love be real											383		
g	Lord Christ, the Father's mighty Son	386						568						
g	Now is eternal life	402	114		351		203	432			152		470	
g	O thou who at thy eucharist / O Christ at your first eucharist	265	302	420	391		779			492	318		540	476

Year C
The Seventh Sunday of Easter (Sunday after Ascension Day)

Acts 16: 16-34; Psalm 97; Revelation 22: 12-14, 16-17, 20-21; John 17: 20-26

		AMS	NEH	HTC	HON	MP	H&P	R&S	BPW	CH3	CP	SG	ONC	MPC
s	All hail the power of Jesus' name	140	332	587/203	13	13	252		29	382	163	24	16	13
s	Alleluia! sing to Jesus	262	271	170	26	207	592		270		278	458	12	207
s	At the name of Jesus	148	338	172	46	41	74	261	370	300	380	317	54	
s	Christ is the King! O friends rejoice	345	345	492				571	475	474	165	31		
s	Christ triumphant, ever reigning			173	81	77			306		398	319	104	74
s	Eternal Monarch, King most high		128											
s	Hail the day that sees him rise	87	130	176	191	202	197	252	272		167	434	255	202
s	Heaven's throne ascending											840		
s	Lord, enthroned in heavenly splendour	263	296	416	309	431	616			583	311	52	408	
s	See the Conqueror mounts in triumph	88	132	181	441								591	
s	Songs of praise the angels sang	196	451	350			512	667		38	574		608	
s	The golden gates are lifted up							256						
s	The head that once was crowned with thorns	141	134	182	480	647	209	257	274	286	172	442		644
s	The Lord ascendeth up on high		135				210			287	173			
o	Breathe on me, Breath of God	157	342	226	69	67	280	295	282	103	174	554	84	67
o	O for a heart to praise my God	230	74	483	361	495	536	514	538	85	533	149	484	495
p	The Lord is king! With joyful sound PR97													
e	Christ is the world's true light	346	494	323	78		456	601	618	505	396	432	100	
e	Come with the sound of trumpet										15			
e	Come, let us join our cheerful songs	144	349	206	94	93	810	382	6		401	33	120	93
e	Crown him with many crowns	147	352	174	103	109	255	262	37	298	166	321	137	109
e	God is our strength from days of old				171								220	
e	Hark what a sound, and too divine for hearing						236	660		314	28			
e	Heaven is open wide											271		
e	Rejoice! the Lord is King	139	443	180	432	575	243	657	317	296	563	440	580	575
e	Through the darkness of the ages										538			
e	Thy/Your kingdom come, O God	177	499	334	519		783	638	644	322	607	269	691	949
g	Exult, archangels bright										402			
g	Will you come and follow me				560			558	363		622	634	752	

Year A
Day of Pentecost (Whit Sunday)

Acts **2**: 1-21 or Numbers **11**: 24-30; Psalm **104**: 24-34, 35b; 1 Corinthians **12**: 3b-13 or Acts **2**: 1-21; John **20**: 19-23 or John **7**: 37-39

		AMS	NEH	HTC	HON	MP	H&P	R&S	BPW	CH3	CP	SG	ONC	MPC
ls	Away with our fears, our troubles and tears			224			296	323	279					
ls	Come down, O Love Divine	156	137	231	90	89	281	294	283	115	170	663	114	89
ls	Come, gracious Spirit, heavenly dove	153	347							116	176		116	
ls	Come, Holy Spirit, heavenly dove						297	299						
ls	Creator Spirit, by whose aid						285		286	118				
ls	Sing to him in whom creation		142				324							
ls	Spirit of God within me			243			294	304	296		196	677	612	
ls	Spirit of God, unseen as the wind								295			233		
ls	Spirit of the living God, fall afresh on me			S23	454	612	295	308	298				615	613
ls	There's a spirit in the air	515		245			326	329	300			69	661	
o	Come, Holy Ghost, our hearts inspire (Wesley)	448	348		91		469	312	97	122	177		117	
p	O worship the King all glorious above	101	433	24	393	528	28	47	63	35	546	90	551	528
æ	Born in song						486					28		
al	Christians, lift up your hearts … Praise for the Spirit	444		229							399		95	
a	A mighty wind invades the world									365				
a	God as Fire, send your Spirit: SS52													
a	O joy, because the circling year / Rejoice! the year upon its way		136		433					329/ 330			581	
a	On the day of Pentecost	504									192			
a	Our Lord, his passion ended	91					323	328			194			
a	Rushing wind that fills: SS51													
a	Spirit of mercy, truth and love	89	143		453					338	197		613	
a	The Lord is King! He set the stars in space										67			
e	Holy Spirit, ever dwelling/living		141				303	324	290	334				
e	Let every Christian pray	478		230			305					576		
e	Lord God, the Holy Ghost						306			332				
e	Name of all majesty			218		481					525	324	465	481
e	O Holy Ghost, thy people bless / O Holy Spirit, come to bless	155		238	370						187		500	
e	Skills and abilities										279			
e	What shall our greeting be						806					584		

continued on next page

		AMS	NEH	HTC	HON	MP	H&P	R&S	BPW	CH3	CP	SG	ONC	MPC
g	Breathe on me breath of God	157	342	226	69	67	280	295	282	103	174	554	84	67
g	Come, Holy Ghost, our souls inspire	93	138	589	92	90	283	751		342	178	555	118	90
g	Come, Holy Spirit, come inflame				93						179		119	
g	Come, thou/most Holy Spirit, come / Come, thou Holy Paraclete	92	139	227	97		284	297		105		180	127	
g	Jesus, the gift divine I know						318							
g	Like the murmur of the dove's song	185	17											
g	O King enthroned on high	158	421		373		311	296			180		504	
g	Our blest /great Redeemer	151		241	410	548	312	330		336	193	448	543	548

Year B
Day of Pentecost (Whit Sunday)

Acts **2**: 1-21 or Ezekiel **37**: 1-14; Psalm **104**: 24-34, 35b; Romans **8**: 22-27 or Acts **2**: 1-21; John **15**: 26-27, **16**: 4b-15

		AMS	NEH	HTC	HON	MP	H&P	R&S	BPW	CH3	CP	SG	ONC	MPC
ls	Away with our fears, our troubles and tears			224			296	323	279					
ls	Come down, O Love Divine	156	137	231	90	89	281	294	283	115	170	663	114	89
ls	Sing to him in whom creation		142				324							
ls	There's a spirit in the air	515		245			326	329	300			69	661	
o	Breathe on me, Breath of God	157	342	226	69	67	280	295	282	103	174	554	84	67
o	O Breath of life, come sweeping / O Breath of love, come breathe			237	356	488	777	302	293	339			476	488
o	O Spirit of the living God			513			322	577	579	496	190	605		
p	O worship the King all glorious above	101	433	24	393	528	28	47	63	35	546	90	551	528
ag	Wind of God, dynamic Spirit										681			
al	Christians, lift up your hearts … Praise for the Spirit	444		229							399		95	
a	A mighty wind invades the world									365				
a	Creator Spirit, by whose aid						285		286	118				
a	God as Fire, send your Spirit: SS52													
a	Holy Spirit, ever dwelling/living		141				303	324	290	334				
a	Let every Christian pray	478		230			305					576		
a	O Holy Ghost, thy people bless / O Holy Spirit, come to bless	155		238	370						187		500	
a	On the day of Pentecost	504									192			
a	Our Lord, his passion ended	91					323	328			194			
a	Rushing wind that fills: SS51													
a	Spirit of God, unseen as the wind								295			233		

continued on next page

		AMS	NEH	HTC	HON	MP	H&P	R&S	BPW	CH3	CP	SG	ONC	MPC
a	Spirit of mercy, truth and love	89	143		453					338	197		613	
a	Upon the day of Pentecost						328							
e	Born by the Holy Spirit's breath			225		61	279		281			446		
e	Holy Spirit, will you be										239			
e	I will pour out my Spirit						292							
g	Come, gracious Spirit, heavenly dove	153	347							116	176		116	
g	Come, Holy Ghost, our souls inspire	93	138	589	92	90	283	751		342	178	555	118	90
g	Come, Holy Spirit, come inflame				93						179		119	
g	Come, Holy Spirit, heavenly dove						297	299						
g	Come, thou/most Holy Spirit, come / Come, thou Holy Paraclete	92	139	227	97		284	297		105		180	127	
g	Gift of Christ from God our Father										447			
g	Hidden Christ, alive for ever										530			
g	Like the murmur of the dove's song	185	17											
g	Spirit of God within me			243			294	304	296		196	677	612	
g	Spirit of the living God, fall afresh on me			S23	454	612	295	308	298				615	613

Year C
Day of Pentecost (Whit Sunday)

Acts **2**: 1-21 or Genesis **11**: 1-9; Psalm **104**: 24-34, 35b; Romans **8**: 14-17 or Acts **2**: 1-21; John **14**: 8-17 [25-27]

		AMS	NEH	HTC	HON	MP	H&P	R&S	BPW	CH3	CP	SG	ONC	MPC
s	Away with our fears, our troubles and tears			224			296	323	279					
s	Come down, O Love Divine	156	137	231	90	89	281	294	283	115	170	663	114	89
s	O Holy Ghost, thy people bless / O Holy Spirit, come to bless	155		238	370						187		500	
s	O King enthroned on high	158	421		373		311	296			180		504	
s	Sing to him in whom creation		142				324							
s	There's a spirit in the air	515		245			326	329	300			69	661	
p	Creator of the earth and skies	351		320			419	82			410	296		
al	Christians, lift up your hearts ... Praise for the Spirit	444		229							399		95	
a	A mighty wind invades the world								365					
a	Come, Holy Ghost, our souls inspire	93	138	589	92	90	283	751		342	178	555	118	90
a	Creator Spirit, by whose aid						285		286	118				
a	God as Fire, send your Spirit: SS52													

continued on next page

		AMS	NEH	HTC	HON	MP	H&P	R&S	BPW	CH3	CP	SG	ONC	MPC
a	I will pour out my Spirit						292							
a	Let every Christian pray	478		230			305					576		
a	On the day of Pentecost	504									192			
a	Our Lord, his passion ended	91					323	328			194			
a	Rushing wind that fills: SS51													
a	Spirit of God, unseen as the wind								295			233		
a	Spirit of holiness, wisdom and faithfulness			246		611					576	449		611
a	Spirit of mercy, truth and love	89	143		453					338	197		613	
a	The Spirit came as promised			244					297			450		
a	Upon the day of Pentecost						328							
a	Wind who makes all winds that blow BL29													
e	Born by the Holy Spirit's breath			225		61	279		281			446		
e	Eternal Spirit of the living Christ							300						
e	Holy Spirit, ever dwelling/living		141				303	324	290	334				
g	Come, gracious Spirit, heavenly dove	153	347							116	176		116	
g	Come, Holy Spirit, come inflame				93						179		119	
g	Come, Holy Spirit, heavenly dove						297	299						
g	Come, light of the world										21			
g	Come, thou/most Holy Spirit, come / Come, thou Holy Paraclete	92	139	227	97		284	297		105		180	127	
g	Gift of Christ from God our Father										447			
g	Holy Spirit, come, confirm us	471	140		214		288	298	289		183		288	
g	Like the murmur of the dove's song	185	17											
g	Spirit of God within me			243			294	304	296		196	677	612	
g	Spirit of the living God, fall afresh on me			S23	454	612	295	308	298				615	613

Years A, B, C
Ordinary Time: Trinity Sunday

Year A: Isaiah **40**: 12-17, 27-31; Psalm **8**; 2 Corinthians **13**: 11-13;
Matthew **28**: 16-20
Year B: Isaiah **6**: 1-8; Psalm **29**; Romans **8**: 12-17; John **3**: 1-17
Year C: Proverbs **8**: 1-4, 22-31; Psalm **8**; Romans **5**: 1-5; John **16**: 12-15

		AMS	NEH	HTC	HON	MP	H&P	R&S	BPW	CH3	CP	SG	ONC	MPC
s	Affirm anew the three-fold name									200				
s	All hail, adored Trinity		145											
s	Bright the vision / Round the Lord	96	343	578	70		445	665	71	353	392	29	86	
s	Eternal God, your love's tremendous glory							33						822
s	Father all-powerful, thine is the kingdom	355												
s	Father eternal, Lord of the ages		356	1										
s	Father in heaven, grant to your children			2			3		38			200		
s	Father in whom we live						4				417			
s	Father most holy, merciful and loving/tender	94	144	3	123		5			31	419			
s	Father of heaven, whose love profound	97	358	359	124		519			77	421	144		827
s	Father, we adore you			S5	125	139		29	39				166	139
s	Glory be to God the Father									354				
s	God lies beyond us										301			
s	God the Father, throned in splendour								50					
s	Holy Trinity of Love									463				
s	Holy, holy, holy, Lord God almighty	95	146	7/594	212	237	594	34	51	352	202	290	286	237
s	How shall I sing that majesty	472	373				8	661			466		296	
s	I bind unto myself / myself to God today / Christ be with me		159	5	225		695	36		402	203		302	
s	May the grace of Christ our Saviour	181		370	333		762		110	634	520	579	446	
s	Meekness and majesty			335	465			58				395	448	465
s	Most ancient of all mysteries		147											
s	O God, by whose almighty plan	406					396	651			204			

continued on next page

		AMS	NEH	HTC	HON	MP	H&P	R&S	BPW	CH3	CP	SG	ONC	MPC
s	O Trinity, O Trinity			6								291		
s	Praise the Father, God of justice			8										
s	Rejoice in God, let trumpets sound										60			
s	Restore in us, O God									564				
s	This day God gives me	516					79				205			
s	Thou/God whose almighty word	180	466	506	514	699	29	38	591	494	267	684	597	699
s	Three in One and One in Three			12	515								685	
s	We believe in God almighty, Maker			10								285		
s	We give immortal praise	520		11			18	37	72		206	331	713	
l	Sing of a God in majestic divinity										292			
l	Today I awake										293			
o	'How shall they hear?', who have not heard				250							598		250
o	Do you not know? This is our God										297			
o	Inspired by love and anger				252								325	
o	We will run and not grow weary										552			
ps	How excellent in all the earth									138				
p	Holy, holy, holy One AFJ2													
p	The God of heaven thunders										315			
e	Born by the Holy Spirit's breath			225		61	279		281			446		
e	Let us rejoice: God's gift to us is peace											389		
e	Spirit of truth, essential God						480	313						
gl	Go forth for God		321								438			
gs	Sing glory to God the Father										1	599		
g	All authority is yours										590			
g	Christ is alive! Let Christians sing						190	260	244		140	32	96	
g	Come, Father, Son and Holy Ghost						580							
g	God who created light										288			
g	Holy Spirit, Truth divine			235			289	301	292	106	184		289	
g	I will pour out my Spirit						292							
g	Spirit of God within me			243			294	304	296		196	677	612	

It is intended that churches should follow either the Continuous or Related scheme of readings in any one year. Hymns selected for the Continuous scheme are marked o1 or p1, and those for the Related scheme are marked o2 or p2.

Year A
Proper 4

Continuous: Genesis **6**: 9-22, **7**: 24, **8**: 14-19 and Psalm **46**
or *Related:* Deuteronomy **11**: 18-21, 26-28 and Psalm **31**: 1-5, 19-24;
Romans **1**: 16-17, **3**: 22b-28 [29-31]; Matthew **7**: 21-29

		AMS	NEH	HTC	HON	MP	H&P	R&S	BPW	CH3	CP	SG	ONC	MPC
o1	Creatures, once in safety held: SS5													
o1	Lord of our life, and God of our salvation		404	529	315	441				491			417	441
o1	Now in the name of him who sent						590	425						
o1	What Adam's disobedience cost	524					430							
o	Born of Adam, torn from Eden PR685													
p1	A safe stronghold/fortress/refuge	114		523		2	661	585	375	406/7				2
p1	Be still and know that I am God			52	48			347	280			18& 242	66	
p1	God is our refuge and our strength							691			24			
p1	God is our strength and refuge			527		188			308		443	650	219	188
p2g	Rock of ages	135	445	593	437	582	273	365	545	83	565	150	584	582
p2	Open, Lord, my inward ear						540							
e	And can it be			588	30	33	216	136	328	409	376	168	32	
e	Come, ye faithful / Alleluia, raise the anthem	145	351	205	99	103			269		409	25	131	103
e	Father, whose everlasting love						520				107			
e	Great is the gospel of our glorious God CHH120													
e	I'm not ashamed to own/name my Lord			448	240	323	677	428	343	591		532	316	323
e	Jesus, our Lord and King							429						
g	Christ be my leader by night as by day						709							
g	City of God, how broad and far	173	346		85		809			422	400		106	
g	Come, let us to the Lord our God						33	81		69	402			
g	How firm a foundation			430	216	243		589	380				292	243
g	My hope is built on nothing less			462		473				411		537		473
g	The right hand of God						408	91						

Year B
Proper 4

Continuous: 1 Samuel **3**: 1-10 [11-20] and Psalm **139**: 1-6, 13-18
or *Related:* Deuteronomy **5**: 12-15 and Psalm **81**: 1-10; 2 Corinthians **4**: 5-12;
Mark **2**:23 — **3**:6

		AMS	NEH	HTC	HON	MP	H&P	R&S	BPW	CH3	CP	SG	ONC	MPC
o1 p1	Lord, speak to me, that I may speak			510		444	553	613	611	485	512			444
o1	Hushed was the evening hymn					253	523	526		123				253
o1	Master, speak! Thy servant heareth / Your servant's listening					459	535		536					459
o1	Speak, Lord, in the stillness			253		608			105					608
o1	When heaven's voice was still: SS71													
o2	Can we/man by searching find out God	438					76	80			201	496		
o2	Come, divine interpreter						468							
o2	Father of all, whose laws have stood			539					335			664		
o2	Help us, O Lord, to learn	373	370	493			474				460	226		
o2	Lord, be thy word my rule / Lord, make your word	232		250										
o2	Powerful in making us wise			252			479					228		
p1	In all my vast concerns with thee						72							
p1	Lord, you have searched and known my ways						71	70	564					
p1	There is no moment of my life						428		133			185		
p1	Thou art / You are before me, Lord						543	731		68				
p1	You know me, you formed me										696			
p2	I sing the almighty power of God					293	334	43						293
p	Lord all-knowing, you have found me										683			
p	My Lord, you called my name										203			
p	O God you search me										514			
p	To God our strength come, sing aloud PR81													
el	Christ, whose glory fills the skies	4	234	266	82	79	457	380		114	2	170	105	79
e	Lord, the light of your love [Shine, Jesus, shine]				317	445			347		513	614	419	445
e	O God, enthroned in majesty											490		
e	O splendour of God's glory						461	537			7			
e	Out of darkness let light shine			447										
g	Come, let us with our Lord arise	449	254	375			575	383			142			
g	First of the week and finest day			376								2		
g	Jesus calls us here to meet him								12				346	
g	Sweet is the work, my God			377		620	514				580	97		620
g	The first day of the week	424					576							
g	This is the day the Lord hath/has made	22	257	379			577	376			9	70	677	

Year C
Proper 4

Continuous: 1 Kings **18**: 20-21 [22-29] 30-39 and Psalm **96**
or *Related:* 1 Kings **8**: 22-23, 41-43 and Psalm **96**: 1-9; Galatians **1**: 1-12;
Luke **7**: 1-10

		AMS	NEH	HTC	HON	MP	H&P	R&S	BPW	CH3	CP	SG	ONC	MPC
s	Lord we know that we have failed you													
o1	The God of Abraham praise	331	148	9	478	645	452	121	131	358	586	66	642	645
o2	God of light and life's creation			561										
o2	O God, in whom we live and move							409						
o2	Saviour, and can it be						541						587	
o2	The heaven of heavens / Where the appointed		312				78							
p1& 2	Sing, sing, sing to the Lord WAM74													
p	In beauty of his holiness									311				
p	Let all the world in every corner sing	202	394	342	296	404	10	114	54	361	497	47	382	404
p	O sing a new song to the Lord									22				
p	O worship / Worship the Lord in the beauty of holiness	49	52	344	394	529	505	187	22	40	89	204	552	529
e	Come, Holy Ghost, our hearts inspire (Wesley)	448	348		91		469	312	97	122	177		117	
g	At even[ing], ere/when the sun was/had set	9	243	315	43	43	142	644	616	52	12	487	50	
g	I am not worthy, holy Lord			407						570				
g	Into our world from God he came: SS78													
g	Jesus, my Lord, how rich thy grace / Fountain of good	381					147			459				
g	Jesus, thy far-extended fame						148							
g	O changeless Christ, for ever new			108					206			374		

Continuous: Genesis **12**: 1-9 and Psalm **33**: 1-12
or *Related:* Hosea **5**:15 — **6**:6 and Psalm **50**: 7-15;
Romans **4**: 13-25; Matthew **9**: 9-13, 18-26

		AMS	NEH	HTC	HON	MP	H&P	R&S	BPW	CH3	CP	SG	ONC	MPC
s	Here on the threshold of a new beginning										506	280		
o1	Deep in the shadows of the past						447							
o1	The God of Abraham praise	331	148	9	478	645	452	121	131	358	586	66	642	645
o1	Through all the changing scenes of life	209	467	46	516	702	73	685	544		604	654	686	702
o1	Thy/Your way, not mine			555	521								692	950
o1	To Abraham and Sarah							553						
o2	Brightest and best of the sons of the morning	47	49	338	71	65	123	183	190	201	84	346	85	65
o2	Come, let us to the Lord our God						33	81		69	402			
o2	How do we start to touch the broken hearts										613		847	
o2	O worship / Worship the Lord in the beauty of holiness	49	52	344	394	529	505	187	22	40	89	204	552	529
o p1	O God, thou art the Father						52	73		397				
o	Born of Adam, torn from Eden PR685													
p1	Lift up your heads, ye/you mighty gates	483	8				240			12	30			
p1	Rejoice, O land, in God thy might / your Lord	296	493	331	431						227		579	
p1	Songs of praise the angels sang	196	451	350			512	667		38	574		608	
p1	Thanks/Praise to God whose word	423	439	255			483	319	106		584	229		
e	Father of Jesus Christ, my Lord						693	351						
e	From the apple in the garden										528			
e	Gracious God in adoration											244		
e	How deep the Father's love for us										193		988	
e	See how great a flame aspires						781							
g	At the name of Jesus	148	338	172	46	41	74	261	370	300	380	317	54	
g	He gave his life in selfless love			405		214			435			467		214
g	He sat to watch o'er customs paid		189											
g	Heal us, Immanuel! Hear our prayer						390	335						

continued on next page

		AMS	NEH	HTC	HON	MP	H&P	R&S	BPW	CH3	CP	SG	ONC	MPC
g	Immortal Love, for ever full	133	378	105	243	328	392	267	198	306	475	176	315	328
g	Jesus calls us: o'er/in the tumult	312	200	104	266	359	141	355		211	233	668	347	359
g	Jesus came — the heavens adoring			195										
g	Jesus' hands were kind hands						393	197		228				
g	Jesus, my Lord, how rich thy grace / Fountain of good	381					147			459				
g	Lord, I was blind			437		433	423	358	558					433
g	O Christ the healer, we have come						395					346	489	395
g	Shout for joy, loud and long			348										
g	The Kingdom of God is justice and joy			333		651	139	200	321			591	184	646	651
g	We give God thanks for those who knew			318										
g	When our God came to earth				552								740	
g	Where shall my wondering soul begin						706							

Year B
Proper 5

Continuous: 1 Samuel **8**: 4-11 [12-15] 16-20 [**11**: 14-15] and Psalm **138**
or *Related:* Genesis **3**: 8-15 and Psalm **130**; 2 Corinthians **4**:13 — **5**:1;
Mark **3**: 20-35

		AMS	NEH	HTC	HON	MP	H&P	R&S	BPW	CH3	CP	SG	ONC	MPC
o1	It is God who holds the nations						404					304		
o1	Lift up your heads, ye/you mighty gates	483	8				240			12	30			
o1	Lord of lords and King eternal	396										357		
o1	O day of God, draw near/nigh In beauty	405						632	635	511	33			
o2p1	All hail the power of Jesus' name	140	332	587/ 203	13	13	252		29	382	163	24	16	13
o2	In Adam we have all been one	474					420							
o2	Jesus, the name high over all			213		385	264					323		385
o2	Join all the glorious names			214		392	78	280	557	304	493	46		392
o2	Lift high the cross	72		508	303	417	170	422	575	550	499	601	394	417
o2	Lord your voice in Eden's garden											426		

continued on next page

		AMS	NEH	HTC	HON	MP	H&P	R&S	BPW	CH3	CP	SG	ONC	MPC
o2	O lift us up, strong Son of God						427	337						
o2	Praise to the Holiest in the height	117	439	140	426	563	231	103	562	238	557	58	572	563
o2	The Lord made man, the Scriptures tell			143										
o2	Walking in a garden	518	123					334					705	
o2	What Adam's disobedience cost	524					430							
o	Born of Adam, torn from Eden PR685													
p1	Thy/Your hand, O God, has guided	171	485	536	518	705	784	567	398	424	606	649	689	705
p1	With undivided heart												963	
p2	Out of our failure to create							88					549	
p2	Out of the depths I cry to thee						429	331						
p2	Souls of men / Restless souls / There's a wideness	251	461	443	501	607, 683	230	353	573	218	598	188	662	607
p2	What is our calling's glorious hope						749							
p	With undivided heart												963	
e1	Here, O my Lord, I see thee/you	274		406		230	608		436	573	304	468	279	230
e	All my ways, all our hearts										685			
e	Behold the temple of the Lord						808							
e	Fight the good fight	220	359	526	128	143	710	496	524	442	423	635	169	143
e	From the apple in the garden										528			
e	O Lord, I would delight in thee							593					510	
e	Spirit of faith, come down						325							
g	God is love: his the care			311	169		220	274	45	416			216	
g	In Christ there is no east or west	376	480	322	244	329	758	647	482	425	477	575	319	329
g	Love is his word			481	322				445			180	429	
g	O God, by whose almighty plan	406					396	651			204			
g	When Jesus walked upon this earth		317											
g	Who would true valour / He who would valiant / Who honours courage	212	372	537, 590	205	224	688	557	362	443	621	639	281	224

Continuous: 1 Kings **17**: 8-16 [17-24] and Psalm **146** or *Related:*
1 Kings **17**: 17-24 and Psalm **30**; Galatians **1**: 11-24; Luke **7**: 11-17

		AMS	NEH	HTC	HON	MP	H&P	R&S	BPW	CH3	CP	SG	ONC	MPC
oe	Thou art / You are the way	128	464	113	512	695	234	554		121	600		682	695
og	Eternal light, shine in my heart			339							415			
og	Thine arm, O Lord, in days of old	285	324		502		397			214		671		
op1g	Jesus, the name high over all			213		385	264					323		385
op1g	Lord, I was blind			437		433	423	358	558					433
op1g	O for a thousand tongues to sing	125	415	219	362	496	744	285	59	371	534	55	485	495
op1	O Father, whose creating hand						349							
op2g	All shall be well			149				243				397		
o	'How shall they hear?', who have not heard				250							598		250
o	Guide me, O thou/my great Redeemer/Jehovah	214	368	528	188	201	437	345	593	89	455	638	252	201
o	Sometimes a light surprises	108					571	595			572			
p1	I'll praise my Maker while I've breath			20		320	439	734	127		473	84		320
p1	Judge eternal, throned in splendour		490	329	285	395	409	626	627	519	356	600	372	395
p1	Sing praise to God who reigns above	193	447				511	75		142	569			
p1	The Lord is King! lift up thy/your voice	107		183	485	656	58	76	322	36	592	98	650	656
p2	Lord Jesus, think on/of me	129	70	316	312		533	363		80	97		412	
p2	O love that will/wilt not let me go			486	384	515	685	511	541	677	542		517	515
p2	O worship / Worship the Lord in the beauty of holiness	49	52	344	394	529	505	187	22	40	89	204	552	529
p2	The Church's one foundation	170	484	501	473	640	515	566	393	420	585	581	636	640
p2	Where there once was only hurt										140			
e	A heavenly splendour from on high		154											
e	Captains of the saintly band / Christian soldiers	299	215							539	212		91	
e	Disposer supreme and judge of the earth	298	216		110						214		149	
e	How beauteous/gracious are their feet	301					449	133			220			
e	The eternal gifts of Christ the King	297	213		476					540			639	
e	We have a gospel to proclaim	431	486	519	532	728	465		585		612		716	728
g	Join all the glorious names			214		392	78	280	557	304	493	46		392
g	Life-giving Christ, our hope and head LUTR90													
g	O bless the God of Israel			599										

Year A
Proper 6

Continuous: Genesis **18**: 1-15 [**21**: 1-7] and Psalm **116**: 1-2, 12-19 or *Related:* Exodus **19**: 2-8a and Psalm **100**; Romans **5**: 1-8; Matthew **9**:35 — **10**:8 [9-23]

		AMS	NEH	HTC	HON	MP	H&P	R&S	BPW	CH3	CP	SG	ONC	MPC
o2	Church of God, elect and glorious			504					406			592		
o2	Forth in the peace of Christ we go	458	361	542	142			602	607	589	429	594	187	
o2	Ye that know the Lord is gracious	175	477								628			
o	The God of Abraham praise	331	148	9	478	645	452	121	131	358	586	66	642	645
p1e1	Draw nigh and take / Draw near and take		281	401							296			
p1e	Being of beings, God of love						690							
p1	All my hope on God is founded	336	333	451	15	16	63	586	327	405	368	525	19	16
p1	Awake, my soul, and with the sun	1	232	264	50		632	378		42	1	618	58	804
p1	O God beyond all praising			36	363							53	489	
p1	What shall I render to my God						703							
p2e	Born in song						486					28		
p2	All praise to thee/Christ, for thou / our Lord and King divine	337	335	204	18		253	750		297	372		22	
p2	Before Jehovah's aweful/awesome throne / Sing to the Lord	197		15			61	119		2	387			
p2	Come, rejoice before your Maker			17					35			81		
eg	Love divine, all loves excelling	131	408	217	321	449	267	663	559	437	516	179	428	449
eg	The Kingdom of God is justice and joy			333		651	139	200	321		591	184	646	651
e	Come down, O Love Divine	156	137	231	90	89	281	294	283	115	170	663	114	89
e	God of all human history											223		
e	Hail thou/our once-despisèd/rejected Jesus			175	192	203	222		273		168		258	203
e	I hear the words of love			436										
e	Jesus, thine all-victorious love / My God, I know, I feel thee mine						740							
e	Let us rejoice: God's gift to us is peace											389		
e	Morning glory, starlit sky	496						99			259			
e	Not what these hands / I bless the Christ of God			435		487				410		175		
e	O Love divine, how sweet thou art	124	424					372			541			

continued on next page

		AMS	NEH	HTC	HON	MP	H&P	R&S	BPW	CH3	CP	SG	ONC	MPC
e	O thou/Lord who came[st]	233	431	552/ 596	392	525	745	433	355	110	191	560	541	525
e	One there is above all others					542	149		560					542
e	Thank you for saving me										137		937	
e	We give immortal praise	520		11			18	37	72		206	331	713	
g	Go in Jesus' name										611			
g	How shall they hear the word of God			507		250						599		250
g	Jesus, thy wandering sheep behold						772							
g	Lord, you give the great commission							580						
g	Send out/forth the gospel			517		593			584					593

Year B
Proper 6

Continuous: 1 Samuel **15**:34 — **16**:13 and Psalm **20** or *Related:* Ezekiel **17**: 22-24 and Psalm **92**: 1-4, 12-15; 2 Corinthians **5**: 6-10 [11-13] 14-17; Mark **4**: 26-34

		AMS	NEH	HTC	HON	MP	H&P	R&S	BPW	CH3	CP	SG	ONC	MPC
o1g	Hail to the Lord's anointed	142	55	190	193	204	125	127	142	317	87		259	204
o1	Blest are the pure in heart	238	341	110	63	58	724		588	113	391	372	77	58
o1	O Spirit of the living God			513			322	577	579	496	190	605		
o1	Rejoice, O people, in the mounting years						657							
o1	What does the Lord require	432					414							
p1	Be thou my vision / Lord be my vision	343	339	545	56	51	378	489	521	87	386	669	70	51
p1	Lord of our life, and God of our salvation		404	529	315	441				491			417	441
p1	Onward, Christian soldiers/pilgrims	333	435	532	(408)	543	718			480	549		531	543
p1	Soldiers of Christ, arise	219	449	533	449	604	719	370	580	441	571	643	606	604
p1	Stand up, stand up for Jesus	221	453	535	457	617	721			481	578	644	617	617
p1	The Lord be near us as we prayPR20													
p1	The royal banners forward go / As royal banners are unfurled	58	79		492		179	216	228	257	122		663	

continued on next page

		AMS	NEH	HTC	HON	MP	H&P	R&S	BPW	CH3	CP	SG	ONC	MPC
p2	For the music of creation										36			
p2	Sweet is the work, my God, my King			377		620	514				580	97		620
e	All who believe and are baptized							421	402		373			
e	Christ on whom the Spirit rested			228										
e	Come, thou/O fount of every blessing			337			517	360			406			
e	For ourselves no longer living							520					183	
e	For the might of thine/your arm we bless thee/you					154	435		479	365				154
e	Glory to God, the source of all our mission										595			
e	Great God, what do I see and hear			189										
e	How can we sinners know						728							
e	Lord Christ, when first thou cam'st to men	387						270		255				
e	Lord/Great God, your love has called us here	489		480			500	339	442		133		246	
e	Love divine, all loves excelling	131	408	217	321	449	267	663	559	437	516	179	428	449
e	My God, I love thee/you; not because	65	73	479	344		171	357		379	524		458	
e	No weight of gold or silver			138								181		
e	The Church's one foundation	170	484	501	473	640	515	566	393	420	585	581	636	640
e	We give immortal praise	520		11			18	37	72		206	331	713	
e	We were not there to see you come			121										
gl	Lord Jesus, once you spoke	392		112					598					
gl	Rise and hear! the Lord is speaking	509									321			
g	Almighty God, thy word is cast						466			635				
g	For the fruits of his/all creation	457		286	138	153	342	42	123		254	299	185	153
g	The Kingdom of God is justice and joy			333		651	139	200	321		591	184	646	651

Year C
Proper 6

Continuous: 1 Kings **21**: 1-10 [11-14] 15-21a and Psalm **5**: 1-8
or *Related:* 2 Samuel **11**:26 — **12**:10, **12**: 13-15 and Psalm **32**;
Galatians **2**: 15-21; Luke **7**:36 — **8**:3

		AMS	NEH	HTC	HON	MP	H&P	R&S	BPW	CH3	CP	SG	ONC	MPC
l	Awake, my soul, and with the sun	1	232	264	50		632	378		42	1	618	58	804
l	Now let us from this table rise	403		419	352		619	463	451		315	475	472	
o1&2	Teach us how grave a thing it is										151			
o1	Father, we have sinned against you										158			
o1	Show mercy to us, loving Father										164			
o2	Who sees it all, before whose gaze										165			
o	Almighty Father, who for us thy Son didst give	338					401	621			374			
o	Come, O thou all-victorious Lord / O come, our all-victorious			441			418							
o	Drop, drop, slow tears		82		112					106			151	
o	Father of all, whose laws			539				335			664			
o	Forgive our sins as we forgive	362	66	111	141		134	84	83		428	145	180	
o	Give praise for famous men			568										
o	Lead us, heavenly Father, lead us	224	393	595	293	400	68	543	597	90	496	640	379	400
o	O Christ the Lord, O Christ the King		496				406	630						
p2	Happy are those, beyond all measure blessed										172			
e	And can it be			588	30	33	216	136	328	409	376	168	32	
e	Come, O thou traveller unknown	243	350				434				407			
e	God made me for himself			361										
e	Great is thy/your faithfulness			260	186	200	66	96	553		453	39	249	200
e	Hail thou/our once-despisèd/rejected Jesus			175	192	203	222		273		168		258	203
e	Lord for the years				310	428		603	535		81	602	409	428
e	Lord, as I wake I turn to you	485	236	267			634	534				561		
e	No weight of gold or silver			138								181		
e	None other Lamb						271							
e	These are the facts			162		687					347	284		687
e	Who is there like you										141		1017	
g	How sweet the name of Jesus sounds	122	374	211	220	251	257	277	339	376	467	42	297	251
g	I bind unto myself / myself to God today / Christ be with me		159	5	225		695	36			402	203	302	
g	Jesus loves me, this I know			303							418			
g	Jesus, Lord of life and glory		68											
g	Jesus, lover of my soul	123	383	438	261	372	528	332	345	78	96	201	343	372
g	Rock of ages	135	445	593	437	582	273	365	545	83	565	150	584	582
g	Thou hidden love of God						544			96	602			
g	Ye that know the Lord is gracious	175	477								628			

134

Continuous: Genesis **21**: 8-21 and Psalm **86**: 1-10, 16-17
or *Related:* Jeremiah **20**: 7-13 and Psalm **69**: 7-10 [11-15] 16-18;
Romans **6**: 1b-11; Matthew **10**: 24-39

		AMS	NEH	HTC	HON	MP	H&P	R&S	BPW	CH3	CP	SG	ONC	MPC
o2	My God, I know, I feel thee mine						740							
p1	O Lord, hear my prayer				379			398	600			246	938	
p1	The Lord will come and not be slow	29	15		489		245	128		321	37		655	
p2	Help me, O God, and hear my cry PR69B													
p2	How firm a foundation			430	216	243		589	380				292	243
p2	When the waters cover me										268			
el	Bread of the world in mercy broken	270	277	396	68		599	443	428	574	285	465	83	
el	Now let us from this table rise	403		419	352		619	463	451		315	475	472	
e	A mighty mystery we set forth								403					
e	All shall be well			149				243				397		
e	Baptized in water			381								492		
e	Born of the water			382										
e	Christians, lift up your hearts … Here God's life-giving word	446		383										
e	Come, ye faithful / Alleluia, raise the anthem	145	351	205	99	103			269		409	25	131	103
e	Have you not heard?			386										
e	Jesus, we follow thee						583							
e	Lord, for the years			328	310	428		603	535		51	602	409	428
e	My God, accept my heart this day	279	318	551	341		701			429	338	559	455	
e	Now is eternal life	402	114		351		203	432			152		470	
e	Now lives the Lamb of God			159					255			413		
e	O for a heart to praise my God	230	74	483	361	495	536	514	538	85	533	149	484	495
e	Praise to God, almighty Maker						582	430	414					
e	The strife is o'er/past	78	119	163	495	670	214	250	261	266	159	416	667	670
e	This day above all days			164										
e	We know that Christ is raised and dies no more			389				426						
e	With Christ we share a mystic grave		317											
g	Christ for the world we sing	344					789	599			500	394		
g	Go, labour on						794				483			
g	I'm not ashamed to own/name my Lord			448	240	323	677	428	343	591		532	316	323
g	Light of the minds that know him		400	477				529			501	626	397	
g	Take up thy/your cross	237	76	114	465					430	582	645	626	935

Year B
Proper 7

Continuous: 1 Samuel **17**: [1a, 4-11, 19-23] 32-49 and Psalm **9**: 9-20 or 1 Samuel **17**:57 — **18**:5, **18**: 10-16 and Psalm **133** or *Related:* Job **38**: 1-11 and Psalm **107**: 1-3, 23-32; 2 Corinthians **6**: 1-13; Mark **4**: 35-41

		AMS	NEH	HTC	HON	MP	H&P	R&S	BPW	CH3	CP	SG	ONC	MPC
o1e	Be thou / Lord be my vision	343	339	545	56	51	378	489	521	87	386	669	70	51
o1e	Christian, seek not yet repose			355										
o1e	Fight the good fight	220	359	526	128	143	710	496	524	442	423	635	169	143
o1e	Soldiers of Christ, arise	219	449	533	449	604	719	370	580	441	571	643	606	604
o1e	Stand up, stand up for Jesus	221	453	535	457	617	721			481	578	644	617	617
o1	Lift up your heads, ye gates of brass						227			471				
o1	Through all the changing scenes	209	467	46	516	702	73	685	544		604	654	686	702
o1	Who can bind the raging sea: STG 181													
o1	Who would true valour / He who would valiant / Who honours courage	212	372	537, 590	205	224	688	557	362	443	621	639	281	224
o2	Lord, as I wake I turn to you	485	236	267			634	534				561		
o2	Songs of praise the angels sang	196	451	350			512	667		38	574		608	
o2g	Eternal Father, strong to save	292	354	285	114	122	379	58	587	527	413	235	153	122
p1	How good a thing it is			497								587		
p1	How good and how pleasant it is											587		
p2g	Fierce raged the tempest	225					144							
p2g	I cannot tell why/how he			194	226	266	238	265	381		54	437	303	266
p2g	Jesus calls us: o'er/in the tumult	312	200	104	266	359	141	355		211	233	668	347	359
p2g	O changeless Christ, for ever new			108					206			374		
p2g	O Jesus, I have promised	235	420	531	372	501	704	509	352	434	538	676	503	501
p2g	Son of God, eternal Saviour	132	498	102				605	639	454	573			
p2g	Timeless love! we sing the story			47		707	60					100		707
p2	Lord, thy word abideth / Lord, your word	166	407	251	318	446	476	317	102	130	515		420	446
e	God of all human history											223		
e	I bind unto myself / myself to God today / Christ be with me		159	5	225		695	36		402	203		302	
e	Oft in danger, oft in woe / Christian soldiers, onward go	210	434	524	396	533	715				547		487	533
e	Preachers of the God of grace LUTR139													
e	This day God gives me	516						79			205			
g1	This is the day of light	21		380						46				

continued on next page

		AMS	NEH	HTC	HON	MP	H&P	R&S	BPW	CH3	CP	SG	ONC	MPC
g	Begone, unbelief						667							
g	Bless the Lord, creation sings			604										
g	Commit thou all thy griefs / Put thou thy trust / Give to the winds	223			429		672	550		669	562		576	
g	Holy Spirit, Truth divine			235			289	301	292	106	184		289	
g	Jesus, Saviour of the world			607										
g	Light of the minds that know him		400	477				529			501	626	397	
g	O sing a song of Bethlehem	413						201		220	545		536	
g	Seed, secret sown in the earth: SS26													

Year C
Proper 7

Continuous: 1 Kings **19**: 1-4 [5-7] 8-15a and Psalms **42**, **43** or *Related:* Isaiah **65**: 1-9 and Psalm **22**: 19-28; Galatians **3**: 23-29; Luke **8**: 26-39

		AMS	NEH	HTC	HON	MP	H&P	R&S	BPW	CH3	CP	SG	ONC	MPC
o1g	Dear Lord and Father of mankind	115	353	356	106	111	673	492	84	76	411	497	144	111
o1	Be still for the presence / Spirit of the Lord				53	50			5		383	7	67	
o1	Come, living God, when least expected							354			403			
o1	I searched so long and hard: SS58													
o1	Lord Jesus, let these eyes of mine			549										
o1	Lord, you sometimes speak in wonders							101						
o1	My Lord, I did not choose you			107										
o1	O Jesus, I have promised	235	420	531	372	501	704	509	352	434	538	676	503	501
o1	Open, Lord, my inward ear						540							
o1	Speak, Lord, in the stillness			253		608			105					608
o1	Thanks/Praise to God whose word	423	439	255			483	319	106		584	229		
o1	There is a name I love to hear					672								
o	A still, small voice											46		
p1	As pants the hart	226	337		38		416	689			379	44		
p1	As the deer pants for the water				39	37						45		37
p1	As the fainting deer cries out PR42													
p1	Father of mercies, in thy/your word	167		247					99			224		
p1	I hunger and I thirst			409			730	449			306	470		
p1	If thou but trust in God / suffer God to guide thee						713			668				

continued on next page

		AMS	NEH	HTC	HON	MP	H&P	R&S	BPW	CH3	CP	SG	ONC	MPC
p1	Jesus, priceless treasure			461	262		259				484	535	344	
p1	Jesus, thou/the joy of loving hearts	255	292	413	265	383	258	389	439	571	486	471		
p1	O send thy/your light forth						537	690	18	7				
p1	Send out your light, Lord										231			
p2	Ye/You servants of God, your Master proclaim	149	476	520	565	784	278	293	76	372	627	75	784	756
e	For the healing of the nations	361			139		402	620	621		427	261	186	
e	He went to the top of a mountain: SS63													
e	In Christ there is no east or west	376	480	322	244	329	758	647	482	425	477	575	319	329
e	Jesus is the Lord of living			309										
e	Jesus, the very thought of thee/you is sweet	120	291, 385	478	264	386	265	509	352	377	486	471, 534	368	
e	Living God, your word has called us											404		
e	The great love of God						45	105		415				
e	To him we come			518		709			547			679		709
e	We worship God in harmony										583			
g	Lord Jesus, think on/of me	129	70	316	312		533	363		80	97		412	
g	To God be the glory			584	522	708	463	289	566	374	609	71	695	708
g	When Jesus walked upon this earth			317										

Year A
Proper 8

26 JUNE → 2 JULY

Continuous: Genesis **22**: 1-14 and Psalm **13** or *Related:* Jeremiah **28**: 5-9 and Psalm **89**: 1-4, 15-18; Romans **6**: 12-23; Matthew **10**: 40-42

		AMS	NEH	HTC	HON	MP	H&P	R&S	BPW	CH3	CP	SG	ONC	MPC
o1	Begone, unbelief						667							
o1	God moves in a mysterious way	112	365		173	193	65	59	122	147	445		222	193
o1	Teach me thy way, O Lord				626								629	626
o1	The God of Abraham praise	331	148	9	478	645	452	121	131	358	586	66	642	645
o1	Though troubles assail and dangers affright: BHB 588; HF 397													
o2	God has spoken — by his prophets			248			64		100			225		831
p1	How long, O Lord, will you forget											651	848	

continued on next page

		AMS	NEH	HTC	HON	MP	H&P	R&S	BPW	CH3	CP	SG	ONC	MPC
p1	How long, O Lord, will you quite forget me							671						
p1	Timeless love! we sing the story			47		707	60					100		707
e1	And now, O Father, mindful of the love	260	273	392	32		593			580	279	459	34	
e	Father, Son, and Holy Ghost						791							
e	Freedom and life are ours			544					528			171		
e	How can I be free from sin										518		846	
e	In full and glad surrender			557	245	330							322	330
e	Jesus, Master, whose I am									431	342			
e	Make me a captive, Lord					455	714	505		445	518			455
e	Now lives the Lamb of God			159					255			413		
e	O for a heart to praise my God	230	74	483	361	495	536	514	538	85	533	149	484	495
e	Take my life, and let it be	249		554	464	624	705	371	358	462	581	678	625	624
e	Who is on the Lord's side?					769	722		615	479				769
e	Ye/You servants of God, your Master proclaim	149	476	520	565	784	278	293	76	372	627	75	784	756
g	Where cross the crowded ways of life						431	606	626	512	620			

Year B
Proper 8

Continuous: 2 Samuel **1**: 1, 17-27 and Psalm **130** or *Related:* Wisdom **1**: 13-15, **2**: 23-24; (Canticle or substitute OT reading) Lamentations **3**: 23-33; or Psalm **30**; 2 Corinthians **8**: 7-15; Mark **5**: 21-43

		AMS	NEH	HTC	HON	MP	H&P	R&S	BPW	CH3	CP	SG	ONC	MPC
o12	Teach us how grave a thing it is										151			
o2l	New every morning is the love	2	238	270	349	480	636	536		47	6		467	480
o2	Immortal honours rest: CHH 125; GH 152													
o2	Jesus, thou/the joy of loving hearts	255	292	413	265	383	258	389	439	571	486	471		
o2	Not the grandeur of the mountains										182			
o2	You can't stop rain from falling down							567						
o	We cannot measure how you heal							653			348	490	712	
p1	Out of our failure to create						88						549	

continued on next page

		AMS	NEH	HTC	HON	MP	H&P	R&S	BPW	CH3	CP	SG	ONC	MPC
p1	Out of the depths I cry to thee						429	331						
p2e	Jesus, if still the same thou art						529							
p2g	Father of Jesus Christ, my Lord						693	351						
p2	O love that will/wilt not let me go			486	384	515	685	511	541	677	542		517	515
p2	Souls of men / Restless souls / There's a wideness	251	461	443	501	607, 683	230	353	573	218	598	188	662	607
p2	The Church's one foundation	170	484	501	473	640	515	566	393	420	585	581	636	640
a	The gifts we bring express our love										278			
e	Before the heaven and earth			612										
e	Eternal God, we bring our praise FF p80													
e	God is the giver of all things that are FF p84													
e	How privileged we are FF p88													
e	Jesus, most generous Lord FF p97													
e	Jesus, the very thought of thee/you is sweet	120	291, 385	478	264	386	265	509	352	377	486	471, 534	368	
e	My Lord, you wore no royal crown			118							628			
e	Thou didst leave thy throne	250	465		513	697	154	192	179		601		683	697
e	Thou who wast rich / Lord, you were rich			63		700					72	356		700
e	What will you give the Lord today? FF p110													
g	A stranger once did bless the earth	335						198						
g	Heal me, hands of Jesus			319								488		
g	Heal us, Immanuel! Hear our prayer						390	335						
g	Immortal Love, for ever full	133	378	105	243	328	392	267	198	306	475	176	315	328
g	Inspired by love and anger				252							325		
g	Jesus' hands were kind hands						393	197		228				
g	Lord of all, to whom alone	492												
g	Lord, I was blind			437		433	423	358	558					433
g	O Christ the healer, we have come						395				346	489		395
g	O for a thousand tongues to sing	125	415	219	362	496	744	285	59	371	534	55	485	495
g	She was made in God's image: SS92													
g	Thine arm, O Lord, in days of old	285	324		502		397			214		671		
g	Thou to whom the sick and dying		325											
g	We give God thanks for those who knew			318										
g	Woman in the night: SS76													

Year C
Proper 8

Continuous: 2 Kings **2**: 1-2, 6-14 and Psalm **77**: 1-2, 11-20 or *Related:* 1 Kings **19**: 15-16, 19-21 and Psalm **16**; Galatians **5**: 1, 13-25; Luke **9**: 51-62

		AMS	NEH	HTC	HON	MP	H&P	R&S	BPW	CH3	CP	SG	ONC	MPC
o1e	The prophets spoke in days of old	513									327			
o1g	O happy band of pilgrims	208	418	530	368								497	
o1	Children of the heavenly King	213	344	566	63									
o1	Christians, lift up your hearts … Praise for the Spirit	444		229							399		95	
o1	Come, thou/most Holy Spirit, come / Come, thou Holy Paraclete	92	139	227	97		284	297		105		180	127	
o1	Jerusalem on high			565										
o1	Ye/You holy angels bright	198	475	353	564	783	20	125	23	363	626	76	755	783
o2	Cry 'freedom' in the name of God				104								138	
o2	When God almighty came to earth				545								733	
p1	God moves in a mysterious way	112	365		173	193	65	59	122	147	445		222	193
p1	How firm a foundation			430	216	243		589	380				292	243
p1	I cried out to God to help me PR77													
p1	Through all the changing scenes of life	209	467	46	516	702	73	685	544		604	654	686	702
p2e	Holy Spirit, Truth divine			235			289	301	292	106	184		289	
p2e	Lead us, heavenly Father, lead us	224	393	595	293	400	68	543	597	90	496	640	379	400
p2	Jesus, thou/the joy of loving hearts	255	292	413	265	383	258	389	439	571	486	471		
p2	O Lord, you are the centre of my life										543			
e	Dost thou truly seek renown		81											
e	For the fruits of his/all creation	457		286	138	153	342	42	123		254	299	185	153
e	Freedom and life are ours			544					528			171		
e	Give me joy in my heart / oil in my lamp	459		S11	153	167	492	523	530		433		201	167
e	Give me/us the wings of faith	324	225		156		815	664			216		202	
e	Here within this house of prayer			563										
e	Jesus, the very thought of thee/you is sweet	120	291, 385	478	264	386	265	509	352	377	486	471, 534	368	
e	Let saints on earth / Come let us join our friends above	182	396	574	297	409	812	472		543	222	578	384	409
e	May we, O Holy Spirit, bear your fruit			236								672		
e	Now the fruit of the Spirit												903	
e	O Holy Spirit, giver of life			239										
e	Of all the Spirit's gifts to me	503					320							
e	Spirit of holiness, wisdom and faithfulness			246		611					576	449		611
g	Filled with the Spirit's power	359		233	131		314				425	593	170	
g	Jesus, good above all other	378	387	96	269		732	528		111	487		350	
g	Lord, who left the highest heaven			97										
g	My song is love unknown	63	86	136	346	478	173	207	204	224	112	384	463	478
g	Thou didst leave thy throne	250	465		513	697	154	192	179		601		683	697

141

Year A
Proper 9

Continuous: Genesis **24**: 34-38, 42-49, 58-67 and Psalm **45**: 10-17 or (Canticle) Song of Solomon **2**: 8-13 or *Related:* Zechariah **9**: 9-12 and Psalm **145**: 8-14; Romans **7**: 15-25a; Matthew **11**: 16-19, 25-30

		AMS	NEH	HTC	HON	MP	H&P	R&S	BPW	CH3	CP	SG	ONC	MPC
c	Jesus, lover of my soul	123	383	438	261	372	528	332	345	78	96	201	343	372
c	Loved with everlasting love			482		452								452
lp2	The day thou gavest / you gave us, Lord, is ended	16	252	280	475	641	648	584	319	646	22	65	641	638
o1	Be thou my vision / Lord be my vision	343	339	545	56	51	378	489	521	87	386	669	70	51
o1	Come, see, the winter in past PR712													
o1	Have faith in God, my heart	372		431	201		675	499	336		458		268	
o1	I do not know tomorrow's way										531			
o1	Lord, be thy word my rule / Lord, make your word	232		250										
o2	There's a light upon the mountains				679	246		149			198			679
op2	Hail to the Lord's anointed	142	55	190	193	204	125	127	142	317	87		259	204
p1	My heart is full of admiration										128		898	
p1	Wake, O wake / Sleepers, wake	32	16	199	529		249	132		315	39		703	
p1	With hearts in love abounding PR45													
p2e	The strife is o'er/past	78	119	163	495	670	214	250	261	266	159	416	667	670
p2	All glory, honour, blessing and power: SS2													
p2	My God, my King, thy various praise						12	115						
e	Dear Master, in whose life I see						522	493	337	691				
e	O lift us up, strong Son of God						427	337						
g	'Come to me' says Jesus									408				
g	All ye who seek a comfort / for sure relief	64	63		22						101		26	
g	Alleluia! sing to Jesus	262	271	170	26	207	592		270		278	458	12	207
g	Father in heaven, grant to your children			2			3	38				200		
g	Father of mercy, God of consolation		323					645						
g	Forth in thy/your name, O Lord	239	235	306	143	159	381	521	526	463	430	623	188	159
g	Hark what a sound, and too divine for hearing						236	660		314	28			

continued on next page

		AMS	NEH	HTC	HON	MP	H&P	R&S	BPW	CH3	CP	SG	ONC	MPC
g	Here within this house of prayer			563										
g	Here, O my Lord, I see thee/you	274		406		230	608		436	573	304	468	279	230
g	How sweet the name of Jesus sounds	122	374	211	220	251	257	277	339	376	467	42	297	251
g	I cannot tell why/how he			194	226	266	238	265	381		54	437	303	266
g	I heard the voice of Jesus say	247	376		231	275	136	349		212	469		310	275
g	Jesus shall reign where'er the sun	143	388	516	277	379	239	269	313	413	490	45	359	379
g	Just as I am, without one plea	246	294	440	287	396	697	364	346	79	308	507	374	396
g	O Christ the same		258	263										477
g	One there is above all others				542	149			560					542
g	So dies this man, this carpenter: SS41													
g	Thou art / You are the way	128	464	113	512	695	234	554		121	600		682	695
g	What a friend we have in Jesus			373	541	746	559	413	603			646	727	746
g	When the Son of Mary: SS80 HSN82													

Year B
Proper 9

Continuous: 2 Samuel **5**: 1-5, 9-10 and Psalm **48** or *Related:* Ezekiel **2**: 1-5 and Psalm **123**; 2 Corinthians **12**: 2-10; Mark **6**: 1-13

		AMS	NEH	HTC	HON	MP	H&P	R&S	BPW	CH3	CP	SG	ONC	MPC
o1	God is our strength and refuge			527		188			308		443	650	219	188
o1	God save and bless our nation			325										
o1	Thy/Your hand, O God, has guided	171	485	536	518	705	784	567	398	424	606	649	689	705
o2e	Thanks/Praise to God whose word	423	439	255			483	319	106		584	229		
o2l	The prophets spoke in days of old	513									327			
o2	Come with all joy to sing to God			16										
o2	God has spoken — by his prophets			248			64		100			225		831
p1e	Jesus, thy boundless love to me						696	506						
p1	City of God, Jerusalem			187										
p1	Glorious things of thee/you are spoken	172	362	494	158	173	817	560	480	421	435	35	205	173

continued on next page

		AMS	NEH	HTC	HON	MP	H&P	R&S	BPW	CH3	CP	SG	ONC	MPC
p1	Great is our redeeming Lord						438							
p1	Great is the Lord, his praise is great PR48													
p1	Now thank we all our God	205	413	33	354	486	566	72	128	368	530	54	474	486
p2	Holy Lord, have mercy on us all										159			
p2	Up to you I lift my eyes PR123													
e	Almighty God, my redeemer										102			
e	Captain of Israel's host						62							
e	Dear Lord, for all in pain: AHB 396													
e	Enthrone thy God within thy heart						692							
e	Father, hear the prayer we offer	113	357	360	120	132	436	495	523		416	237	161	132
e	God of almighty love						793							
e	I could not do without thee: AMR353													
e	Lord of all power, I give you my will / Lord of creation, to you be all praise	395		547		440	699	532		428	508			
e	Still near me, O my Saviour			464										
g	God's Spirit is in my heart (Go tell everyone)				180		315	576					231	
g	Join all the glorious names			214		392	78	280	557	304	493	46		392
g	Lord of all hopefulness	394	239	101	313		552	531	517	92	507	509	413	882
g	O Christ, the master carpenter			135								673		
g	Songs of thankfulness and praise	53	56	98	451			191			90	376	609	
g	When the Lord in glory comes			201		758								758

Year C
Proper 9

Continuous: 2 Kings **5**: 1-14 and Psalm **30** or *Related:* Isaiah **66**: 10-14 and Psalm **66**: 1-9; Galatians **6**: [1-6] 7-16; Luke **10**: 1-11, 16-20

		AMS	NEH	HTC	HON	MP	H&P	R&S	BPW	CH3	CP	SG	ONC	MPC
o1	Jesu(s), Lover of my soul	123	383	483	261	372	528	332	345	78	96	201	343	372
o1	Just as I am, without one plea	246	294	440	287	396	697	364	346	79	308	507	374	396

continued on next page

		AMS	NEH	HTC	HON	MP	H&P	R&S	BPW	CH3	CP	SG	ONC	MPC
o1	There is a fountain			144		671								671
o2	Like a mighty river flowing			32		419			632			51	400	419
o2	Like a river glorious			463		421								421
o2	Sing praise to God who reigns above	193	447				511	75		142	569			
op2e	When peace like a river					757								757
p2	By every nation, race and tongue			579								30		
p2	How firm a foundation			430	216	243		589	380				292	243
p2	Let all the world in every corner sing	202	394	342	296	404	10	114	54	361	497	47	382	404
p2	Praise our God with shouts of joy LUTR224													
p2	Sing glory to God the Father										1	599		
e	As now the sun's declining rays		242		37						11		43	
e	Beneath the cross of Jesus				59	55	165			684	105		65	55
e	Help us to help each other / Jesus, united by thy grace	374		540	208		773	500			461		275	
e	I'm not ashamed to own/name my Lord			448	240	323	677	428	343	591		532	316	323
e	In the Cross of Christ I glory		379		249	338	167	224	344	259	480		327	338
e	Jesus, Lord, we look to thee	380	481				759	564			489			
e	No weight of gold or silver			138								181		
e	We sing the praise of him who died	138	94	146	536	738	182	229	231	258	125	390	723	738
e	When I survey the wondrous cross	67	95	147	549	755	180	217	233	254	127	680	738	755
ge	Go, labour on						794			483				
gl	Christ is risen! Alleluia					74			245				423	74
g	Glorious things of thee/you are spoken	172	362	494	158	173	817	560	480	421	435	35	205	173
g	Go forth and tell			505	164	178	770	574	570		437	596	238	178
g	He that is down need fear no fall	218				676								
g	How can we sinners know					728								
g	How deep the Father's love for us										193		988	
g	I cannot forget them: SS82													
g	Join all the glorious names			214		392	78	280	557	304	493	46		392
g	Lord, you give the great commission							580						
g	Love divine, all loves excelling	131	408	217	321	449	267	663	559	437	516	179	428	449
g	The Kingdom of God is justice and joy			333		651	139	200	321		591	184	646	651

Year A
Proper 10

Continuous: Genesis **25**: 19-34 and Psalm **119**: 105-112 or *Related:* Isaiah **55**: 10-13 and Psalm **65**: [1-8] 9-13; Romans **8**: 1-11; Matthew **13**: 1-9, 18-23

		AMS	NEH	HTC	HON	MP	H&P	R&S	BPW	CH3	CP	SG	ONC	MPC
o2g	Christ's Church shall glory in his power			522										
o2l	At even[ing], ere/when the sun was/had set	9	243	315	43	43	142	644	616	52	12	487	50	
o2	To God be the glory			584	522	708	463	289	566	374	609	71	695	708
o2	You shall go out with joy				571	796		415					766	796
p1e	Come down, O Love Divine	156	137	231	90	89	281	294	283	115	170	663	114	89
p1	Father of mercies, in thy/your word	167		247					99			224		
p1	Help us, O Lord, to learn	373	370	493			474				460	226		
p1	Jesus, Jesus, holy and anointed one				271							215	353	872
p1	Lamp of our feet: AHB 302													
p1	Lord, I have made thy word my choice	490					475	316			504			
p1	Lord, thy word abideth / Lord, your word shall guide us	166	407	251	318	446	476	317	102	130	515		420	446
p1	O Word of God incarnate					527	478				531			527
p1	Powerful in making us wise to salvation			252			479					228		
p1	The will of God to mark my way: CFW 607													
p1	When we walk with the Lord				553	760	687		548				741	750
p1	Your word is a lamp unto my feet										234			
p2	The earth is yours, O God			290								313		
e	And can it be			588	30	33	216	136	328	409	376	168	32	
e	Born by the Holy Spirit's breath			225		61	279		281			446		
e	Father of heaven, whose love profound	97	358	359	124		519			77	421	144		827
e	Give to our God immortal praise	460		31	155	171	22	94	47		434	83	203	171
e	He lives in us, the Christ of God			457					554			173		
e	He stood before the court			129										
e	Holy Spirit, Truth divine			235			289	301	292	106	184		289	
e	Spirit of faith, by faith be mine: WAM 75													
e	Spirit of God within me			243			294	304	296		196	677	612	
e	The Spirit lives to set us free				494	664							666	664

continued on next page

		AMS	NEH	HTC	HON	MP	H&P	R&S	BPW	CH3	CP	SG	ONC	MPC
e	These are the facts			162		687					347	284		687
e	We give immortal praise	520		11			18	37	72		206	331	713	
g	Almighty God, thy word is cast						466			635				
g	Faith and truth and life bestowing										223			
g	Gift of Christ from God our Father										447			
g	Lord, we know that we have failed you											423		
g	Rise and hear! the Lord is speaking	509									321			
g	Seed, secret sown in the earth: SS26													
g	The sower went forth sowing: AMR 486; AHB 652													

Year B
Proper 10

Continuous: 2 Samuel **6**: 1-5, 12b-19 and Psalm **24** or *Related:* Amos **7**: 7-15 and Psalm **85**: 8-13; Ephesians **1**: 3-14; Mark **6**: 14-29

		AMS	NEH	HTC	HON	MP	H&P	R&S	BPW	CH3	CP	SG	ONC	MPC
o1e	Thy/Your hand, O God, has guided	171	485	536	518	705	784	567	398	424	606	649	689	705
o1	Bless the Lord, our fathers' God			610										
o2g	Give praise for famous men			568										
o2	God has spoken — by his prophets			248			64		100			225		831
p1el	All-holy Father, King of endless glory			391										
p1e	Souls of men / Restless souls / There's a wideness	251	461	443	501	607, 683	230	353	573	218	598	188	662	607
p1	At the name of Jesus	148	338	172	46	41	74	261	370	300	380	317	54	
p1	Crown him with many crowns	147	352	174	103	109	255	262	37	298	166	321	137	109
p1	God in his love for us lent us this planet						343	85				300		832
p1	Lift up your heads, ye gates of brass						227				471			
p1	Lift up your heads, ye/you mighty gates	483	8				240				12	30		
p1	Make way, make way, for Christ the King				329	457		141					438	457
p1	Our Lord is risen from the dead						206							
p1	The earth belongs unto the Lord									566				

continued on next page

		AMS	NEH	HTC	HON	MP	H&P	R&S	BPW	CH3	CP	SG	ONC	MPC
p1	The eternal gates lift up their heads / are lifted up		133							288				
p1	The golden gates are lifted up							256						
p1	This earth belongs to God Church Family Worship 584											99		
p1	Ye/You gates, lift up your heads on high						516	681	276	566				
p2	Lord, thine heart in love hath yearned							704		75				
p2	When this land knew God's gracious love PR85													
el	Again the Lord's own day is here	20												
es	Hidden Christ, alive for ever										530			
e	Come, thou/O fount of every blessing			337			517	360			406			
e	Come, ye faithful / Alleluia, raise the anthem	145	351	205	99	103			269		409	25	131	103
e	Eternal Light! Eternal Light!			454			458	83	85	357	414	527		
e	Father in heaven, grant to your children			2			3		38			200		
e	Great God of wonders! All thy ways					197	38				452			197
e	Jesus my Lord, my God, my all		384	476							483			
e	Lead us, heavenly Father, lead us	224	393	595	293	400	68	543	597	90	496	640	379	400
e	My Lord, I did not choose you			107										
e	O how the grace of God amazes me PR749													
e	O the mercy of God, the glory of grace										195			
e	Praise be to Christ in whom we see			220										
e	Through the darkness of the ages										538			
e	To God be the glory			584	522	708	463	289	566	374	609	71	695	708
e	We worship God in harmony										583			
g	Lo, in the wilderness a voice	384	170											

Year C
Proper 10

Continuous: Amos **7**: 7-17 and Psalm **82** or *Related:* Deuteronomy **30**: 9-14 and Psalm **25**: 1-10; Colossians **1**: 1-14; Luke **10**: 25-37

		AMS	NEH	HTC	HON	MP	H&P	R&S	BPW	CH3	CP	SG	ONC	MPC
o2	Immortal Love, for ever full	133	378	105	243	328	392	267	198	306	475	176	315	328
o2	Not far beyond the sea	401					477	318			528			
p1g	The God who rules this earth	425												
p1g	Who can sound the depths of sorrow					766						257	747	766
p1	God is king - be warned, you mighty PR82													
p1	The Lord will come and not be slow	29	15		489		245	128		321	37		655	
p1	Thy/Your kingdom come, O God	177	499	334	519		783	638	644	322	607	269	691	949
p1	Who can sound the depths of sorrow					766						257		766
p2g	Lord Christ, who on thy heart didst bear	388			308		394						407	
p2	Remember, remember your mercy, Lord										154			
p2	Show me thy ways, O Lord									74				
p2	Teach me thy way, O Lord					626							629	626
p2	Thy/Your way, not mine			555	521								692	950
p2	To you, O Lord, I lift up my soul										545			
eg	Father in heaven, grant to your children		2				3		38			200		
eg	Gracious Spirit, dwell with me						286							
eg	Help us to help each other / Jesus, united by thy grace	374		540	208		773	500			461		275	
eg	O God of mercy, God of might							615		461				
el	When morning gilds the skies	146	473	223	551	756	276	292	73	370				
e	All-holy Father, King of endless glory			391										
e	Come, ye faithful / Alleluia, raise the anthem	145	351	205	99	103			269		409	25	131	103
e	Gracious Spirit, Holy Ghost / Holy Spirit, gracious Guest	154	367	474	184	198	301	310	288	438	182	556	245	198
e	Lord, teach us how to pray aright	227	406	367	316		551				98		418	
e	Soldiers of Christ, arise	219	449	533	449	604	719	370	580	441	571	643	606	604
e	Speak, Lord, in the stillness			253		608			105					608
e	Ye that know the Lord is gracious	175	477								628			
gl	Welcome to another day			272								483		
g	Almighty Father, who for us thy Son didst give	338					401	621			374			
g	Father of all, whose laws have stood			539					335			664		
g	Hark, my soul, it is the Lord / Christian, do you hear the Lord	244		472	197	209	521	348		676	264		457	209
g	I was lying in the roadway: SS98													
g	Jesus, Lord, we look to thee	380	481				759	564			489			
g	My God, accept my heart this day	279	318	551	341		701				429	338	559	455
g	Thou to whom the sick and dying		325											

Year A
Proper 11

Continuous: Genesis **28**: 10-19a and Psalm **139**: 1-12, 23-24 or *Related:*
Wisdom **12**: 13, 16-19 or Isaiah **44**: 6-8 and Psalm **86**: 11-17;
Romans **8**: 12-25; Matthew **13**: 24-30, 36-43

		AMS	NEH	HTC	HON	MP	H&P	R&S	BPW	CH3	CP	SG	ONC	MPC
o1l	God, that madest earth and heaven	12	245		178		641				15		232	
o1	As Jacob with travel was weary one day	435			36		444				378		775	
o1	Beneath the cross of Jesus				59	55	165			684	105		65	55
o1	Blessed assurance				62	59	668		329		390		74	59
o1	God has spoken — by his prophets			248			64		100			225		831
o1	Lo, God is here! let us adore		209				531							
o1	Nearer, my God, to thee				348	482	451			689	526		466	482
o1	O God of Bethel / O God of Jacob	216	416	35	364		442	71	599	72	536	241	491	907
o1	O happy band of pilgrims	208	418	530	368								497	
o1	Timeless love! we sing the story			47		707	60					100		707
o2	How good is the God we adore / This, this is the God			450	217	244	277	542	338		464	41	293	244
o2	None other Lamb						271							
oe	Creation sings! Each plant and tree										295			
p1l	Saviour, again to thy/your dear name	15	250	281	438	584	643	640		649	20		587	584
p1	Awake, my soul, and with the sun	1	232	264	50		632	378		42	1	618	58	804
p1	Lord all-knowing you have found me										683			
p1	Lord, you have searched						71	70	564					
p1	My Lord, you called my name										203			
p1	O God, you search me										514			
p1	Search me, O God, my actions try: AHB 148													
p1	There is no moment of my life						428		133			185		
p1	Thou art / You are before me, Lord, thou art behind						543	731		68				
p1	When I watch a child at play: SS9													
p2	Lord of all, to whom alone	492												
p2	Not the grandeur of the mountains: CFW382											182		
p2	Teach me thy way, O Lord					626							629	626
e	Arise, my soul, arise						217							
e	Born by the Holy Spirit's breath			225		61	279		281			446		
e	He lives in us, the Christ of God			457					554			173		
e	Holy Spirit, come, confirm us	471	140		214		288	298	289		183		288	
e	Lord God, the Holy Ghost						306			332				
e	O God, enthroned in majesty											490		
g	Almighty God, thy word is cast						466			635				
g	Happy are they, they that/who love God	176	369	473	195		711			408	456		262	
g	Lord Jesus, once you spoke to men	392		112					598					

Continuous: 2 Samuel **7**: 1-14a and Psalm **89**: 20-37 or *Related:* Jeremiah **23**: 1-6 and Psalm **23**; Ephesians **2**: 11-22; Mark **6**: 30-34, 53-56

		AMS	NEH	HTC	HON	MP	H&P	R&S	BPW	CH3	CP	SG	ONC	MPC
o1	Lord, you need no house			546					349					
o1l	The day thou gavest / you gave us, Lord, is ended	16	252	280	475	641	648	584	319	646	22	65	641	638
o1	The Lord, my shepherd, rules my life			45										
o2	All hail the power of Jesus' name	140	332	587/203	13	13	252		29	382	163	24	16	13
o2	The God of Abraham praise	331	148	9	478	645	452	121	131	358	586	66	642	645
o2	Thy/Your kingdom come, O God	177	499	334	519		783	638	644	322	607	269	691	949
p2	Because the Lord is my shepherd										513			
p2	Faithful Shepherd, feed me		282	29	117							498	156	
p2	My God, and/now is thy table spread	259		418	342						313	474	456	
p2	The God of love my shepherd is	110	77		479		43	677			587		643	649
p2	The King of love my shepherd is	126	457	44	484	649	69	552	394	388	589	205	649	649
p2	The Lord is King! lift up thy/your voice	107		183	485	656	58	76	322	36	592	98	650	656
p2	The Lord's my shepherd, I'll not want	426	459	591/45	490	660	70	679	395	387	594	207	654	660
el	I come with joy to meet my Lord	473		408	227		610	447	437		365	469	304	
e	Christ is made the sure foundation / Blessed city, heavenly Salem	283/332	204-5	559	76	73	485	559	474	10	208	572	97	73
e	Christ is our corner-stone	161		564	77						395		98	
e	Christ is the world's light	440		321			455	600	34		213	591	99	
e	Christ is the world's true light	346	494	323	78		456	601	618	505	396	432	100	
e	Church of God, elect and glorious			504					406			592		
e	He/they want/lack not friends	183	371				495	481			459			
e	In Christ there is no east or west	376	480	322	244	329	758	647	482	425	477	575	319	329
e	Peace, perfect peace, in this dark world of sin			467	413	555			561		553		554	555
e	Sing together on our journey										580			
e	The Church's one foundation	170	484	501	473	640	515	566	393	420	585	581	636	640
e	The Spirit came, as promised			244					297			450		
e	To God be the glory			584	522	708	463	289	566	374	609	71	695	708
g	Behold us, Lord, a little space						376			453				
g	Come ye yourselves apart: AHB375													
g	Immortal Love, for ever full	133	378	105	243	328	392	267	198	306	475	176	315	328
g	Thine arm, O Lord, in days of old	285	324		502		397			214		671		

Year C
Proper 11

Continuous: Amos **8**: 1-12 and Psalm **52** or *Related:* Genesis **18**: 1-10a and Psalm **15**; Colossians **1**: 15-28; Luke **10**: 38-42

		AMS	NEH	HTC	HON	MP	H&P	R&S	BPW	CH3	CP	SG	ONC	MPC
o1e	How firm a foundation			430	216	243		589	380				292	243
o1	Father of mercies, in thy/your word	167		247					99			224		
o1	Hail to the Lord's anointed	142	55	190	193	204	125	127	142	317	87		259	204
o2e	My God, how wonderful thou art / you are	102	410	369	343	468	51	408		356	523	202	457	468
o2	The God of Abraham praise	331	148	9	478	645	452	121	131	358	586	66	642	645
o	Inspired by love and anger				252							325		
p1e	Praise to the Lord, the Almighty	207	440	40	427	564	16	74	68	9	558	59	573	564
p2	God be in my head	236	328	543	166		694	498	592	433	439	666	211	
p2	Lord, who may dwell within your house										684			
p2	Within thy tabernacle, Lord									5				
el	I come with joy to meet my Lord	473		408	227		610	447	437		365	469	304	
el	Lord, enthroned in heavenly splendour	263	296	416	309	431	616			583	311	52	408	
el	The Son of God proclaim	427		415			627	458	455		328			
e	At the name of Jesus	148	338	172	46	41	74	261	370	300	380	317	54	
e	Come, let us worship the Christ of creation			207										
e	God's glory fills the universe							275				283		
e	Jesus, our hope, our hearts' desire	86		178							169			
e	Lord of the Church, we pray for our renewing			499		442			486			577		442
e	Nature with open volume stands	497	87				174	219			113			
e	O Christ the same, through all our story's pages		258	263									477	
e	O firstborn of the unseen Lord										326			
e	O Spirit of the living God			513			322	577	579	496	190	605		
e	O the mercy of God, the glory of grace										195			
e	Of the Father's love/heart begotten / God of God	33	33	56	395		79	181	145	198	64,65		486	
e	Peace, perfect peace, in this dark world of sin			467	413	555			561		553		554	555
e	Praise be to Christ in whom			220										
e	The brightness of God's glory			221										
e	With glorious clouds encompassed round						184				623			
g	Hail thou/our once-despisèd/ rejected Jesus			175	192	203	222		273		168		258	203
g	O Lord of life, thy quickening voice						637			48				
g	O love divine, how sweet thou art	124	424					372			541			
g	Seek ye first the Kingdom of God				442	590	138	512	357				590	590
g	When we walk with the Lord				553	760	687		548				741	750
g	Woman in the night: SS76													

Year A
Proper 12

Continuous: Genesis **29**: 15-28 and Psalm **105**: 1-11, 45b or Psalm **128**
or *Related:* 1 Kings **3**: 5-12 and Psalm **119**: 129-136; Romans **8**: 26-39;
Matthew **13**: 31-33, 44-52

		AMS	NEH	HTC	HON	MP	H&P	R&S	BPW	CH3	CP	SG	ONC	MPC
o2	Be it my only wisdom here						786							
o	Be thou my vision / Lord be my vision	343	339	545	56	51	378	489	521	87	386	669	70	51
o	God of grace and God of glory	367		324	174	192	712	344	572	88	448	574	225	192
o	God, you have / who hast given us power	469					345				256			
o	Happy the man that finds the grace						674							
p1	Blessed are those who fear the Lord PR128													
p2	The will of God to mark my way: Church Family Worship 607													
p	As man and woman we were made						364	466	506					
p	O God of Bethel / O God of Jacob	216	416	35	364		442	71	599	72	536	241	491	907
p	The God of Abraham praise	331	148	9	478	645	452	121	131	358	586	66	642	645
e	Born by the Holy Spirit's breath			225		61	279		281			446		
e	Eternal Spirit of the living Christ							300						
e	God moves in a mysterious way	112	365		173	193	65	59	122	147	445		222	193
e	Have faith in God, my heart	372		431	201		675	499	336		458		268	
e	He lives in us, the Christ of God			457					554			173		
e	Holy Spirit, will you be										239			
e	Mercy in our time of failure										240			
e	Now is eternal life	402	114		351		203	432			152		470	
e	Shepherd divine, our wants relieve	228					558				566			
e	Spirit of God within me			243			294	304	296		196	677	612	
e	Spread, O spread, thou mighty word		482											
e	The Saviour died, but rose again						233	597		293				
e	We do not know how to pray AFJ38													
e	We do not know how to pray as we ought						545	400						
gl	Lord, thy word abideth / Lord, your word shall guide us	166	407	251	318	446	476	317	102	130	515		420	446
g	'The Kingdom is upon you!'	512									590			
g	Jesus, priceless treasure			461	262		259				484	535	344	
g	Now let us learn of Christ			503										
g	Seed, secret sown in the earth: SS26													
g	The Kingdom of God is justice and joy			333		651	139	200	321		591	184	646	651

Year B
Proper 12

Continuous: 2 Samuel **11**: 1-15 and Psalm **14** or *Related:* 2 Kings **4**: 42-44 and Psalm **145**: 10-18; Ephesians **3**: 14-21; John **6**: 1-21

		AMS	NEH	HTC	HON	MP	H&P	R&S	BPW	CH3	CP	SG	ONC	MPC
se	Gather around for the table is spread				152								199	
o1	Christ's is the world in which we move				83							252		
o1	Creator of the earth and skies	351		320			419	82			410	296		
o1	How can we sing with joy to God			362					86			147		
o1	I want a principle within						422							
o2	Praise and thanksgiving be to our creator	506												
o2	The Church of Christ in every age						804	636	613					
p1	As if you were not there: LFB 72													
p1	The fool whose heart declares in pride PR14													
p2	All glory, honour, blessing and power: SS2													
p2	Let us, with a gladsome mind / Let us gladly with one mind	204	397	23	302	415	27		56	33	498	312	392	415
p2	Sing to the Lord a joyful song						17	77		366	570			929
e	Come dearest Lord, descend and dwell						725	381	284	637	291		113	
e	Father and God, from whom our world derives			357										
e	It passeth / Beyond all knowledge, that dear love of thine			471		349	526							349
e	Not far beyond the sea	401					477	318			528			
e	O Love divine, how sweet thou art	124	424					372			541			
e	That priceless gift, what tongue can tell									329				
g	A rich young man came seeking FF p78													
g	Bread of heaven, on thee we feed	271	276	398	67			442			284	464	82	
g	Eternal Father, strong to save	292	354	285	114	122	379	58	587	527	413	235	153	122
g	For the fruits of his/all creation	457		286	138	153	342	42	123		254	299	185	153
g	Guide me, O thou/my great Redeemer/Jehovah	214	368	528	188	201	437	345	593	89	455	638	252	201
g	Here comes Jesus: SS79													
g	I saw the man from Galilee: SS88													
g	I sought the Lord, and afterward						368							
g	Just as I am, without one plea	246	294	440	287	396	697	364	346	79	308	507	374	396
g	Let us break bread together	480			299	414	615	452	443				387	414
g	Let us talents and tongues employ	481		414	301			453					391	
g	O bread to pilgrims given / O food of men wayfaring		300				620	456	317					
g	When the Son of Mary: SS80 HSN82													

Year C
Proper 12

Continuous: Hosea **1**: 2-10 and Psalm **85** or *Related:* Genesis **18**: 20-32 and Psalm **138**; Colossians **2**: 6-15 [16-19]; Luke **11**: 1-13

		AMS	NEH	HTC	HON	MP	H&P	R&S	BPW	CH3	CP	SG	ONC	MPC
o1	Father of heaven, whose love profound	97	358	359	124		519			77	421	144		827
o1	Hark, my soul, it is the Lord / Christian, do you hear the Lord	244		472	197	209	521	348		676	264		457	209
o1	O lift us up, strong Son of God						427	337						
o1	Our cities cry to you, O God											251		
o2	Beauty for brokenness										263	60	806	
o2	Lord, save thy world; in bitter need	397					425							
o2	Lord, teach us how to pray aright	227	406	367	316		551				98		418	
o2	The God who sent the prophets						454							
p1	Lord, thine heart in love hath yearned							704		75				
p1	O Spirit of the living God			513			322	577	579	496	190	605		
p1	The Lord will come and not be slow	29	15		489		245	128		321	37		655	
p2	God is in his temple					186	494	32	7					186
p2	Jesus, where'er thy people meet / Lord Jesus, when your people	162	390	371	282		549	476			492	16	367	
p	With undivided heart												963	
a	Rejoice, the Lord of life ascends										441			
e	All who believe and are baptized							421	402		373			
e	At the name of Jesus	148	338	172	46	41	74	261	370	300	380	317	54	
e	Christ above all glory seated						189				164			
e	Head of the Church, our risen Lord						547	562						
e	Lift high the cross	72		508	303	417	170	422	575	550	499	601	394	417
g	Beyond the mist and doubt							490						
g	Father God in heaven, hallowed						518							
g	Father God in heaven, Lord			358								236		
g	Forgive our sins as we forgive	362	66	111	141		134	84	83		428	145	180	
g	Now let us learn of Christ			503										
g	Our Father who art/is in heaven				411	552		247	544	552				
g	Prayer is the soul's sincere/supreme desire		442	372		567	557				561			567
g	Thy/Your kingdom come, O God	177	499	334	519		783	638	644	322	607	269	691	949
g	Who's that knocking?: SS99													

Year A
Proper 13

Continuous: Genesis **32**: 22-31 and Psalm **17**: 1-7, 15 or *Related:* Isaiah **55**: 1-5 and Psalm **145**: 8-9, 14-21; Romans **9**: 1-5; Matthew **14**: 13-21

		AMS	NEH	HTC	HON	MP	H&P	R&S	BPW	CH3	CP	SG	ONC	MPC
se	Gather around for the table is spread				152								199	
l	When morning gilds the skies	146	473	223	551	756	276	292	73	370				
o1	Come, O thou traveller unknown	243	350				434				407			
o1	My name was Jacob: SS65													
o1	Shepherd divine, our wants relieve	228					558				566			
o2	Glorious things of thee/you are spoken	172	362	494	158	173	817	560	480	421	435	35	205	173
o2	Hear our cry, O hear our cry										253			
o2	I hunger and I thirst			409			730	449			306	470		
p1	Be thou / O Lord, my/our guardian	217	64	374	55	385		68			385		68	
p2	All glory, honour, blessing and power: SS2													
p2	Good unto all men is the Lord									617				
p2	Praise to the Lord, the Almighty	207	440	40	427	564	16	74	68	9	558	59	573	564
p2	We would extol thee	206												
e	The God of Abraham praise	331	148	9	478	645	452	121	131	358	586	66	642	645
e	To Abraham and Sarah							553						
g	Bread of heaven, on thee we feed	271	276	398	67			442			284	464	82	
g	Guide me, O thou/my great Redeemer/Jehovah	214	368	528	188	201	437	345	593	89	455	638	252	201
g	How lovely is thy dwelling place — my soul					247								247
g	How lovely is thy dwelling place — tabernacles							703		4				
g	I saw the man from Galilee: SS88													
g	O bread to pilgrims given / O food of men wayfaring		300				620	456	317					
g	O Father, whose creating hand						349							
g	O God, unseen yet ever near	272		421	367								496	

Year B
Proper 13

Continuous: 2 Samuel **11**:26 — **12**:13a and Psalm **51**: 1-12
or *Related:* Exodus **16**: 2-4, 9-15 and Psalm **78**: 23-29; Ephesians **4**: 1-16;
John **6**: 24-35

		AMS	NEH	HTC	HON	MP	H&P	R&S	BPW	CH3	CP	SG	ONC	MPC
o1	Come, O thou all-victorious Lord / O come, our all-victorious			441			418							
o1	Rise and hear! the Lord is speaking	509									321			
o2	Guide me, O thou/my great Redeemer/Jehovah	214	368	528	188	201	437	345	593	89	455	638	252	201
o2	I hunger and I thirst			409			730	449			306	470		
o	Our hunger cries from plenty, Lord							341			551			
p1	God, be merciful to me										153			
p1	Just as I am, without one plea	246	294	440	287	396	697	364	346	79	308	507	374	396
p1	My Lord, what love is this										194	462		
p1	O for a heart to praise my God	230	74	483	361	495	536	514	538	85	533	149	484	495
p1	O God, be gracious to me in thy/your love							695		64				
p1	Rock of ages	135	445	593	437	582	273	365	545	83	565	150	584	582
p2	O bread to pilgrims given / O food of men wayfaring		300				620	456	317					
p2	O God, unseen yet ever near	272		421	367								496	
p2	O praise our great and glorious Lord		116											
eg	O thou who at thy eucharist / O Christ at your first eucharist	265	302	420	391		779				492	318		540	476
el	Come, risen Lord, and deign to be our guest	349	279		96		605				572	293		126
e	Christ from whom all blessings flow			491			764	561						
e	Christ is the King! O friends rejoice	345	345	492				571	475	474	165	31		
e	Come build the church											111		
e	Father, Lord of all creation	356			122				620		418		163	

continued on next page

		AMS	NEH	HTC	HON	MP	H&P	R&S	BPW	CH3	CP	SG	ONC	MPC
e	He went to the top of a mountain: SS63													
e	Head of the Church, our risen Lord						547	562						
e	In Christ there is no east or west	376	480	322	244	329	758	647	482	425	477	575	319	329
e	Jesus, the very thought of thee/you is sweet	120	291, 385	478	264	386	265	509	352	377	486	471, 534	368	
e	Living God, your word has called us											404		
e	One is the body										280			
e	The Saviour, when to heaven he rose						211							
e	Through the night of doubt and sorrow	211	468	466	517		441		546	423	605	544	687	948
e	Thy/Your hand, O God, has guided	171	485	536	518	705	784	567	398	424	606	649	689	705
e	We need each other's voice to sing										582			
e	We worship God in harmony										583			
g	As we break the bread			393				439				460	48	
g	Bread is blessed and broken				66							81		
g	Bread of heaven, on thee we feed	271	276	398	67			442			284	464	82	
g	Bread of the world in mercy broken	270	277	396	68		599	443	428	574	285	465	83	
g	I am the bread of life			S10	222	261	611						299	261
g	Jesus the Lord said/says, I am the Bread					384	137	199	202					384
g	Jesus, the broken bread											363		
g	Jesus, thou/the joy of loving hearts	255	292	413	265	383	258	389	439	571	486	471		
g	Lord Jesus Christ, you have come to us	391	297	417	311	435	617	373	444		505	670	411	435

Year C
Proper 13

Continuous: Hosea **11**: 1-11 and Psalm **107**: 1-9, 43
or *Related:* Ecclesiastes **1**: 2, 12-14, **2**: 18-23 and Psalm **49**: 1-12;
Colossians **3**: 1-11; Luke **12**: 13-21

		AMS	NEH	HTC	HON	MP	H&P	R&S	BPW	CH3	CP	SG	ONC	MPC
o1	God is love: let heaven adore him	365	364		170	187	36	95	374		442		217	187
o1	My God, how wonderful thou art / you are	102	410	369	343	468	51	408		356	523	202	457	468
o1	Sing praise to God who reigns above	193	447				511	75		142	569			
o1	Thy ceaseless, unexhausted love						48	106					688	
o1	When Israel was young, you loved him LUTR56													
o2	As if you were not there: LFB72													
o2	Blest are the saints/is the man / How blest are they						670	541		324				
o2	Put thou thy trust / Commit thou all thy griefs	223			429		672	550		669	562		576	
o2	Stay with us, God							338						
o	How long, O Lord, will you quite forget me?							671						
p1	Now thank we all our God	205	413	33	354	486	566	72	128	368	530	54	474	486
p1	When all thy/your mercies	109	472	39	544	751	573	109		150	617	73	732	751
p2	All my hope on God is founded	336	333	451	15	16	63	586	327	405	368	525	19	16
p2	God of grace and God of glory	367		324	174	192	712	344	572	88	448	574	225	192
p2	Hast thou not known						446	61						
e	Christ is alive! Let Christians sing						190	260	244		140	32	96	
e	Christ is the world's true light	346	494	323	78		456	601	618	505	396	432	100	
e	Come, let us with our Lord arise	449	254	375			575	383			142			
e	Here on the threshold of a new beginning										506	280		
e	In Christ there is no east or west	376	480	322	244	329	758	647	482	425	477	575	319	329
e	Sing we the song of those who stand						821	666						
e	Ye faithful souls who Jesus know						751							
g	Be thou my vision / Lord be my vision	343	339	545	56	51	378	489	521	87	386	669	70	51
g	He that is down need fear no fall	218					676							
g	Jesus, priceless treasure			461	262		259				484	535	344	
g	O worship / Worship the Lord in the beauty of holiness	49	52	344	394	529	505	187	22	40	89	204	552	529
g	Take my life, and let it be	249		554	464	624	705	371	358	462	581	678	625	624

159

Year A
Proper 14

Continuous: Genesis **37**: 1-4, 12-28 and Psalm **105**: 1-6, 16-22, 45b
or *Related:* 1 Kings **19**: 9-18 and Psalm **85**: 8-13; Romans **10**: 5-15;
Matthew **14**: 22-33

		AMS	NEH	HTC	HON	MP	H&P	R&S	BPW	CH3	CP	SG	ONC	MPC
o1	Creator of the earth and skies	351		320			419	82			410	296		
o1	O crucified Redeemer	404					424	604						
o2	A still, small voice											46		
o2	Dear Lord and Father of mankind	115	353	356	106	111	673	492	84	76	411	497	144	111
o2	I searched so long and hard: SS58													
o2	Open, Lord, my inward ear						540							
p1	O God of Bethel / O God of Jacob	216	416	35	364		442	71	599	72	536	241	491	907
p1	The God of Abraham praise	331	148	9	478	645	452	121	131	358	586	66	642	645
p	The Lord will come and not be slow	29	15		489		245	128		321	37		655	
e	'How shall they hear?', who have not heard										598			
e	At the name of Jesus	148	338	172	46	41	74	261	370	300	380	317	54	
e	Christ is the world's true light	346	494	323	78		456	601	618	505	396	432	100	
e	Go forth and tell			505	164	178	770	574	570		437	596	238	178
e	How beauteous/gracious are their feet	301					449	133			220			
e	How shall they hear the word of God			507		250						599		250
e	How sweet the name of Jesus sounds	122	374	211	220	251	257	277	339	376	467	42	297	251
e	I'm not ashamed to own/name my Lord			448	240	323	677	428	343	591		532	316	323
e	Name of all majesty			218		481					525	324	465	481
e	Not far beyond the sea	401					477	318			528			
e	To the Name of our / that brings salvation	121	470	222	523		80	291		373	610	72	698	
g	Have faith in God, my heart	372		431	201		675	499	336		458		268	
g	I sought the Lord, and afterward							368						
g	Light of the minds that know him		400	477				529			501	626	397	
g	My dear Redeemer and my Lord							205	205					
g	Pray when the morn is breaking: EH473													

Year B
Proper 14

Continuous: 2 Samuel **18**: 5-9, 15, 31-33 and Psalm **130** or *Related:* 1 Kings **19**: 4-8 and Psalm **34**: 1-8; Ephesians **4**:25 — **5**:2; John **6**: 35, 41-51

		AMS	NEH	HTC	HON	MP	H&P	R&S	BPW	CH3	CP	SG	ONC	MPC
o1	Abide with me	13	331	425	6	4	665	336	515	695	10	495	2	4
o1	My faith looks up to thee		72		339	469	683			81	522		453	469
o1	O love that will/wilt not let me go			486	384	515	685	511	541	677	542		517	515
o2	Put thou thy trust / Commit thou all thy griefs	223			429		672	550		669	562		576	
o2	When our confidence is shaken						686							
o2	When, O God, our faith is tested							343						
p1	Lord, from the depths to thee I cried									65				
p1	Out of our failure to create							88					549	
p1	Out of the depths I cry to thee						429	331						
p1	Souls of men / Restless souls / There's a wideness	251	461	443	501	607, 683	230	353	573	218	598	188	662	607
p2	God will I bless at all times									391				
p2	Through the night of doubt and sorrow	211	468	466	517		441		546	423	605	544	687	948
e	God is love, and where true love is / Here in Christ we gather	465	513				757	473			441			
e	Jesus, Lord, we look to thee	380	481				759	564			489			
e	Make me a channel of your peace			S19	328	456	776	629	634		519	691	437	456
e	May the mind of Christ my Saviour			550	334	463	739		537	432	521	671	447	463
e	O Jesus, King most wonderful	120	386	484			269	356	353	378	539			
e	Where love and loving-kindness dwell	528												
g	Author of life divine	258	274	395	48		596	440		587	281		56	
g	Bread is blessed and broken				66								81	
g	Bread of heaven, on thee we feed	271	276	398	67			442			284	464	82	
g	Bread of the world in mercy broken	270	277	396	68		599	443	428	574	285	465	83	
g	Father, we thank thee, who hast planted / you now for planting	357	284					444	434	586	298			
g	I am the bread of life			S10	222	261	611						299	261
g	Jesus, the broken bread											363		
g	O bread to pilgrims given / O food of men wayfaring		300				620	456	317					

Year C
Proper 14

Continuous: Isaiah **1**: 1, 10-20 and Psalm **50**: 1-8, 22-23 or *Related:* Genesis **15**: 1-6 and Psalm **33**: 12-22; Hebrews **11**: 1-3, 8-16; Luke **12**: 32-40

		AMS	NEH	HTC	HON	MP	H&P	R&S	BPW	CH3	CP	SG	ONC	MPC
o1	Inspired by love and anger				252								325	
o1	Jesus, lover of my soul	123	383	438	261	372	528	332	345	78	96	201	343	372
o1	Jesus, thou soul of all our joys						761							
o1	Just as I am, without one plea	246	294	440	287	396	697	364	346	79	308	507	374	396
o1	My Lord, what love is this										194		462	
o1	Not for our sins alone	229												
o2	Creatures, once in safety held: SS5													
o2	Father of Jesus Christ, my Lord						693	351						
o2	The God of Abraham praise	331	148	9	478	645	452	121	131	358	586	66	642	645
p1	Lift up your heads, ye/you mighty gates	483	8				240				12	30		
p1	The Lord will come and not be slow	29	15		489		245	128			321	37		655
p2	God of love and truth and beauty	368					403					5		
p2	Lord, for the years			328	310	428		603	535		51	602	409	428
p2	Rejoice, O land, in God thy might / your Lord	296	493	331	431						227		579	
e	Author of faith, eternal Word						662				381			
e	How beauteous/gracious are their feet	301					449	133			220			
e	Jerusalem the golden	184	381	573	259			662	312	537	482		340	
e	Jerusalem, my happy home / thou city blest	187	225	569	258						481		339	
e	Leader of faithful souls and guide						819							
e	My soul, there is a country	191	412							693	261		464	
e	O what their joy / What of those sabbaths	186	432					659		535	225		550	
e	One more step along the world I go				405		746	549	356		548		525	
e	To Abraham and Sarah						553							
g	Children of the heavenly King	213	344	566	63									
g	He that is down need fear no fall	218					676							
g	Thanks be to God for his saints										64			
g	Wake, O wake / Sleepers, wake	32	16	199	529		249	132		315	39		703	
g	Ye/You servants of the Lord	150	18	598	566		248			319	40		757	

Year A
Proper 15

Continuous: Genesis **45**: 1-15 and Psalm **133** or *Related:* Isaiah **56**: 1, 6-8 and Psalm **67**; Romans **11**: 1-2a, 29-32; Matthew **15**: [10-20] 21-28

		AMS	NEH	HTC	HON	MP	H&P	R&S	BPW	CH3	CP	SG	ONC	MPC
o1g	In Christ there is no east or west	376	480	322	244	329	758	647	482	425	477	575	319	329
o1	Jesus, Lord, we look to thee	380	481				759	564			489			
o1	O Holy Spirit, Lord of grace	152	419		371		310				188		501	
o1	Where love and loving-kindness dwell	528												
o2	I cannot tell why/how he whom angels worship			194	226	266	238	265	381		54	437	303	266
o2	O Lord, all the world belongs to you				378			90	136				509	
p1	Happy are they, they that/who love God	176	369	473	195		711			408	456		262	
p1	How good a thing it is			497								585		
p1	How good and how pleasant it is										587			
p1	Pray that Jerusalem may have		441				510	727			560			
p2	God of mercy, God of grace	179	366	293	175			575	48	497	449		227	
p2	Lord, bless us and pity us									493				
e	And can it be			588	30	33	216	136	328	409	376	168	32	
e	Come, O thou all-victorious Lord / O come, our all-victorious			441			418							
e	Father of everlasting grace						300				420			
e	Father, whose everlasting love						520				107			
e	Souls of men / Restless souls / There's a wideness	251	461	443	501	607, 683	230	353	573	218	598	188	662	607
e	We have a gospel to proclaim	431	486	519	532	728	465		585		612		716	728
e	When Christ was lifted from the earth	525		335			655						142	
g	All hail! the power of Jesus' name	140	332	587/ 203	13	13	252		29	382	163	24	16	13
g	Jesus shall reign where'er the sun	143	388	516	277	379	239	269	313	413	490	45	359	379

163

Year B
Proper 15

Continuous: 1 Kings **2**: 10-12, **3**: 3-14 and Psalm **111** or *Related:*
Proverbs **9**: 1-6 and Psalm **34**: 9-14; Ephesians **5**: 15-20; John **6**: 51-58

		AMS	NEH	HTC	HON	MP	H&P	R&S	BPW	CH3	CP	SG	ONC	MPC
o1 &2	Listen, Wisdom cries aloud LUTR35													
o1	Be it my only wisdom here						786							
o1	Be thou my vision / Lord be my vision	343	339	545	56	51	378	489	521	87	386	669	70	51
o1	Give to me, Lord, a thankful heart						548	497	531			501		
o1	Lord of all power, I give you my will / Lord of creation, to you be all praise	395		547		440	699	532		428	508			
o2	Happy the man that finds the grace						674							
o2	My God, and/now is thy table spread	259		418	342						313	474	456	
o	Who can measure heaven and earth			27										
p1	Lord, as I wake I turn to you	485	236	267			634	534				561		
p1	We praise you, Lord, for all that's true and pure							516						
p2	Father, who on man dost shower						341			515				
p2	God of love and truth and beauty	368					403					5		
p2	Put peace into each other's hands							635	637			479	575	
p2	Tell his praise in song and story			41					563				630	
e	Angel-voices ever singing	163	336	307	33	34	484	405	1	455	377	27	37	34
e	Awake, awake, fling off the night	342			49				404		334		57	
e	For the music of creation										36			
e	Glory in highest heaven	277												
e	Glory to thee who safe hast kept (*See also* Awake, my soul)	1	233		550						1	618	58	804
e	Glory, love, and praise, and honour	461	287		160		35				436		207	
e	Now / Sing, my tongue / Of the glorious body	252	268		353		624	457	449	578	316		473	
e	Songs of praise the angels sang	196	451	350			512	667		38	574		608	
e	When morning gilds the skies	146	473	223	551	756	276	292	73	370				
e	When, in our music, God is glorified				550		388	414			618		737	
g	Bread of heaven, on thee we feed	271	276	398	67			442			284	464	82	
g	Bread of the world in mercy broken	270	277	396	68		599	443	428	574	285	465	83	
g	Draw nigh and take / Draw near and take		281	401							296			
g	Here, Lord, we take the broken bread			404			604	448	440				278	
g	I am the bread of life			S10	222	261	611						299	261
g	Jesus, the broken bread											363		
g	O bread to pilgrims given / O food of men wayfaring		300				620	456	317					

Year C
Proper 15

Continuous: Isaiah **5**: 1-7 and Psalm **80**: 1-2, 8-19 or *Related:* Jeremiah **23**: 23-29 and Psalm **82**; Hebrews **11**:29 — **12**:2; Luke **12**: 49-56

		AMS	NEH	HTC	HON	MP	H&P	R&S	BPW	CH3	CP	SG	ONC	MPC
o1	Awake, awake, fling off the night	342			49				404		334		57	
o1	Awake, my soul, and with the sun	1	232	264	50		632	378		42	1	618	58	804
o2	Come, Holy Ghost, our hearts inspire (Wesley)	448	348		91		469	312	97	122	177		117	
o2	Come, O thou all-victorious Lord / O come, our all-victorious			441			418							
o2	Now in reverence and awe										232		902	
p1	For the might of thine/your arm we bless thee/you					154	435		479	365				154
p1	O God of Bethel / O God of Jacob	216	416	35	364		442	71	599	72	536	241	491	907
p2	Judge eternal, throned in splendour		490	329	285	395	409	626	627	519	356	600	372	395
p2	The Lord will come and not be slow	29	15		489		245	128		321	37		655	
p2	What Adam's disobedience cost	524					430							
p2	Who can sound the depths of sorrow				766							257		766
e	A cloud of witnesses: BWF72													
e	A glorious company we sing						787	570		426				
e	Ahead of us a race to run PR892													
e	Awake, my soul, stretch every nerve							487						
e	Behold what witnesses unseen									531				
e	Fight the good fight	220	359	526	128	143	710	496	524	442	423	635	169	143
e	Give me/us the wings of faith	324	225		156		815	664			216		202	
e	Sing for God's glory											598		
e	The head that once was crowned with thorns	141	134	182	480	647	209	257	274	286	172	442		644
e	We are called to stand together										607			
g	Forgive our sins as we forgive	362	66	111	141		134	84	83		428	145	180	
g	Help us to help each other / Jesus, united by thy grace	374		540	208		773	500			461		275	
g	O God, your love's undying flame							327						
g	O thou/Lord who came[st]	233	431	552/ 596	392	525	745	433	355	110	191	560	541	525
g	See how great a flame aspires						781							

Continuous: Exodus **1**:8 — **2**:10 and Psalm **124** or *Related:* Isaiah **51**: 1-6 and Psalm **138**; Romans **12**: 1-8; Matthew **16**: 13-20

		AMS	NEH	HTC	HON	MP	H&P	R&S	BPW	CH3	CP	SG	ONC	MPC
o1 &2	Cry 'freedom' in the name of God				104								138	
o1	'Moses, I know you're the man'				338		450	547	489				451	
o1	God moves in a mysterious way	112	365		173	193	65	59	122	147	445		222	193
o1	When Israel was in Egypt's land							643						
o2	God is the refuge of his saints						53				218			
o2	To Abraham and Sarah							553						
p1	Had not the Lord, let Israel say PR 124													
p1	Now Israel may say and that truly									392				
p1	With undivided heart												963	
p2	God is in his temple					186	494	32	7					186
p2	Jesus, where'er thy people meet / Lord Jesus, when your people	162	390	371	282		549	476			492	16	367	
e	All that I am										686		801	
e	Almighty Father of all things that be						375	485		451				
e	Born in song						486					28		
e	Christ from whom all blessings flow			491			764	561						
e	God is love, and where true love is / Here in Christ we gather	465	513				757	473			441			
e	Help us to help each other / Jesus, united by thy grace	374		540	208		773	500			461		275	
e	I will offer up my life										565			
e	Let him to whom we now belong						698							
e	Lord of all good, our gifts we bring to thee	393					797	404			458			
e	Lord, for tomorrow and its needs											410		
e	O thou who at thy eucharist / O Christ at your first eucharist	265	302	420	391		779			492	318		540	476
e	Take my life, and let it be	249		554	464	624	705	371	358	462	581	678	625	624
e	Where love and loving-kindness dwell	528												
g	From the very depths of darkness				151								198	
g	God, your glory we have seen in your Son						459	746			469			
g	It was easy up to Caesarea Philippi: SS27													
g	Join all the glorious names			214		392	78	280	557	304	493	46		392
g	The Church's one foundation	170	484	501	473	640	515	566	393	420	585	581	636	640
g	Thou art the Christ, O Lord	317	172								236			

Year B
Proper 16

Continuous: 1 Kings **8**: [1, 6, 10-11] 22-30, 41-43 and Psalm **84**
or *Related:* Joshua **24**: 1-2a, 14-18 and Psalm **34**: 15-22; Ephesians **6**: 10-20;
John **6**: 56-69

		AMS	NEH	HTC	HON	MP	H&P	R&S	BPW	CH3	CP	SG	ONC	MPC
o1	Christ is made the sure foundation / Blessed city, heavenly Salem	283/ 332	204-5	559	76	73	485	559	474	10	208	572	97	73
o1	Christ is our corner-stone	161		564	77						395		98	
o1	Great Shepherd of thy/your people, hear	164		363			490	387			454	238	250	
o1	Open now the gates of beauty						390							
o2	Jesus calls us: o'er/in the tumult	312	200	104	266	359	141	355		211	233	668	347	359
o2	Thine/Yours for ever	234	463	556	504						599		673	992
o2	Who is on the Lord's side?					769	722		615	479				769
p1	How lovely is thy dwelling place — tabernacles							703		4				
p1	Lord of the worlds above	165										511		
p1	O Lord of hosts, how lovely is your dwelling place PR84													
p2	Come, we that love the Lord						487	384	525					
p2	God will I bless at all times, his praise									391				
p2	O God of Bethel / O God of Jacob	216	416	35	364		442	71	599	72	536	241	491	907
p2	Thee will I praise with all my heart						41							
p2	Through all the changing scenes of life	209	467	46	516	702	73	685	544		604	654	686	702
p2	Who honours courage here		537									647		
e	Christian soldiers in the fight PR882													
e	Give me, O Christ, the strength							524						
e	Oft in danger, oft in woe / Christian soldiers, onward go	210	434	524	396	533	715				547		487	533
e	Soldiers of Christ, arise	219	449	533	449	604	719	370	580	441	571	643	606	604
e	Stand up, stand up for Jesus	221	453	535	457	617	721			481	578	644	617	617
g	As we break the bread			393				439				460	48	
g	Bread of the world in mercy broken	270	277	396	68		599	443	428	574	285	465	83	
g	How sweet the name of Jesus sounds	122	374	211	220	251	257	277	339	376	467	42	297	251
g	I am the bread of life			S10	222	261	611						299	261
g	Jesus the Lord said/says, I am the Bread					384	137	199	202					384
g	Jesus, the broken bread											363		
g	Lord Jesus, once you spoke to men	392		112					598					
g	O bread to pilgrims given / O food of men wayfaring		300				620	456	317					
g	Your words to me are life and health						482	321						

Year C
Proper 16

Continuous: Jeremiah **1**: 4-10 and Psalm **71**: 1-6 or *Related:* Isaiah **58**: 9b-14
and Psalm **103**: 1-8; Hebrews **12**: 18-29; Luke **13**: 10-17

		AMS	NEH	HTC	HON	MP	H&P	R&S	BPW	CH3	CP	SG	ONC	MPC
o1	Come, living God, when least expected							354			403			
o1	Come, Lord, to our souls come down	348					470	361			335		122	
o1	Master, speak! Thy servant heareth / Your servant's listening				459		535		536					459
o1	Speak, Lord, in the stillness			253		608			105					608
o2	Come, let us to the Lord our God						33	81		69	402			
o2	King of glory, King of peace	194	391	603	288	397	499	97	53	364	494	178	375	
p1	A safe stronghold/fortress/refuge	114		523		2	661	585	375	406/7				2
p1	Rock of ages	135	445	593	437	582	273	365	545	83	565	150	584	582
p2	Fill thou/now my/our life	200		541	129	146	792	406	569	457	424	665	171	146
p2	My soul, repeat his praise						716							
p2	O bless the Lord, my soul, let all			34										
p2	Praise the Lord! My soul is singing PR103A													
p2	Praise to the Lord, the Almighty	207	440	40	427	564	16	74	68	9	558	59	573	564
p2	Praise, my soul, the King of heaven	192	436	38	422	560	13	104	65	360	555		565	560
e	Come let us go, up to the mountain of the Lord										9			
e	God is a name my soul adores						24	31			255			
e	Join all the glorious names			214		392	78	280	557	304	493	46		392
e	Leader of faithful souls and guide						819							
e	O God of our forefathers, hear / With solemn faith		314				554							
e	Rejoice! the Lord is King	139	443	180	432	575	243	657	317	296	563	440	580	575
e	Victim divine, thy grace we claim		309				629							
g	Hark the glad sound! The Saviour comes	30	6	193	198	210	82	137	143	160	27	435	265	210
g	Lord, we come to ask your healing				319								422	
g	She was made in God's image: SS92													
g	The first day of the week	424					576							
g	Thine arm, O Lord, in days of old	285	324		502		397			214		671		

Year A
Proper 17

Continuous: Exodus **3**: 1-15 and Psalm **105**: 1-6, 23-26, 45c or *Related:*
Jeremiah **15**: 15-21 and Psalm **26**: 1-8; Romans **12**: 9-21; Matthew **16**: 21-28

		AMS	NEH	HTC	HON	MP	H&P	R&S	BPW	CH3	CP	SG	ONC	MPC
o1	'Moses, I know you're the man'				338		450	547	489				451	
o1	Be still for the presence / Spirit of the Lord				53	50			5		383	7	67	
o1	Deep in the shadows of the past						447							
o1	Take off your shoes: SS66													
o1	The bush in flame BL27													
o2	A safe stronghold/fortress/refuge	114		523		2	661	585	375	406/7				2
o2	Inspired by love and anger				252							325		
o2	Lord, thy word abideth / Lord, your word shall guide us	166	407	251	318	446	476	317	102	130	515		420	446
o2	Your words to me						482	321						
op1	The God of Abraham praise	331	148	9	478	645	452	121	131	358	586	66	642	645
p1	When Israel was in Egypt's land						643							
p2	In judgement, Lord, arise PR26													
p2	Lord of the worlds above	165									511			
p2	Mine hands in innocence, O Lord									564				
p2	O praise the Lord, ye servants of the Lord		426											
p2	We love the place, O God	160	471	558	533	731				15	211		718	731
e	Christ from whom all blessings flow			491			764	561						
e	Go forth for God		321								438			
e	God is love, and where true love is / Here in Christ we gather	465	513				757	473			441			
e	Gracious Spirit, Holy Ghost / Holy Spirit, gracious Guest	154	367	474	184	198	301	310	288	438	182	556	245	198
e	Holy Spirit, Truth divine			235			289	301	292	106	184		289	
e	I was lying in the roadway: SS98													
e	Jesus, Lord, we look to thee	380	481				759	564			489			
e	Lord, to you we bring our treasure	495												
e	Now in view of all God's mercies LUTR129													
e	O God of hope										493			
e	Of all the Spirit's gifts to me	503					320							
e	Where love and loving-kindness dwell	528												
g	Beneath the cross of Jesus				59	55	165			684	105		65	55
g	Father, hear the prayer we offer	113	357	360	120	132	436	495	523		416	237	161	132
g	Jesus, prince and saviour				274	377						410	358	377
g	Never further than thy cross							507						
g	Take up thy/your cross	237	76	114	465					430	582	645	626	935
g	Take up your cross, he says											627		
g	The head that once was crowned with thorns	141	134	182	480	647	209	257	274	286	172	442		644

Year B
Proper 17

Continuous: Song of Solomon **2**: 8-13 and Psalm **45**: 1-2, 6-9
or *Related:* Deuteronomy **4**: 1-2, 6-9 and Psalm **15**; James **1**: 17-27;
Mark **7**: 1-8, 14-15, 21-23

		AMS	NEH	HTC	HON	MP	H&P	R&S	BPW	CH3	CP	SG	ONC	MPC
o1	Christian people, raise your song	443					601	435	430		289			
o1	Jesus, we thus / Now Jesus we obey	477					614	450	446		307			
o2	Before Jehovah's aweful/awesome throne / Sing to the Lord	197		15			61	119		2	387			
o2	God is my great desire											218		
o2	The Lord is King! lift up thy/your voice	107		183	485	656	58	76	322	36	592	98	650	656
p1	My heart is full of Christ, and longs						799							
p1	No other prophet ever spoke										325			
p2	Almighty Father, who for us thy Son didst give	338					401	621			374			
p2	Enthrone thy God within thy heart						692							
p2	Lord, who may dwell within your house										684			
p2	My God, accept my heart this day	279	318	551	341		701			429	338	559	455	
p2	Within thy tabernacle, Lord									5				
e	For the beauty of the earth	104	285	298	137	152	333	41	121	367	253	298	184	152
e	Help us, O Lord, to learn	373	370	493			474				460	226		
e	In an age of twisted values											317		
e	Of all the Spirit's gifts to me	503					320							
e	Teach me, my God and King	240	456		466		803	538		692	583		629	
g	Almighty God, we come to make confession											27		
g	Come, O thou all-victorious Lord / O come, our all-victorious			441			418							
g	God who created this Eden of earth	369												
g	In Adam we have all been one	474					420							
g	O lift us up, strong Son of God						427	337						
g	Purify my heart/Refiner's fire				428							163	574	921

Year C
Proper 17

Continuous: Jeremiah **2**: 4-13 and Psalm **81**: 1, 10-16 or *Related:*
Ecclesiasticus **10**: 12-18 or Proverbs **25**: 6-7 and Psalm **112**;
Hebrews **13**: 1-8, 15-16; Luke **14**: 1, 7-14

		AMS	NEH	HTC	HON	MP	H&P	R&S	BPW	CH3	CP	SG	ONC	MPC
o1	Glorious things of thee/you are spoken	172	362	494	158	173	817	560	480	421	435	35	205	173
o1	Jesus, lover of my soul	123	383	438	261	372	528	332	345	78	96	201	343	372
o1	Lord we know that we have failed you											423		
o2	Come down, O Love Divine	156	137	231	90	89	281	294	283	115	170	663	114	89
o2	Lord, that I may learn of thee						737							
o2	O for a heart to praise my God	230	74	483	361	495	536	514	538	85	533	149	484	495
p1	God in his love for us lent us this planet						343	85				300		832
p1	O Father, whose creating hand						349							
p1	Praise and thanksgiving, Father, we offer	415					350	48			272		558	
p1	We plough the fields and scatter	290	262	292	534	732	352	124	135	620	275	311	719	732
p2	Jesus, my Lord, how rich thy grace / Fountain of good	381					147			459				
p2	Lord Christ, who on thy heart didst bear	388			308		394						407	
p2	We find thee, Lord, in others' need	430												
e	Jesus, these eyes have never seen	245	389					592		674	491		365	
e	Jesus, thy far-extended fame						148							
e	Leader of faithful souls and guide						819							
e	O Christ the same, through all our story's pages		258	263									477	
e	Praise to Christ, the Lord incarnate										327			
gl	My God, and /now is thy table spread	259		418	342						313	474	456	
g	All praise to thee/Christ, for thou / our Lord and King divine	337	335	204	18		253	750		297	372		22	
g	Jesus, humble was your birth	379					196			488				
g	Lord God, we see thy power displayed	390												
g	Tell out, my soul, the greatness of the Lord	422	186	42	467	631	86	740	391	164	362	62	631	631

Year A
Proper 18

Continuous: Exodus **12**: 1-14 and Psalm **149** or *Related:* Ezekiel **33**: 7-11 and Psalm **119**: 33-40; Romans **13**: 8-14; Matthew **18**: 15-20

		AMS	NEH	HTC	HON	MP	H&P	R&S	BPW	CH3	CP	SG	ONC	MPC
o1	At the Lamb's high feast we sing	81	104		45						138	53		
o1	If our God had simply saved us: SS35													
o1	Lord, enthroned in heavenly splendour	263	296	416	309	431	616			583	311	52	408	
o1	Now lives the Lamb of God			159				255				413		
o2	Come, let us to the Lord our God						33	81		69	402			
o2	Go, tell it on the mountains				165		179	135	164	571			243	179
o2	Here is the risen Son										443			
o2	Lord, speak to me, that I may speak			510		444	553	613	611	485	512		444	
o2	My God, how wonderful thou art / you are	102	410	369	343	468	51	408		356	523	202	457	468
p1	Be it my only wisdom here						786							
p1	Captains of the saintly band / Christian soldiers	299	215							539	212		91	
p1	Ye/You servants of God, your Master proclaim	149	476	520	565	784	278	293	76	372	627	75	784	756
p2	Thou art / You are the way	128	464	113	512	695	234	554		121	600		682	695
e	Awake, awake, fling off the night	342			49				404		334		57	
e	Father of all, whose laws have stood			539				335				664		
e	O day of God, draw near/nigh In beauty	405						632	635	511	33			
e	Soldiers of Christ, arise	219	449	533	449	604	719	370	580	441	571	643	606	604
e	Thy kingdom come! on bended knee	178	500		520					323	608		690	
e	Ye/You servants of the Lord	150	18	598	566		248			319	40		757	
g	Brother, sister, let me serve you			73				474	473		393	619	88	
g	Forgive our sins as we forgive	362	66	111	141		134	84	83		428	145	180	
g	O thou not made with hands	174	430				656	617						
g	Rejoice, the Lord of life ascends										441			

Year B
Proper 18

Continuous: Proverbs **22**: 1-2, 8-9, 22-23 and Psalm **125** or *Related:* Isaiah **35**: 4-7a and Psalm **146**; James **2**: 1-10 [11-13] 14-17; Mark **7**: 24-37

		AMS	NEH	HTC	HON	MP	H&P	R&S	BPW	CH3	CP	SG	ONC	MPC
o1	Happy are they who walk in God's wise way							669						
o1	Help us to help each other / Jesus, united by thy grace	374		540	208		773	500			461		275	
o2g	O for a thousand tongues to sing	125	415	219	362	496	744	285	59	371	534	55	485	495
o2	Christ brings the kingdom where barrenness blooms										430			
o2	Let the desert sing			198										
o2	Lord, we your Church						775							
o2	The day of the Lord shall come							637						
o2	The Saviour will come resplendent in joy											664		
o2	The voice of God goes out to all the world						140	131						
o2	When the King shall come again			200										
p1	Glorious things of thee/you are spoken	172	362	494	158	173	817	560	480	421	435	35	205	173
p1	God is love: let heaven adore him	365	364		170	187	36	95	374		442		217	187
p1	Those who rely on the Lord are unshakable PR125													
p2	All glory, honour, blessing and power: SS2													
p2	I'll praise my Maker while I've breath			20		320	439	734	127		473	84		320
p2	O Christ the Lord, O Christ the King		496				406	630						
e	Father all-loving, thou rulest in majesty	355ii												
e	For ourselves no longer living							520					183	
e	Jesus, my Lord, how rich thy grace / Fountain of good	381					147			459				
e	Son of God, eternal Saviour	132	498	102				605	639	454	573			
e	Teach us how grave a thing it is										151			
e	The Church of Christ in every age						804	636	613					
e	The love of God comes close							107				186		940

continued on next page

		AMS	NEH	HTC	HON	MP	H&P	R&S	BPW	CH3	CP	SG	ONC	MPC
e	When Christ was lifted from the earth	525		335				655					142	
g	A stranger once did bless the earth	335						198						
g	Father of mercy, God of consolation		323					645						
g	O Christ the healer, we have come						395				346	489		395
g	O Lord, whose saving name												910	
g	Soundless were the tossing trees: SS93													
g	The Kingdom of God is justice and joy			333		651	139	200	321		591	184	646	651
g	We cannot measure how you heal							653			348	490	712	

Year C
Proper 18

Continuous: Jeremiah **18**: 1-11 and Psalm **139**: 1-6, 13-18 or *Related:* Deuteronomy **30**: 15-20 and Psalm **1**; Philemon 1-21; Luke **14**: 25-33

		AMS	NEH	HTC	HON	MP	H&P	R&S	BPW	CH3	CP	SG	ONC	MPC
o1	Before Jehovah's aweful/awesome throne / Sing to the Lord	197		15			61	119		2	387			
o1	Behold the servant of the Lord						788							
o2	I heard the voice of Jesus say	247	376		231	275	136	349		212	469		310	275
o2	Lord, I have made thy word my choice	490					475	316			504			
o2	O happy day that fixed my choice			442	369	499	702	359	539				498	499
p1	In all my vast concerns with thee						72							
p1	Lord, you have searched and known my ways						71	70	564					
p1	My Lord, you called my name										203			
p1	O God, you search me and you know me										514			
p1	Thou art / You are before me, Lord, thou art behind						543	731		68				
p1	Walk the hills and you will find him										309			
p2	Happy are they who walk in God's wise way							669						
p2	Lord, as I wake I turn to you	485	236	267			634	534				561		

continued on next page

		AMS	NEH	HTC	HON	MP	H&P	R&S	BPW	CH3	CP	SG	ONC	MPC
e	Brother, sister, let me serve you				73			474	473		393	619	88	
e	When Christ was lifted from the earth	525		335			655						142	
g	God be in my head	236	328	543	166		694	498	592	433	439	666	211	
g	I bind unto myself / myself to God today / Christ be with me		159	5	225		695	36		402	203		302	
g	Let him to whom we now belong						698							
g	O Jesus, I have promised	235	420	531	372	501	704	509	352	434	538	676	503	501
g	Take up your cross, he says											627		

Year A
Proper 19

Continuous: Exodus **14**: 19-31 and Psalm **114** or (Canticle) Exodus **15**: 1b-11, 20-21; or *Related:* Genesis **50**: 15-21 and Psalm **103**: [1-7] 8-13; Romans **14**: 1-12; Matthew **18**: 21-35

		AMS	NEH	HTC	HON	MP	H&P	R&S	BPW	CH3	CP	SG	ONC	MPC
o1, c	I will sing the Lord's high triumph LUTR13													
o1	At the dawning of creation							424				52		
o1	Be thou / O Lord, my/our guardian	217	64	374	55	385		68			385		68	
o1	Lead us, heavenly Father, lead us	224	393	595	293	400	68	543	597	90	496	640	379	400
o1	O God of Bethel / O God of Jacob	216	416	35	364		442	71	599	72	536	241	491	907
o1	O/Our God, our help in ages past	99	417	37	366	498	358	705	389	611	537	542	494	498
o1	The God of Abraham praise	331	148	9	478	645	452	121	131	358	586	66	642	645
o1	Through the night of doubt and sorrow	211	468	466	517		441		546	423	605	544	687	948
op1	Guide me, O thou/my great Redeemer/Jehovah	214	368	528	188	201	437	345	593	89	455	638	252	201
p1	Be still for the presence / Spirit of the Lord				53	50			5		383	7	67	
p1	Glorious things of thee/you are spoken	172	362	494	158	173	817	560	480	421	435	35	205	173
p2g	Praise, my soul, the King of heaven	192	436	38	422	560	13	104	65	360	555		565	560
p2	Bless the Lord, my soul				61							105		
e	At the name of Jesus	148	338	172	46	41	74	261	370	300	380	317	54	
e	Jesus lives! Thy/Your terrors now	82	112	156	272	373	198	239	253	605	148	409	354	373
e	Teach us how grave a thing it is											151		
g	Almighty God, we come to make confession											27		
g	Amazing grace			28	27	31	215	92	550		375	26	29	

continued on next page

		AMS	NEH	HTC	HON	MP	H&P	R&S	BPW	CH3	CP	SG	ONC	MPC
g	And can it be			588	30	33	216	136	328	409	376	168	32	
g	Dear Lord and Father of mankind	115	353	356	106	111	673	492	84	76	411	497	144	111
g	Father of heaven, whose love profound	97	358	359	124		519			77	421	144		827
g	Forgive our sins as we forgive	362	66	111	141		134	84	83		428	145	180	
g	God is love: let heaven adore him	365	364		170	187	36	95	374		442		217	187
g	Great is thy/your faithfulness			260	186	200	66	96	553		453	39	249	200
g	I heard the voice of Jesus say	247	376		231	275	136	349		212	469		310	275
g	Jesus, where'er thy people meet / Lord Jesus, when your people	162	390	371	282		549	476			492	16	367	
g	Just as I am, without one plea	246	294	440	287	396	697	364	346	79	308	507	374	396
g	Make me a channel of your peace			S19	328	456	776	629	634		519	691	437	456
g	O God beyond all praising			36	363							53	489	
g	O love that will/wilt not let me go			486	384	515	685	511	541	677	542		517	515
g	Oh, the deep, deep, love of Jesus			465		522						183	538	522
g	Rock of ages	135	445	593	437	582	273	365	545	83	565	150	584	582
g	The price is paid					663								663
g	Timeless love! we sing the story			47		707	60					100		707
g	When all thy/your mercies	109	472	39	544	751	573	109		150	617	73	732	751

Year B
Proper 19

Continuous: Proverbs **1**: 20-33 and Psalm **19**
or (Canticle) Wisdom **7**:26 — **8**:1
or *Related:* Isaiah **50**: 4-9a and Psalm **116**: 1-9; James **3**: 1-12; Mark **8**: 27-38

		AMS	NEH	HTC	HON	MP	H&P	R&S	BPW	CH3	CP	SG	ONC	MPC
o1	Be thou my vision / Lord be my vision	343	339	545	56	51	378	489	521	87	386	669	70	51
o1	Can we/man by searching find out God	438					76	80			201	496		
o1	O Lord of every shining constellation	411		314					130	141	263		512	
o1	Thou/God whose almighty / Father your mighty word	180	466	506	514	699	29	38	591	494	267	684	597	699
o2	He lives in us, the Christ of God			457					554			173		
o2	I heard the voice of Jesus say	247	376		231	275	136	349		212	469		310	275

continued on next page

		AMS	NEH	HTC	HON	MP	H&P	R&S	BPW	CH3	CP	SG	ONC	MPC
o2	O sacred head	68	90	139	389	520	176	220	223	253	120	385	535	520
p1	Father, Lord of all creation	356			122				620		418		163	
p1	O worship the King all glorious above	101	433	24	393	528	28	47	63	35	546	90	551	528
p1	The heavens declare thy/your glory, Lord	168		254			481	320			264	230		
p1	The spacious firmament	103	267		493		339			143	265		665	
p1	The stars declare his glory										314			
p2	God of mercy, God of grace	179	366	293	175			575	48	497	449		227	
p2	When all thy/your mercies	109	472	39	544	751	573	109		150	617	73	732	751
e	Lord, speak to me, that I may speak			510		444	553	613	611	485	512			444
e	Teach us how grave a thing it is										151			
g	Be thou / O Lord, my/our guardian	217	64	374	55	385		68			385		68	
g	God our Father and Creator			562										
g	I danced in the morning	375	375		228			195			468		305	
g	I'm not ashamed to own/name my Lord			448	240	323	677	428	343	591		532	316	323
g	It was easy up to Caesarea Philippi: SS27													
g	Jesus our Lord, our King and our God	382												
g	Just as I am, without one plea	246	294	440	287	396	697	364	346	79	308	507	374	396
g	Light of the minds that know him		400	477				529			501	626	397	
g	Lord Jesus Christ, you have come to us	391	297	417	311	435	617	373	444		505	670	411	435
g	O Jesus, I have promised	235	420	531	372	501	704	509	352	434	538	676	503	501
g	Praise to the Holiest in the height	117	439	140	426	563	231	103	562	238	557	58	572	563
g	Take my life, and let it be	249		554	464	624	705	371	358	462	581	678	625	624
g	Take up thy/your cross	237	76	114	465					430	582	645	626	935
g	Take up your cross, he says											627		
g	There is a Redeemer				500	673						396	658	673
g	Thou art the Christ, O Lord	317	172								236			
g	Will you come and follow me?				560			558	363		622	634	752	

Year C
Proper 19

Continuous: Jeremiah **4**: 11-12, 22-28 and Psalm **14** or *Related:*
Exodus **32**: 7-14 and Psalm **51**: 1-10; 1 Timothy **1**: 12-17; Luke **15**: 1-10

		AMS	NEH	HTC	HON	MP	H&P	R&S	BPW	CH3	CP	SG	ONC	MPC
o1p	The Lord will come and not be slow	29	15		489		245	128		321	37		655	
o1	Rejoice, O land, in God thy might / your Lord	296	493	331	431						227		579	
o2e	King of glory, King of peace	194	391	603	288	397	499	97	53	364	494	178	375	
o2g	When all thy/your mercies	109	472	39	544	751	573	109		150	617	73	732	751
o2	Jesus calls us: o'er/in the tumult	312	200	104	266	359	141	355		211	233	668	347	359
o2	Through all the changing scenes of life	209	467	46	516	702	73	685	544		604	654	686	702
p1	Come down, O Love Divine	156	137	231	90	89	281	294	283	115	170	663	114	89
p1	The fool whose heart declares in pride PR14													
p2	Create in us clean hearts, O God										682			
p2	God be merciful to me										153			
p2	Heal me, hands of Jesus			319								488		
p2	My God, how wonderful thou art / you are	102	410	369	343	468	51	408		356	523	202	457	468
p2	O for a heart to praise my God	230	74	483	361	495	536	514	538	85	533	149	484	495
e	Immortal, invisible, God only wise	199	377	21	242	327	9	67	383	32	474	44	314	327
e	Jesus, lover of my soul	123	383	438	261	372	528	332	345	78	96	201	343	372
e	My song is love unknown	63	86	136	346	478	173	207	204	224	112	384	463	478
e	Name of all majesty			218		481					525	324	465	481
e	O God of Bethel / O God of Jacob	216	416	35	364		442	71	599	72	536	241	491	907
e	Praise, my soul, the King of heaven	192	436	38	422	560	13	104	65	360	555		565	560
g	All people that on earth do dwell	100	334	14	17	20	1	712	2	1	369	77	21	20
g	Amazing grace			28	27	31	215	92	550		375	26	29	31
g	Be thou / O Lord, my/our guardian	217	64	374	55	385		68			385	68		
g	Before Jehovah's aweful/awesome throne / Sing to the Lord	197		15			61	119		2	387			
g	Christ who knows all his sheep	347						470		672				
g	Faithful Shepherd, feed me		282	29	117							498	156	
g	Father of heaven, whose love profound	97	358	359	124		519			77	421	144		827
g	I will sing the wondrous story			212	237	315	223		382	381		43	337	315
g	In heavenly love abiding			458	246	331	678	590	555	681	478		323	331
g	Loving Shepherd of thy/your sheep	134		305	325					93	517		424	
g	O thou who at thy eucharist / O Christ at your first eucharist	265	302	420	391		779			492	318		540	476
g	O where, O where's my silver piece: SS97													
g	Oh, the deep, deep, love of Jesus			465		522						183	538	522
g	The King of love my shepherd is	126	457	44	484	649	69	552	394	388	589	205	649	649
g	Thine/Yours for ever	234	463	556	504						599		673	992

Year A
Proper 20

Continuous: Exodus **16**: 2-15 and Psalm **105**: 1-6, 37-45 or *Related:* Jonah **3**:10 — **4**:11 and Psalm **145**: 1-8; Philippians **1**: 21-30; Matthew **20**: 1-16

		AMS	NEH	HTC	HON	MP	H&P	R&S	BPW	CH3	CP	SG	ONC	MPC
o1e	Jesus, thou/the joy of loving hearts	255	292	413	265	383	258	389	439	571	486	471		
o1e	Light of the minds that know him		400	477				529			501	626	397	
o1	Bread is blessed and broken				66								81	
o1	Bread of heaven, on thee we feed	271	276	398	67			442			284	464	82	
o1	Deck thyself/yourself, my soul	257	280	400	108		606	446		567	295		146	
o1	Guide me, O thou/my great Redeemer/Jehovah	214	368	528	188	201	437	345	593	89	455	638	252	201
o1	I hunger and I thirst			409			730	449			306	470		
o1	Lord, enthroned in heavenly splendour	263	296	416	309	431	616			583	311	52	408	
o1	Lord, speak to me, that I may speak			510		444	553	613	611	485	512			444
p2	King of glory, King of peace	194	391	603	288	397	499	97	53	364	494	178	375	
p2	O Lord, thou art my God and King							732		346				
e	Fight the good fight	220	359	526	128	143	710	496	524	442	423	635	169	143
e	For me to live is Christ								410					
e	He/they want/lack not friends	183	371				495	481			459			
e	Jesus lives! Thy/Your terrors now	82	112	156	272	373	198	239	253	605	148	409	354	373
e	Jesus, the very thought of thee/you	120	291, 385	478	264	386	265	509	352	377	486	471, 534	368	
e	Lord, for the years			328	310	428		603	535		51	602	409	428
e	Lord, we thank you for the promise											424		
e	My gracious Lord, I own thy right						741	535					459	
e	Pray for the church afflicted						556	634			559	267		
e	Souls of men / Restless souls / There's a wideness	251	461	443	501	607, 683	230	353	573	218	598	188	662	607
e	The saints in Christ are one										629			
g	Father, hear the prayer we offer	113	357	360	120	132	436	495	523		416	237	161	132
g	Forth in the peace of Christ we go	458	361	542	142			602	607	589	429	594	187	
g	From heaven you came (The servant King)				148	162		522	529		432	632	195	16
g	God makes his rain to fall: SS96													
g	Great is thy/your faithfulness			260	186	200	66	96	553		453	39	249	200
g	Lead us, heavenly Father, lead us	224	393	595	293	400	68	543	597	90	496	640	379	400
g	Lord/Great God, your love has called us here	489		480			500	339	442		133		246	
g	May the mind of Christ my Saviour			550	334	463	739		537	432	521	671	447	463
g	Take my life, and let it be	249		554	464	624	705	371	358	462	581	678	625	624
g	The Lord is King! lift up thy/your voice	107		183	485	656	58	76	322	36	592	98	650	656
g	Through all the changing scenes	209	467	46	516	702	73	685	544		604	654	686	702
g	To him we come			518		709			547			679		709
g	With joy we meditate the grace	530				774	235	206	275		624			774

Continuous: Proverbs **31**: 10-31 and Psalm **1** or *Related:* Wisdom **1**:16 — **2**:1, 12-22 or Jeremiah **11**: 18-20 and Psalm **54**; James **3**:13 — **4**:3, 7-8a; Mark **9**: 30-37

		AMS	NEH	HTC	HON	MP	H&P	R&S	BPW	CH3	CP	SG	ONC	MPC
o1	Eternal Father, Lord of life			295										
o1	For the beauty of the earth	104	285	298	137	152	333	41	121	367	253	298	184	152
o1	O perfect love	280	320		387	517	370		509		343		533	517
o2e	All my hope on God is founded	336	333	451	15	16	63	586	327	405	368	525	19	16
o2	Led like a lamb / You're alive, you have risen					294	402	241	254					402
o2	Lord, we know that we have failed you											423		
op2	Behold, the mountain of the Lord						50	130	617	312				
op2	The Lord will come and not be slow	29	15		489		245	128		321	37		655	
p1	Lord, be thy word my rule / Lord, make your word	232		250										
p1	Thy/Your way, not mine			555	521								692	950
eg	Praise to the Holiest in the height	117	439	140	426	563	231	103	562	238	557	58	572	563
e	God of grace and God of glory	367		324	174	192	712	344	572	88	448	574	225	192
e	Jesus, lover of my soul	123	383	438	261	372	528	332	345	78	96	201	343	372
e	Lord, teach us how to pray aright	227	406	367	316		551				98		418	
e	O God of hope, your prophets spoke											493		
e	Put thou thy trust / Commit thou all thy griefs	223			429		672	550		669	562		576	
g	A man there lived in Galilee	334			3								28	
g	And now, O Father, mindful of the love	260	273	392	32		593			580	279	459	34	
g	Christ who welcomed little children								497					
g	From heaven you came (The servant King)				148	162		522	529		432	632	195	16
g	Jesus, Friend of little children						146			100				
g	Lord/Great God, your love has called us here	489		480			500	339	442		133		246	
g	Meekness and majesty				335	465			58			395	448	465
g	Morning glory, starlit sky	496						99			259			
g	My song is love unknown	63	86	136	346	478	173	207	204	224	112	384	463	478
g	O Master, let me walk with thee						802				436			
g	O sing a song of Bethlehem	413						201			220	545		536
g	Once, only once, and once for all	261	304		404								522	
g	Teach me, my God and King	240	456		466		803	538			692	583	629	
g	We sing the praise of him who died	138	94	146	536	738	182	229	231	258	125	390	723	738
g	What a friend we have in Jesus			373	541	746	559	413	603			646	727	746
g	Ye/You servants of the Lord	150	18	598	566		248			319	40		757	

Year C
Proper 20

Continuous: Jeremiah **8**:18 — **9**:1 and Psalm **79**: 1-9 or *Related:* Amos **8**: 4-7 and Psalm **113**; 1 Timothy **2**: 1-7; Luke **16**: 1-13

		AMS	NEH	HTC	HON	MP	H&P	R&S	BPW	CH3	CP	SG	ONC	MPC
o1	Abide with me	13	331	425	6	4	665	336	515	695	10	495	2	4
o1	Stay with us, God							338						
o2e	Thy/Your kingdom come, O God	177	499	334	519		783	638	644	322	607	269	691	949
o2	Inspired by love and anger				252								325	
o2	Judge eternal, throned in splendour		490	329	285	395	409	626	627	519	356	600	372	395
o2	The Kingdom of God is justice and joy			333		651	139	200	321			591	184	646	651
p1	Hark, my soul, it is the Lord / Christian, do you hear the Lord	244		472	197	209	521	348			676	264		457	209
p2	Christ is the world's true light	346	494	323	78		456	601	618	505	396	432	100	
p2	From the rising of the sun				163			43						163
p2	Let all the world in every corner sing	202	394	342	296	404	10	114	54	361	497	47	382	404
p2	O Lord my God, when I in awesome wonder [How great thou art]				380	506		117	62		262	56	511	506
p2	O praise the Lord, ye servants of the Lord		426											
eg	Lord, for the years			328	310	428		603	535		51	602	409	428
e	Father, Lord of all creation	356			122				620		418		163	
e	God of gods, we sound his praises			340					46			504		
e	Jesus, Lord, we look to thee	380	481				759	564			489			
e	Jesus, where'er thy people meet / Lord Jesus, when your people	162	390	371	282		549	476			492	16	367	
e	Lord, teach us how to pray aright	227	406	367	316		551				98		418	
e	Thou art / You are the way	128	464	113	512	695	234	554		121	600		682	695
g	Be thou my vision / Lord be my vision	343	339	545	56	51	378	489	521	87	386	669	70	51
g	Forth in thy/your name, O Lord	239	235	306	143	159	381	521	526	463	430	623	188	159
g	O for a heart to praise my God	230	74	483	361	495	536	514	538	85	533	149	484	495
g	O Jesus, I have promised	235	420	531	372	501	704	509	352	434	538	676	503	501
g	Take my life, and let it be	249		554	464	624	705	371	358	462	581	678	625	624
g	Teach me, my God and King	240	456		466		803	538		692	583		629	
g	The Lord is King! I own his power							543						
g	The Lord is King! lift up thy/your voice	107		183	485	656	58	76	322	36	592	98	650	656
g	To him we come			518		709			547			679		709
g	Who is on the Lord's side?					769	722		615	479				769

Year A
Proper 21

Continuous: Exodus **17**: 1-7 and Psalm **78**: 1-4, 12-16 or *Related:* Ezekiel **18**: 1-4, 25-32 and Psalm **25**: 1-9; Philippians **2**: 1-13; Matthew **21**: 23-32

		AMS	NEH	HTC	HON	MP	H&P	R&S	BPW	CH3	CP	SG	ONC	MPC
o2	O for a heart to praise my God	230	74	483	361	495	536	514	538	85	533	149	484	495
op1	Guide me, O thou/my great Redeemer	214	368	528	188	201	437	345	593	89	455	638	252	201
op1	Rock of ages	135	445	593	437	582	273	365	545	83	565	150	584	582
p2	Lead us, heavenly Father, lead us	224	393	595	293	400	68	543	597	90	496	640	379	400
p2	Praise the Lord! ye heaven(s), adore him	195	437	583	425		15	116	67	37				
p2	Remember, remember your mercy, Lord										154			
p2	Tell out, my soul, the greatness of the Lord	422	186	42	467	631	86	740	391	164	362	62	631	631
p2	To you, O Lord, I lift up my soul										545			
eg	At the name of Jesus	148	338	172	46	41	74	261	370	300	380	317	54	
e	All hail the power of Jesus' name	140	332	587/ 203	13	13	252		29	382	163	24	16	13
e	All praise to thee/Christ, for thou / our Lord and King divine	337	335	204	18		253	750		297	372		22	
e	And can it be			588	30	33	216	136	328	409	376	168	32	
e	Before the heaven and earth			612										
e	Empty he came			127								622		
e	From heaven you came (The servant King)				148	162		522	529		432	632	195	16
e	God is our strength from days of old				171								220	
e	Help us to help each other / Jesus, united by thy grace	374		540	208		773	500			461		275	
e	Here is the risen Son										443			
e	If you are encouraged												861	
e	Jesus is the name we honour											122	870	
e	Jesus shall take the highest honour				278	378						123	360	378
e	May the mind of Christ my Saviour			550	334	463	739		537	432	521	671	447	463
e	Meekness and majesty				335	465			58			395	448	465

continued on next page

		AMS	NEH	HTC	HON	MP	H&P	R&S	BPW	CH3	CP	SG	ONC	MPC
e	O Lord my God, when I in awesome wonder [How great thou art]				380	506		117	62		262	56	511	506
e	O Lord, all the world belongs to you				378			90	136				509	
e	O loving Lord, you are / who art for ever seeking						798		354					
e	That priceless gift, what tongue can tell											329		
e	There's no greater name than Jesus			S27		684			396					
e	Thou who wast rich / Lord, you were rich			63		700					72	356		700
e	What if the One who shapes the stars											364		
g	Christ is the King! O friends rejoice	345	345	492				571	475	474	165	31		
g	Christ triumphant, ever reigning			173	81	77			306		398	319	104	74
g	Crown him with many crowns	147	352	174	103	109	255	262	37	298	166	321	137	109
g	Hark the glad sound! The Saviour comes	30	6	193	198	210	82	137	143	160	27	435	265	210
g	Lo, from the desert homes	316												
g	Lo, in the wilderness a voice	384	170											
g	O Jesus, I have promised	235	420	531	372	501	704	509	352	434	538	676	503	501
g	On Jordan's bank the Baptist's cry	27	12	601	401	538	84	134	147	208	34	339	527	538
g	Rejoice! the Lord is King	139	443	180	432	575	243	657	317	296	563	440	580	575
g	Sing we the praises of the great forerunner / On this high feast day	315	168								234			

Year B
Proper 21

Continuous: Esther **7**: 1-6, 9-10, **9**: 20-22 and Psalm **124**
or *Related:* Numbers **11**: 4-6, 10-16, 24-29 and Psalm **19**: 7-14;
James **5**: 13-20; Mark **9**: 38-50

		AMS	NEH	HTC	HON	MP	H&P	R&S	BPW	CH3	CP	SG	ONC	MPC
o1	Tell out, my soul, the greatness of the Lord	422	186	42	467	631	86	740	391	164	362	62	631	631
o2 p1	A safe stronghold/fortress/refuge	114		523		2	661	585	375	406/7				2

continued on next page

		AMS	NEH	HTC	HON	MP	H&P	R&S	BPW	CH3	CP	SG	ONC	MPC
op1	O/Our God, our help in ages past	99	417	37	366	498	358	705	389	611	537	542	494	498
op1	Through all the changing scenes	209	467	46	516	702	73	685	544		604	654	686	702
op2	Guide me, O thou/my great Redeemer/Jehovah	214	368	528	188	201	437	345	593	89	455	638	252	201
p1	Had not the Lord, let Israel say PR 124													
p2	Lord, thy word abideth / Lord, your word shall guide us	166	407	251	318	446	476	317	102	130	515		420	446
p	O worship the King all glorious above	101	433	24	393	528	28	47	63	35	546	90	551	528
eg	Father of heaven, whose love profound	97	358	359	124		519			77	421	144		827
e	'Lift up your hearts!' We lift them	241	398	366	304		405			440	500		395	
e	Be thou / O Lord, my/our guardian	217	64	374	55	385		68			385		68	
e	Father, hear the prayer we offer	113	357	360	120	132	436	495	523		416	237	161	132
e	I lift my eyes to the quiet hills					281		64	595			515	312	281
e	Lord, teach us how to pray aright	227	406	367	316		551				98		418	
e	New every morning is the love	2	238	270	349	480	636	536		47	6		467	480
e	O God of Bethel / O God of Jacob	216	416	35	364		442	71	599	72	536	241	491	907
e	Prayer is the soul's sincere/supreme desire		442	372		567	557				561			567
g	Be thou my vision / Lord be my vision	343	339	545	56	51	378	489	521	87	386	669	70	51
g	Dear Lord and Father of mankind	115	353	356	106	111	673	492	84	76	411	497	144	111
g	For the beauty of the earth	104	285	298	137	152	333	41	121	367	253	298	184	152
g	Great is thy/your faithfulness			260	186	200	66	96	553		453	39	249	200
g	How sweet the name of Jesus sounds	122	374	211	220	251	257	277	339	376	467	42	297	251
g	I heard the voice of Jesus say	247	376		231	275	136	349		212	469		310	275
g	Jesus, where'er thy people meet / Lord Jesus, when your people	162	390	371	282		549	476			492	16	367	
g	Lord of all hopefulness	394	239	101	313		552	531	517	92	507	509	413	882
g	Lord, I was blind			437		433	423	358	558					433
g	O Lord, whose saving name												910	
g	Praise, my soul, the King of heaven	192	436	38	422	560	13	104	65	360	555		565	560
g	Son of God, eternal Saviour	132	498	102				605	639	454	573			
g	Strengthen for service, Lord, the hands	421	306	423	460		626	461	453	588	323	473	619	
g	The price is paid					663								663
g	When all thy/your mercies	109	472	39	544	751	573	109		150	617	73	732	751

Year C
Proper 21

Continuous: Jeremiah **32**: 1-3a, 6-15 and Psalm **91**: 1-6, 14-16 or *Related:*
Amos **6**: 1a, 4-7 and Psalm **146**; 1 Timothy **6**: 6-19; Luke **16**: 19-31

		AMS	NEH	HTC	HON	MP	H&P	R&S	BPW	CH3	CP	SG	ONC	MPC
p1e	All my hope on God is founded	336	333	451	15	16	63	586	327	405	368	525	19	16
p1	God is our strength and refuge			527		188			308		443	650	219	188
p1	Safe in the shadow of the Lord			445		583						516		583
p2	I'll praise my Maker while I've breath			20		320	439	734	127		473	84		320
p2	Jesus, the name high over all			213		385	264					323		385
e	A rich young man came seeking FF p78													
e	All you have given calls us, Lord, to praise you FF p76													
e	Fight the good fight	220	359	526	128	143	710	496	524	442	423	635	169	143
e	If this is not our world FF p90													
e	Immortal, invisible, God only wise	199	377	21	242	327	9	67	383	32	474	44	314	327
e	In an age of twisted values											317		
e	Rejoice! the Lord is King	139	443	180	432	575	243	657	317	296	563	440	580	575
e	Rise up, O men of God	418												
e	The gifts we bring express our love										278			
e	The head that once was crowned with thorns	141	134	182	480	647	209	257	274	286	172	442		644
e	The Lord is King! lift up thy/your voice	107		183	485	656	58	76	322	36	592	98	650	656
g	'The Kingdom is upon you!'	512									590			
g	Amazing grace			28	27	31	215	92	550		375	26	29	
g	Blest are the pure in heart	238	341	110	63	58	724		588	113	391	372	77	58
g	Brother, sister, let me serve you				73			474	473		393	619	88	
g	Christ is the world's light	440		321			455	600	34		213	591	99	
g	Father of mercies, in thy/your word	167		247					99			224		
g	Father, Lord of all creation	356			122				620		418		163	
g	For the healing of the nations	361			139		402	620	621		427	261	186	
g	God has spoken — by his prophets			248			64		100			225		831
g	God is love: let heaven adore him	365	364		170	187	36	95	374		442		217	187
g	Immortal Love, for ever full	133	378	105	243	328	392	267	198	306	475	176	315	328
g	Inspired by love and anger				252							325		
g	Jesus, Lord, we look to thee	380	481				759	564			489			
g	Lord, speak to me, that I may speak			510		444	553	613	611	485	512			444
g	Tell out, my soul, the greatness of the Lord	422	186	42	467	631	86	740	391	164	362	62	631	631
g	The Kingdom of God is justice and joy			333		651	139	200	321		591	184	646	651
g	We find thee, Lord, in others' need	430												
g	What does the Lord require	432					414							
g	When I needed a neighbour	433			548								736	
g	Ye that know the Lord is gracious	175	477								628			

Year A
Proper 22

Continuous: Exodus **20**: 1-4, 7-9, 12-20 and Psalm **19** or *Related:* Isaiah **5**: 1-7 and Psalm **80**: 7-15; Philippians **3**: 4b-14; Matthew **21**: 33-46

		AMS	NEH	HTC	HON	MP	H&P	R&S	BPW	CH3	CP	SG	ONC	MPC
o1	Father of all, whose laws have stood			539					335			664		
p1	Christ, whose glory fills the skies	4	234	266	82	79	457	380		114	2	170	105	79
p1	The heavens declare thy/your glory, Lord	168		254			481	320			264	230		
p1	The spacious firmament	103	267		493		339			143	265		665	
p1	The stars declare his glory										314			
p2	Creator of the earth and skies	351		320			419	82			410	296		
p2	God of mercy, God of grace	179	366	293	175			575	48	497	449		227	
eg	To him we come			518		709			547			679		709
eg	When I survey the wondrous cross	67	95	147	549	755	180	217	233	254	127	680	738	755
e	All I once held dear										562	18		
e	Come, let us with our Lord arise	449	254	375			575	383			142			
e	Fight the good fight	220	359	526	128	143	710	496	524	442	423	635	169	143
e	Here, O my Lord, I see thee/you	274		406		230	608		436	573	304	468	279	230
e	How deep the Father's love for us										193	988		
e	Jesus, the name high over all			213		385	264					323		385
e	Jesus, the very thought of thee/you is sweet	120	291, 385	478	264	386	265	509	352	377	486	471, 534	368	
e	Jesus, thou/the joy of loving hearts	255	292	413	265	383	258	389	439	571	486	471		
e	Lord of all life and power										414			
e	We sing the praise of him who died	138	94	146	536	738	182	229	231	258	125	390	723	738
g	A man there lived in Galilee	334			3							28		
g	Ah, holy Jesus, how hast thou offended		62	123	8		164	215	215	251	100		5	
g	At the name of Jesus	148	338	172	46	41	74	261	370	300	380	317	54	
g	Christ is made the sure foundation / Blessed city, heavenly Salem	283/332	204-5	559	76	73	485	559	474	10	208	572	97	73
g	Christ is our corner-stone	161		564	77						395		98	
g	How firm a foundation			430	216	243		589	380				292	243
g	I danced in the morning	375	375		228			195			468		305	
g	It is a thing most wonderful	70	84	131	255	346	224	503	219	385	109	557	333	346
g	My Lord, what love is this				345	476					194	462		476
g	My song is love unknown	63	86	136	346	478	173	207	204	224	112	384	463	478
g	Nature with open volume stands	497	87				174	219						
g	O sacred head	68	90	139	389	520	176	220	223	253	120	385	535	520
g	Praise to the Holiest in the height	117	439	140	426	563	231	103	562	238	557	58	572	563
g	The head that once was crowned with thorns	141	134	182	480	647	209	257	274	286	172	442		644
g	The price is paid				663									663
g	We have a gospel to proclaim	431	486	519	532	728	465		585		612		716	728

Year B
Proper 22

Continuous: Job **1**: 1, **2**: 1-10 and Psalm **26** or *Related:* Genesis **2**: 18-24 and Psalm **8**; Hebrews **1**: 1-4, **2**: 5-12; Mark **10**: 2-16

		AMS	NEH	HTC	HON	MP	H&P	R&S	BPW	CH3	CP	SG	ONC	MPC
o1	O for a heart to praise my God	230	74	483	361	495	536	514	538	85	533	149	484	495
o2g	Lord of all hopefulness	394	239	101	313		552	531	517	92	507	509	413	882
o2g	Love divine, all loves excelling	131	408	217	321	449	267	663	559	437	516	179	428	449
p1	In judgement, Lord, arise PR26													
p1	We love the place, O God	160	471	558	533	731				15	211		718	731
p2	How excellent in all the earth									138				
p2	O Lord of every shining constellation	411		314				130		141	263		512	
e	Above the clash of creeds										332			
e	Christ is the world's light	440		321			455	600	34		213	591	99	
e	Christ triumphant, ever reigning			173	81	77			306		398	319	104	74
e	God has spoken — by his prophets			248			64		100			225		831
e	No other prophet ever spoke										325			
e	The brightness of God's glory			221										
e	The Lord is King! lift up thy/your voice	107		183	485	656	58	76	322	36	592	98	650	656
g	Blest are the pure in heart	238	341	110	63	58	724		588	113	391	372	77	58
g	Christ who welcomed little children								497					
g	Father on high, to whom we pray			296					499					
g	Father, Lord of all creation	356			122				620		418		163	
g	Happy are they, they that/who love God	176	369	473	195		711			408	456		262	
g	Happy the home that welcomes you				300		366							
g	He/they want/lack not friends	183	371				495	481			459			
g	It fell upon a summer day				254					213			331	
g	Jesus, good above all other	378	387	96	269		732	528		111	487		350	
g	Lead us, heavenly Father, lead us	224	393	595	293	400	68	543	597	90	496	640	379	400
g	Lord Jesus Christ, you have come to us	391	297	417	311	435	617	373	444		505	670	411	435
g	Lord of the home, your only Son	494					367		500		510			
g	Loving Shepherd of thy/your sheep	134		305	325					93	517		424	
g	May the grace of Christ our Saviour	181		370	333		762		110	634	520	579	446	
g	Now thank we all our God	205	413	33	354	486	566	72	128	368	530	54	474	486
g	Seek ye first the Kingdom of God				442	590	138	512	357				590	590
g	The Lord's my shepherd, I'll not want	426	459	591/45	490	660	70	679	395	387	594	207	654	660
g	Thine/Yours for ever	234	463	556	504						599		673	992
g	Will you come and follow me?				560			558	363		622	634	752	

Year C
Proper 22

Continuous: Lamentations **1**: 1-6; (Canticle) Lamentations **3**: 19-26
or Psalm **137** or *Related:* Habakkuk **1**: 1-4, **2**: 1-4 and Psalm **37**: 1-9;
2 Timothy **1**: 1-14; Luke **17**: 5-10

		AMS	NEH	HTC	HON	MP	H&P	R&S	BPW	CH3	CP	SG	ONC	MPC
I	New every morning is the love	2	238	270	349	480	636	536		47	6		467	480
o1g	Put thou thy trust / Commit thou all thy griefs	223			429		672	550		669	562		576	
o1g	Through all the changing scenes	209	467	46	516	702	73	685	544		604	654	686	702
o1	Because of the Lord's great love										189			
o1	Not the grandeur of the mountains										182			
o1	O come, O come, Emmanuel	26	11	66	358	493	85	126	144	165	32	338	480	493
o2g	Fill thou/now my/our life	200		541	129	146	792	406	569	457	424	665	171	146
o2	God is working his purpose out		495	191	172	189	769	573		303	444	451	221	189
o2	I cannot tell why/how he whom angels worship			194	226	266	238	265	381		54	437	303	266
o2	Thy/Your kingdom come, O God	177	499	334	519		783	638	644	322	607	269	691	949
op1	Lead, kindly light	215	392		292	399	67	544		682	495		378	
op1	Maker of Earth, to thee alone		71											
p1	By rivers of sorrow we sat and remembered PR137													
p1	By the Babylonian rivers										655			
p2	Be thou my vision / Lord be my vision	343	339	545	56	51	378	489	521	87	386	669	70	51
eg	O thou/Lord who came[st]	233	431	552/596	392	525	745	433	355	110	191	560	541	525
e	I know not why God's wondrous grace					279			532					279
e	I'm not ashamed to own/name my Lord			448	240	323	677	428	343	591		532	316	323
e	Spirit of God come dwell within me											611		
e	To God be the glory			584	522	708	463	289	566	374	609	71	695	708
e	We have a gospel to proclaim	431	486	519	532	728	465		585		612		716	728
g	Almighty Father, who for us thy Son didst give	338					401	621			374			
g	Come, praise the name of Jesus			538						331				
g	Dear Lord and Father of mankind	115	353	356	106	111	673	492	84	76	411	497	144	111
g	Father, hear the prayer we offer	113	357	360	120	132	436	495	523		416	237	161	132
g	Fight the good fight	220	359	526	128	143	710	496	524	442	423	635	169	143
g	Firmly I believe and truly	118	360	429	133					400	426	287	174	
g	Give me/us the wings of faith	324	225		156		815	664			216	202		
g	Have faith in God, my heart	372		431	201		675	499	336		458		268	
g	Help us to help each other / Jesus, united by thy grace	374		540	208		773	500			461		275	
g	Safe in the shadow of the Lord			445		583						516		583
g	Strengthen for service, Lord, the hands	421	306	423	460		626	461	453	588	323	473	619	
g	Teach me, my God and King	240	456		466		803	538			692	583	629	

Year A
Proper 23

Continuous: Exodus **32**: 1-14 and Psalm **106**: 1-6, 19-23 or *Related:* Isaiah **25**: 1-9 and Psalm **23**; Philippians **4**: 1-9; Matthew **22**: 1-14

		AMS	NEH	HTC	HON	MP	H&P	R&S	BPW	CH3	CP	SG	ONC	MPC
o1	O for a closer walk with God	231	414	368	360	494		551		663	532		483	494
o2	How bright these glorious spirits shine	306	227	572						533	221			
o2	Jesus, lover of my soul	123	383	438	261	372	528	332	345	78	96	201	343	372
o2	See the feast our God prepares LUTR42													
o2	We trust in you, our shield and our defender		446									510		
p1	Praise the Lord! Give thanks for ever PR106													
p1	The King of love my shepherd is	126	457	44	484	649	69	552	394	388	589	205	649	649
p2	I know that my Redeemer lives, what joy			169	232	278	196	278	251			406	311	278
p2	The Lord's my shepherd, I'll not want	426	459	591/ 45	490	660	70	679	395	387	594	207	654	660
e	Like a mighty river flowing			32		419			632			51	400	419
e	May the mind of Christ my Saviour			550	334	463	739		537	432	521	671	447	463
e	Rejoice! the Lord is King	139	443	180	432	575	243	657	317	296	563	440	580	575
e	Rejoice, rejoice, Christ is in you					572							572	
e	Whatever things are lovely LUTR160													
e	Within the busy rush of life										648			
p2	Because the Lord is my shepherd										513			
g2	God is our strength from days of old				171								220	
g	A rich young man came seeking FF p78													
g	Bread of heaven, on thee we feed	271	276	398	67			442			284	464	82	
g	Christians, lift your hearts and voices	447						431			290			
g	Come, risen Lord, and deign to be our guest	349	279		96		605			572	293		126	
g	Faithful Shepherd, feed me		282	29	117							498	156	

continued on next page

		AMS	NEH	HTC	HON	MP	H&P	R&S	BPW	CH3	CP	SG	ONC	MPC
g	From glory to glory advancing	276	286		147			462		325	299		194	
g	Here, O my Lord, I see thee/you	274		406		230	608		436	573	304	468	279	230
g	I come with joy to meet my Lord	473		408	227		610	447	437		365	469	304	
g	Jerusalem the golden	184	381	573	259			662	312	537	482		340	
g	Light's abode, celestial Salem	185	401		305						502		398	
g	Lord/Great God, your love has called us here	489		480			500	339	442		133		246	
g	My God, and/now is thy table spread	259		418	342						313	474	456	
g	O what their joy / What of those sabbaths	186	432					659		535	225		550	
g	Spread the table of the Lord						625		450					
g	The Kingdom of God is justice and joy			333		651	139	200	321			591	184	646	651
g	To him we come			518		709			547				679		709
g	We come as guests invited			602		723									723
g	Ye watchers and ye holy ones	532	478		567							230		758	

Year B
Proper 23

Continuous: Job **23**: 1-9, 16-17 and Psalm **22**: 1-15 or *Related:* Amos **5**: 6-7, 10-15 and Psalm **90**: 12-17; Hebrews **4**: 12-16; Mark **10**: 17-31

		AMS	NEH	HTC	HON	MP	H&P	R&S	BPW	CH3	CP	SG	ONC	MPC
o1g	Can we/man by searching find out God	438					76	80			201	496		
o2	Eternal Ruler of the ceaseless round	353	355		115			623	477	514	181		154	
o2	The day of the Lord shall come						637							
o2	Thy/Your kingdom come, O God	177	499	334	519		783	638	644	322	607	269	691	949
p1	O Lord my God, O Lord my God										491			
p2e g	God of mercy, God of grace	179	366	293	175			575	48	497	449		227	
p2	Judge eternal, throned in splendour		490	329	285	395	409	626	627	519	356	600	372	395
e	A rich young man came seeking FF p78													
e	Alleluia..Word of God, Jesus Christ										687			
e	Amazing grace			28	27	31	215	92	550		375	26	29	
e	How sure the Scriptures are			249								227		
e	Lord, enthroned in heavenly splendour	263	296	416	309	431	616			583	311	52	408	

continued on next page

		AMS	NEH	HTC	HON	MP	H&P	R&S	BPW	CH3	CP	SG	ONC	MPC
e	Now in reverence and awe										232	902		
e	O God of Bethel / O God of Jacob	216	416	35	364		442	71	599	72	536	241	491	907
e	Where high the heavenly temple stands	130		184				259		295	75			
e	With joy we meditate the grace	530				774	235	206	275		624			774
g	Be thou my vision / Lord be my vision	343	339	545	56	51	378	489	521	87	386	669	70	51
g	Come Holy Spirit, heavenly dove						297	299						
g	Come, praise the name of Jesus			538						331				
g	Glorious things of thee/you are spoken	172	362	494	158	173	817	560	480	421	435	35	205	173
g	God who came in Jesus FF p86													
g	Jesus calls us: o'er/in the tumult	312	200	104	266	359	141	355		211	233	668	347	359
g	Jesus, lover of my soul	123	383	438	261	372	528	332	345	78	96	201	343	372
g	Just as I am, without one plea	246	294	440	287	396	697	364	346	79	308	507	374	396
g	Lord, be thy word my rule / Lord, make your word	232		250										
g	My God, accept my heart this day	279	318	551	341		701			429	338	559	455	
g	O Jesus, I have promised	235	420	531	372	501	704	509	352	434	538	676	503	501
g	O thou/Lord who came[st]	233	431	552/596	392	525	745	433	355	110	191	560	541	525
g	Rejoice, rejoice, Christ is in you				572							572		
g	Safe in the shadow of the Lord			445	583							516		583
g	Take my life, and let it be	249		554	464	624	705	371	358	462	581	678	625	624
g	Thine/Yours for ever	234	463	556	504						599		673	992
g	Will you come and follow me?				560			558	363		622	634	752	
g	Ye/You servants of God, your Master proclaim	149	476	520	565	784	278	293	76	372	627	75	784	756

Year C
Proper 23

Continuous: Jeremiah **29**: 1, 4-7 and Psalm **66**: 1-12 or *Related:* 2 Kings **5**: 1-3, 7-15c and Psalm **111**; 2 Timothy **2**: 8-15; Luke **17**: 11-19

		AMS	NEH	HTC	HON	MP	H&P	R&S	BPW	CH3	CP	SG	ONC	MPC
o2	Just as I am, without one plea	246	294	440	287	396	697	364	346	79	308	507	374	396
o2	Rock of ages	135	445	593	437	582	273	365	545	83	565	150	584	582
p1	All people that on earth do dwell	100	334	14	17	20	1	712	2	1	369	77	21	20
p1	Before Jehovah's aweful/awesome throne / Sing to the Lord	197		15			61	119		2	387			

continued on next page

		AMS	NEH	HTC	HON	MP	H&P	R&S	BPW	CH3	CP	SG	ONC	MPC
p1	Sing glory to God the Father										1			
p1	The Lord is king: tremble, O earth, and fear him PR99													
p2g	Praise to the Lord, the Almighty	207	440	40	427	564	16	74	68	9	558	59	573	564
p2	O praise the Lord, ye servants of the Lord		426											
p2	O sing a new song										89			
p2	Sing a new song of glory and salvation										94			
e	Be thou / O Lord, my/our guardian	217	64	374	55	385		68			385		68	
e	Christ's Church shall glory in his power			522										
e	Grace and peace be ours for ever LUTR164													
e	I'm not ashamed to own/name my Lord			448	240	323	677	428	343	591		532	316	323
e	Lead, kindly light	215	392		292	399	67	544		682	495		378	
e	Lord of our life, and God of our salvation		404	529	315	441				491			417	441
e	Oft in danger, oft in woe / Christian soldiers, onward go	210	434	524	396	533	715				547		487	533
e	Stand up, stand up for Jesus	221	453	535	457	617	721			481	578	644	617	617
e	Take up thy/your cross	237	76	114	465					430	582	645	626	935
e	The head that once was crowned with thorns	141	134	182	480	647	209	257	274	286	172	442		644
e	Through the night of doubt and sorrow	211	468	466	517		441		546	423	605	544	687	948
g	A man there lived in Galilee	334			3								28	
g	As pants the hart	226	337		38		416	689			379		44	
g	Eternal God, we bring our praise FF p80													
g	Give thanks with a grateful heart				154	170						108	202	170
g	How rich and deep God's judgements are FF p89													
g	How sweet the name of Jesus sounds	122	374	211	220	251	257	277	339	376	467	42	297	251
g	I'll praise my Maker while I've breath			20		320	439	734	127		473	84		320
g	Immortal Love, for ever full	133	378	105	243	328	392	267	198	306	475	176	315	328
g	Lord Christ, who on thy heart didst bear	388			308		394						407	
g	Now thank we all our God	205	413	33	354	486	566	72	128	368	530	54	474	486
g	O for a thousand tongues to sing	125	415	219	362	496	744	285	59	371	534	55	485	495
g	Praise, my soul, the King of heaven	192	436	38	422	560	13	104	65	360	555		565	560
g	The crippled hands reached out: SS95													
g	Thine arm, O Lord, in days of old	285	324		502		397			214		671		
g	To God be the glory			584	522	708	463	289	566	374	609	71	695	708
g	When all thy/your mercies	109	472	39	544	751	573	109		150	617	73	732	751

Year A
Proper 24

Continuous: Exodus **33**: 12-23 and Psalm **99** or *Related:* Isaiah **45**: 1-7 and Psalm **96**: 1-9 [10-13]; 1 Thessalonians **1**: 1-10; Matthew **22**: 15-22

		AMS	NEH	HTC	HON	MP	H&P	R&S	BPW	CH3	CP	SG	ONC	MPC
o1	Great is thy/your faithfulness			260	186	200	66	96	553		453	39	249	200
o1	Rock of ages	135	445	593	437	582	273	365	545	83	565	150	584	582
o2g	Jesus shall reign where'er the sun	143	388	516	277	379	239	269	313	413	490	45	359	379
o2	Day of wrath and day of wonder											141		
o2	Immortal, invisible, God only wise	199	377	21	242	327	9	67	383	32	474	44	314	327
o2	Lift up your heads, ye gates of brass						227			471				
o2	Thou/God whose almighty / Father your mighty word	180	466	506	514	699	29	38	591	494	267	684	597	699
p1g	Rejoice! the Lord is King	139	443	180	432	575	243	657	317	296	563	440	580	575
p1g	The Lord is King! lift up thy/your voice	107		183	485	656	58	76	322	36	592	98	650	656
p2	In beauty of his holiness									311				
p2	Join all the glorious names			214		392	78	280	557	304	493	46		392
p2	O sing a new song to the Lord									22				
p2	O worship / Worship the Lord in the beauty of holiness	49	52	344	394	529	505	187	22	40	89	204	552	529
e	Christ is the King! O friends rejoice	345	345	492				571	475	474	165	31		
e	Firmly I believe and truly	118	360	429	133					400	426	287	174	
e	God of gods, we sound his praises			340					46			504		
e	O thou/Lord who came[st]	233	431	552/ 596	392	525	745	433	355	110	191	560	541	525
e	Through all the changing scenes of life	209	467	46	516	702	73	685	544		604	654	686	702
e	We have a gospel to proclaim	431	486	519	532	728	465		585		612		716	728
g2	God is our strength from days of old			171								220		
g	All my hope on God is founded	336	333	451	15	16	63	586	327	405	368	525	19	16
g	At the name of Jesus	148	338	172	46	41	74	261	370	300	380	317	54	
g	Christ triumphant, ever reigning			173	81	77				306	398	319	104	74
g	City of God, how broad and far	173	346		85		809			422	400		106	
g	Crown him with many crowns	147	352	174	103	109	255	262	37	298	166	321	137	109
g	Give to our God immortal praise	460		31	155	171	22	94	47		434	83	203	171
g	Glorious things of thee/you are spoken	172	362	494	158	173	817	560	480	421	435	35	205	173
g	Judge eternal, throned in splendour		490	329	285	395	409	626	627	519	356	600	372	395
g	Name of all majesty			218		481					525	324	465	481
g	The Kingdom of God is justice and joy			333		651	139	200	321		591	184	646	651
g	Thy/Your kingdom come, O God	177	499	334	519		783	638	644	322	607	269	691	949
g	Ye that know the Lord is gracious	175	477								628			
g	Ye/You servants of the Lord	150	18	598	566		248			319	40		757	

Year B
Proper 24

Continuous: Job **38**: 1-7 [34-41] and Psalm **104**: 1-9, 24, 35c or *Related:*
Isaiah **53**: 4-12 and Psalm **91**: 9-16; Hebrews **5**: 1-10; Mark **10**: 35-45

		AMS	NEH	HTC	HON	MP	H&P	R&S	BPW	CH3	CP	SG	ONC	MPC
o1	Lord of beauty, thine the splendour	106	265		314					120	258		415	
o1	The works of the Lord are created			26							266			
o2e	Christ triumphant, ever reigning			173	81	77			306		398	319	104	74
o2e	Hail thou/our once-despisèd/rejected Jesus			175	192	203	222		273		168		258	203
o2e	We sing the praise of him who died	138	94	146	536	738	182	229	231	258	125	390	723	738
o2	Come wounded healer											130		
o2	Creating God, we bring our song											134		
o2	I will sing the wondrous story			212	237	315	223		382	381		43	337	315
o2	Led like a lamb / You're alive				294	402	241	254						402
o2	My song is love unknown	63	86	136	346	478	173	207	204	224	112	384	463	478
o2	No weight of gold or silver			138							181			
o2	O sacred head	68	90	139	389	520	176	220	223	253	120	385	535	520
o2	See, Christ was wounded for our sake			137					229					
o2	The price is paid					663								663
o2	Who believes what we have heard PR451													
op1	O worship the King	101	433	24	393	528	28	47	63	35	546	90	551	528
op1	The spacious firmament	103	267		493		339			143	265		665	
p2	Safe in the shadow of the Lord			445		583						516		583
e	It is a thing most wonderful	70	84	131	255	346	224	503	219	385	109	557	333	346
e	Where high the heavenly temple stands	130		184				259		295	75			
g	All praise to thee/Christ, for thou / our Lord and King divine	337	335	204	18		253	750		297	372		22	
g	Almighty Father, who for us thy Son didst give	338					401	621			374			
g	Come down, O Love Divine	156	137	231	90	89	281	294	283	115	170	663	114	89
g	Father of heaven, whose love profound	97	358	359	124		519			77	421	144		827
g	From heaven you came (The servant King)				148	162		522	529		432	632	195	16
g	God of gods, we sound his praises			340					46		504			
g	He gave his life in selfless love			405		214			435		467			214
g	Help us to help each other / Jesus, united by thy grace	374		540	208		773	500			461		275	
g	Jesus is Lord! creation's voice proclaims it			S17	270	367	260	268	384		170		352	367
g	Lord, speak to me, that I may speak			510		444	553	613	611	485	512			444
g	Lord/Great God, your love has called us here	489		480			500	339	442		133		246	
g	My Lord, you word no royal crown			118								628		
g	Praise, my soul, the King of heaven	192	436	38	422	560	13	104	65	360	555		565	560
g	There is a green hill far away	137	92	148	499	674	178	223	230	241	123	388	657	674

Year C
Proper 24

Continuous: Jeremiah **31**: 27-34 and Psalm **119**: 97-104 or *Related:* Genesis **32**: 22-31 and Psalm **121**; 2 Timothy **3**:14 — **4**:5; Luke **18**: 1-8

		AMS	NEH	HTC	HON	MP	H&P	R&S	BPW	CH3	CP	SG	ONC	MPC
o1g	Immortal, invisible, God only wise	199	377	21	242	327	9	67	383	32	474	44	314	327
o1	A debtor to mercy alone			449										
o1	Hail to the Lord's anointed	142	55	190	193	204	125	127	142	317	87		259	2047
o1	Restore, O Lord, the honour of your name				434	579			324			274	582	579
o1	We are called to be God's people								583					
o2	Here, O my Lord, I see thee/you	274		406		230	608		436	573	304	468	279	230
o2	O love that will/wilt not let me go			486	384	515	685	511	541	677	542		517	515
p1e	Father of mercies, in thy/your word	167		247					99			224		
p2	I to the hills lift up my eyes PR121A													
p2	Unto the hills around			48										
po1	My hope is built on nothing less			462		473				411		537		473
e	Lord, be thy word my rule / Lord, make your word	232		250										
e	Lord, thy word abideth / Lord, your word shall guide us	166	407	251	318	446	476	317	102	130	515		420	446
e	Lord, you sometimes speak in wonders								101					
e	Powerful in making us wise to salvation			252			479					228		
e	Thou/God whose almighty / Father your mighty word	180	466	506	514	699	29	38	591	494	267	684	597	699
g	'Lift up your hearts!' We lift them	241	398	366	304		405			440	500		395	
g	Be thou / O Lord, my/our guardian	217	64	374	55	385		68			385		68	
g	Behold, the mountain of the Lord						50	130	617	312				
g	Father all-loving, thou rulest in majesty	355ii												
g	Father of heaven, whose love profound	97	358	359	124		519			77	421	144		827
g	Father, hear the prayer we offer	113	357	360	120	132	436	495	523		416	237	161	132
g	Give to our God immortal praise	460		31	155	171	22	94	47		434	83	203	171
g	Great Shepherd of thy/your people, hear	164		363			490	387			454	238	250	
g	Lord, for the years			328	310	428		603	535		51	602	409	428
g	Lord, teach us how to pray aright	227	406	367	316		551				98		418	
g	O God beyond all praising			36	363							53	489	
g	Prayer is the soul's sincere/supreme desire		442	372		567	557				561			567
g	Ye that know the Lord is gracious	175	477								628			

Year A
Proper 25

Continuous: Deuteronomy **34**: 1-12 and Psalm **90**: 1-6, 13-17 or *Related:* Leviticus **19**: 1-2, 15-18 and Psalm **1**; 1 Thessalonians **2**: 1-8; Matthew **22**: 34-46

		AMS	NEH	HTC	HON	MP	H&P	R&S	BPW	CH3	CP	SG	ONC	MPC
o1e	Forth in thy/your name, O Lord	239	235	306	143	159	381	521	526	463	430	623	188	159
o1e	Lead, kindly light	215	392		292	399	67	544		682	495		378	
o1	If our God had simply saved us: SS35													
o1	O God of Bethel / O God of Jacob	216	416	35	364		442	71	599	72	536	241	491	907
o1	Put thou thy trust / Commit thou all thy griefs	223			429		672	550		669	562		576	
o1	The God of Abraham praise	331	148	9	478	645	452	121	131	358	586	66	642	645
o1	There is a land of pure delight	190	460	575			822	668	323	536	597			
o1	There was a man who had a dream: SS63													
o2	Beauty for brokenness										263	60	806	
p1	Lord, thou hast been our dwelling-place									102				
p1	O Lord, the refuge												909	
p1	O/Our God, our help in ages past	99	417	37	366	498	358	705	389	611	537	542	494	498
p1	The Church's one foundation	170	484	501	473	640	515	566	393	420	585	581	636	640
p2	Father of mercies, in thy/your word	167		247				99			224			
p2	Lord, be thy word my rule / Lord, make your word	232		250										
p2	Thy/Your way, not mine			555	521								692	950
e	A safe stronghold/fortress/refuge	114		523		2	661	585	375	406/7				2
e	Father, hear the prayer we offer	113	357	360	120	132	436	495	523		416	237	161	132
e	O Jesus, I have promised	235	420	531	372	501	704	509	352	434	538	676	503	501
e	O thou/Lord who came[st]	233	431	552/596	392	525	745	433	355	110	191	560	541	525
e	Through all the changing scenes	209	467	46	516	702	73	685	544		604	654	686	702
e	Through the night of doubt and sorrow	211	468	466	517		441		546	423	605	544	687	948
e	Thy/Your hand, O God, has guided	171	485	536	518	705	784	567	398	424	606	649	689	705
e	Who would true valour / He who would valiant / Who honours courage	212	372	537, 590	205	224	688	557	362	443	621	639	281	224
g	Come down, O Love Divine	156	137	231	90	89	281	294	283	115	170	663	114	89
g	Father of all, whose laws			539				335			664			
g	Firmly I believe and truly	118	360	429	133					400	426	287	174	
g	Hail to the Lord's anointed	142	55	190	193	204	125	127	142	317	87		259	204
g	Lord of all power, I give you my will / Lord of creation, to you be all praise	395		547		440	699	532		428	508			
g	Rejoice! the Lord is King	139	443	180	432	575	243	657	317	296	563	440	580	575
g	Take my life, and let it be	249		554	464	624	705	371	358	462	581	678	625	624

Year B
Proper 25

Continuous: Job **42**: 1-6, 10-17 and Psalm **34**: 1-8, 19-22 or *Related:*
Jeremiah **31**: 7-9 and Psalm **126**; Hebrews **7**: 23-28; Mark **10**: 46-52

		AMS	NEH	HTC	HON	MP	H&P	R&S	BPW	CH3	CP	SG	ONC	MPC
o1	Dear Lord and Father of mankind	115	353	356	106	111	673	492	84	76	411	497	144	111
o1	God moves in a mysterious way	112	365		173	193	65	59	122	147	445		222	193
o2	Hills of the north, rejoice	470	7		209		237		311		29		282	
o2	Praise, my soul, the King of heaven	192	436	38	422	560	13	104	65	360	555		565	560
p1	Holy, holy, holy, Lord God almighty	95	146	7/594	212	237	~~504~~ 7	34	51	352	202	290	286	237
p1	Through all the changing scenes of life	209	467	46	516	702	73	685	544		604	654	686	702
p2	The Lord restored us - we were freed PR126													
p2	To God be the glory			584	522	708	463	289	566	374	609	71	695	708
e	All for Jesus!		272	469	10		251		332		277	661	13	
e	Alleluia! sing to Jesus	262	271	170	26	207	592		270		278	458	12	207
e	Forth in the peace of Christ we go	458	361	542	142			602	607	589	429	594	187	
e	Lord, enthroned in heavenly splendour	263	296	416	309	431	616			583	311	52	408	
e	Mercy in our time of failure										240			
e	Once, only once, and once for all	261	304		404								522	
e	Praise to Christ, the Lord incarnate										327			
e	Priest and victim, Jesus dies										328			
e	That priceless gift, what tongue can tell										329			
e	The Lord ascendeth up on high		135				210			287	173			
e	We hail thy presence glorious	266	310		531								714	
g	Amazing grace			28	27	31	215	92	550		375	26	29	
g	Christ who called disciples to him										620			
g	Come, light of the world										21			
g	Come, Lord, to our souls come down	348					470	361			335		122	

continued on next page

		AMS	NEH	HTC	HON	MP	H&P	R&S	BPW	CH3	CP	SG	ONC	MPC
g	Firmly I believe and truly	118	360	429	133					400	426	287	174	
g	Have faith in God, my heart	372		431	201		675	499	336		458		268	
g	I heard the voice of Jesus say	247	376		231	275	136	349		212	469		310	275
g	I know that my Redeemer lives, and ever prays						731							
g	Immortal Love, for ever full	133	378	105	243	328	392	267	198	306	475	176	315	328
g	Jesus, lover of my soul	123	383	438	261	372	528	332	345	78	96	201	343	372
g	My Lord, I did not choose you			107										
g	O for a thousand tongues to sing	125	415	219	362	496	744	285	59	371	534	55	485	495
g	O God, by whose almighty plan	406					396	651			204			
g	O Master, let me walk with thee						802			436				
g	Put thou thy trust / Commit thou all thy griefs	223			429		672	550		669	562		576	
g	Thine arm, O Lord, in days of old	285	324		502		397			214		671		
g	When all thy/your mercies	109	472	39	544	751	573	109		150	617	73	732	751
g	Ye/You servants of God, your Master proclaim	149	476	520	565	784	278	293	76	372	627	75	784	756

Year C
Proper 25

Continuous: Joel **2**: 23-32 and Psalm **65** or *Related:* Ecclesiasticus **35**: 12-17 or Jeremiah **14**: 7-10, 19-22 and Psalm **84**: 1-7; 2 Timothy **4**: 6-8, 16-18; Luke **18**: 9-14

		AMS	NEH	HTC	HON	MP	H&P	R&S	BPW	CH3	CP	SG	ONC	MPC
o1	Breathe on me, Breath of God	157	342	226	69	67	280	295	282	103	174	554	84	67
o1	Come, Holy Spirit, come inflame				93						179		119	
o1	God as Fire, send your Spirit: SS52													
o1	Help us, O Lord, to learn	373	370	493			474				460	226		
o1	I will pour out my Spirit						292							
o1	O Breath of life, come sweeping / O Breath of love, come breathe			237	356	488	777	302	293	339			476	488
o2g	'Lift up your hearts!' We lift them	241	398	366	304		405			440	500		395	
o2g	Father of heaven, whose love profound	97	358	359	124		519			77	421	144		827
o2	Come, O thou traveller unknown	243	350				434				407			

continued on next page

		AMS	NEH	HTC	HON	MP	H&P	R&S	BPW	CH3	CP	SG	ONC	MPC
o2	O for a closer walk with God	231	414	368	360	494		551		663	532		483	494
p1	Praise waits for thee in Zion, Lord									28				
p2	A sovereign protector I have							54	325	651				
p2	Here, O my Lord, I see thee/you	274		406		230	608		436	573	304	468	279	230
p2	How lovely is thy dwelling place — tabernacles							703		4				
p2	O Lord of hosts, how lovely is your dwelling-place PR84													
eg	And can it be			588	30	33	216	136	328	409	376	168	32	
eg	Ye that know the Lord is gracious	175	477								628			
e	A safe stronghold/fortress/refuge	114		523		2	661	585	375	406/7				2
e	Christ the Lord is risen today / Love's redeeming work is done / All creation	83	113	150	324	76	193	232	246	275	150	412	433	76
e	Fight the good fight	220	359	526	128	143	710	496	524	442	423	635	169	143
e	For all the saints	305	197	567	134	148	814	658	478	534	232	636	177	148
e	Guide me, O thou/my great Redeemer	214	368	528	188	201	437	345	593	89	455	638	252	201
e	Lord, we thank you for the promise											424		
e	Who would true valour / He who would valiant / Who honours courage	212	372	537, 590	205	224	688	557	362	443	621	639	281	224
g	All praise to thee/Christ, for thou / our Lord and King divine	337	335	204	18		253	750		297	372	22		
g	Amazing grace			28	27	31	215	92	550		375	26	29	
g	Come down, O Love Divine	156	137	231	90	89	281	294	283	115	170	663	114	89
g	I will sing the wondrous story			212	237	315	223		382	381		43	337	315
g	Jesus, lover of my soul	123	383	438	261	372	528	332	345	78	96	201	343	372
g	Just as I am, without one plea	246	294	440	287	396	697	364	346	79	308	507	374	396
g	King of glory, King of peace	194	391	603	288	397	499	97	53	364	494	178	375	
g	Name of all majesty			218		481					525	324	465	481
g	Praise, my soul, the King of heaven	192	436	38	422	560	13	104	65	360	555		565	560
g	Tell out, my soul, the greatness of the Lord	422	186	42	467	631	86	740	391	164	362	62	631	631
g	To the Name of our / that brings salvation	121	470	222	523		80	291		373	610	72	698	

Nehemiah **8**: 1-4a [5-6] 8-12; Psalm **119**: 9-16; Colossians **3**: 12-17;
Matthew **24**: 30-35

		AMS	NEH	HTC	HON	MP	H&P	R&S	BPW	CH3	CP	SG	ONC	MPC
sl	Faith and truth and life bestowing										223			
s	Come, Holy Ghost, our hearts inspire (Wesley)	448	348		91		469	312	97	122	177		117	
s	Come, Holy Spirit, come inflame				93						179		119	
s	Father of mercies, in thy/your word	167		247					99			224		
s	God of love, you freely give											226		
s	God who hast caused to be written	467					472							
s	Here on the threshold of a new beginning										506	280		
s	How lovely on the mountains are the feet of him				219	249			310				295	249
s	Lord, you sometimes speak in wonders								101					
s	Now in reverence and awe										232		902	
s	Open our eyes, O Lord, we pray												915	
s	Powerful in making us wise to salvation			252			479					228		
s	Speak, Lord, in the stillness			253		608			105					608
s	Thanks/Praise to God whose word was spoken (5 verse version)	423	438					319			584	229		
s	The heavens declare thy/your glory, Lord	168		254			481	320			264	230		
s	The prophets spoke in days of old	513									327			
s	Thou/God whose almighty / Father your mighty word	180	466	506	514	699	29	38	591	494	267	684	597	699
o	God has spoken — by his prophets			248			64		100			225		831
o	Lord, be thy word my rule / Lord, make your word	232		250										
o	Lord, I have made thy word my choice	490					475	316			504			

continued on next page

		AMS	NEH	HTC	HON	MP	H&P	R&S	BPW	CH3	CP	SG	ONC	MPC
pg	Lord, thy word abideth / Lord, your word shall guide us	166	407	251	318	446	476	317	102	130	515		420	446
e	All for Jesus!		272	469	10		251		332		277	661	13	
e	Angel-voices ever singing	163	336	307	33	34	484	405	1	455	377	27	37	34
e	Come down, O Love Divine	156	137	231	90	89	281	294	283	115	170	663	114	89
e	Forgive our sins as we forgive	362	66	111	141		134	84	83		428	145	180	
e	How sweet the name of Jesus sounds	122	374	211	220	251	257	277	339	376	467	42	297	251
e	Let all the world in every corner sing	202	394	342	296	404	10	114	54	361	497	47	382	404
e	May the mind of Christ my Saviour			550	334	463	739		537	432	521	671	447	463
g	Christ is the King! O friends rejoice	345	345	492				571	475	474	165	31		
g	How sure the Scriptures are			249								227		
g	I cannot tell why/how he whom angels worship			194	226	266	238	265	381		54	437	303	266
g	Lo, he / Jesus comes with clouds descending	28	9	196	307	424	241	656	185	316	31	438	405	424
g	Rejoice! the Lord is King	139	443	180	432	575	243	657	317	296	563	440	580	575
g	Songs of praise the angels sang	196	451	350			512	667		38	574		608	

Year B
Bible Sunday

Isaiah **55**: 1-11; Psalm **19**: 7-14; 2 Timothy **3**:14 — **4**:5; John **5**: 36b-47

		AMS	NEH	HTC	HON	MP	H&P	R&S	BPW	CH3	CP	SG	ONC	MPC
s	Come, Holy Ghost, our hearts inspire (Wesley)	448	348		91		469	312	97	122	177		117	
s	Come, Holy Spirit, come inflame				93						179		119	
s	Father of mercies, in thy/your word	167		247				99				224		
s	God has spoken — by his prophets			248			64		100			225		831

continued on next page

		AMS	NEH	HTC	HON	MP	H&P	R&S	BPW	CH3	CP	SG	ONC	MPC
s	God of love, you freely give											226		
s	God who hast caused to be written	467					472							
s	Here on the threshold of a new beginning										506	280		
s	How lovely on the mountains are the feet of him				219	249			310				295	249
s	Lord, be thy word my rule / Lord, make your word	232		250										
s	Lord, I have made thy word my choice	490					475	316			504			
s	Lord, you sometimes speak in wonders								101					
s	Now in reverence and awe										232		902	
s	Open our eyes, O Lord, we pray											915		
s	Speak, Lord, in the stillness			253		608			105					608
s	Thanks/Praise to God whose word was spoken (5 verse version)	423	438					319			584	229		
s	The heavens declare thy/your glory, Lord	168		254			481	320			264	230		
s	The prophets spoke in days of old	513									327			
s	Thou/God whose almighty / Father your mighty word	180	466	506	514	699	29	38	591	494	267	684	597	699
oeg	Lord, thy word abideth / Lord, your word shall guide us	166	407	251	318	446	476	317	102	130	515		420	446
o	All who are thirsty, come to the Lord										546			
o	At even[ing], ere/when the sun was/had set	9	243	315	43	43	142	644	616	52	12	487	50	
p	Creator of the earth and skies	351		320			419	82			410	296		
p	God be in my head	236	328	543	166		694	498	592	433	439	666	211	
p	God's glory fills the heavens with hymns PR19B													
p	The heavens declare God's glory PR19A													
e	Lord, for the years			328	310	428		603	535		51	602	409	428
e	Powerful in making us wise to salvation			252			479					228		
g	Break thou/now the bread of life					64	467	314	98		286			64
g	How sure the Scriptures are			249								227		
g	Immortal, invisible	199	377	21	242	327	9	67	383	32	474	44	314	327

Isaiah **45**: 22-25; Psalm **119**: 129-136; Romans **15**: 1-6; Luke **4**: 16-24

		AMS	NEH	HTC	HON	MP	H&P	R&S	BPW	CH3	CP	SG	ONC	MPC
s	Come, Holy Ghost, our hearts inspire (Wesley)	448	348		91		469	312	97	122	177		117	
s	Come, Holy Spirit, come inflame				93						179		119	
s	Father of mercies, in thy/your word	167		247					99			224		
s	God has spoken — by his prophets			248			64		100			225		831
s	God of love, you freely give											226		
s	God's Spirit is deep in my heart				180		315	576	574					
s	Here on the threshold of a new beginning										506	280		
s	Now in reverence and awe										232		902	
s	Open our eyes, O Lord, we pray												915	
s	Thanks/Praise to God whose word was spoken (5 verse version)	423	438					319			584	229		
s	The world is full of stories: SS1													
s	Thou/God whose almighty / Father your mighty word	180	466	506	514	699	29	38	591	494	267	684	597	699
o	At the name of Jesus	148	338	172	46	41	74	261	370	300	380	317	54	
o	Come, let us to the Lord our God						33	81		69	402			
o	The prophets spoke in days of old	513									327			
p2	The will of God to mark my way: Church Family Worship 607													
p	Lord, thy word abideth / Lord, your word shall guide us	166	407	251	318	446	476	317	102	130	515		420	446
p	The heavens declare thy/your glory, Lord	168		254			481	320			264	230		
e	Help us, O Lord, to learn	373	370	493			474				460	226		
g	'The Kingdom is upon you!'	512									590			
g	Christ brings the kingdom where barrenness blooms										430			
g	Christ is the world's true light	346	494	323	78		456	601	618	505	396	432	100	
g	Christ on whom the Spirit rested			228										
g	Come to be our hope, Lord Jesus										273			

continued on next page

		AMS	NEH	HTC	HON	MP	H&P	R&S	BPW	CH3	CP	SG	ONC	MPC
g	Come, thou/O long-expected Jesus	31	3	52	98	102	81	138	139	320	24	335	128	102
g	Hail to the Lord's anointed	142	55	190	193	204	125	127	142	317	87		259	204
g	Hark the glad sound! The Saviour comes	30	6	193	198	210	82	137	143	160	27	435	265	210
g	I cannot tell why/how he whom angels worship			194	226	266	238	265	381		54	437	303	266
g	Now is the time, the time of God's favour										341			
g	O changeless Christ, for ever new			108				206				374		
g	O for a thousand tongues to sing	125	415	219	362	496	744	285	59	371	534	55	485	495
g	Son of God, eternal Saviour	132	498	102				605	639	454	573			
g	The Kingdom of God is justice and joy			333	651	139	200	321			591	184	646	651
g	The voice of God goes out to all the world					140	131							
g	There is a Redeemer				500	673						396	658	673
g	When Jesus walked upon this earth			317										

Year A
Dedication Festival

1 Kings **8**: 22-30 or Revelation **21**: 9-14; Psalm **122**; Hebrews **12**: 18-24; Matthew **21**: 12-16

		AMS	NEH	HTC	HON	MP	H&P	R&S	BPW	CH3	CP	SG	ONC	MPC
s	Be thou my vision / Lord be my vision	343	339	545	56	51	378	489	521	87	386	669	70	51
s	Christ is made the sure foundation / Blessed city, heavenly Salem	283/332	204-5	559	76	73	485	559	474	10	208	572	97	73
s	Christ is our corner-stone	161		564	77						395		98	
s	Come, build the church											111		
s	God is here! As we his people	464		560			653				301			
s	Here on the threshold of a new beginning										506	280		
s	Here within this house of prayer			563										
s	Lord, we thank you for the promise											424		

continued on next page

		AMS	NEH	HTC	HON	MP	H&P	R&S	BPW	CH3	CP	SG	ONC	MPC
s	Now thank we all our God	205	413	33	354	486	566	72	128	368	530	54	474	486
s	O praise the Lord, ye servants of the Lord		426											
s	Only-begotten, Word of God eternal		210											
s	Our Father, by whose servants									550				
s	The Church of God a kingdom is	169	483		472						325		635	
s	The Church's one foundation	170	484	501	473	640	515	566	393	420	585	581	636	640
s	Thy/Your hand, O God, has guided	171	485	536	518	705	784	567	398	424	606	649	689	705
s	We have a gospel to proclaim	431	486	519	532	728	465		585		612		716	728
s	Who are we who stand and sing	529												
s	Ye that know the Lord is gracious	175	477								628			
r	Jerusalem, my happy home / thou city blest	187	225	569	258						481		339	
r	Now from the heavens descending									314	439			
og	We love the place, O God	160	471	558	533	731				15	211		718	731
o	Angel-voices ever singing	163	336	307	33	34	484	405	1	455	377	27	37	34
o	Great Shepherd of thy/your people, hear	164		363			490	387			454	238	250	
o	Holy, holy, holy, Lord God almighty	95	146	7/594	212	237	594	34	51	352	202	290	286	237
o	This is the day the Lord hath/has made	22	257	379			577	376			9	70	677	
pr	Jerusalem the golden	184	381	573	259			662	312	537	482		340	
p	Before Jehovah's aweful/awesome throne / Sing to the Lord	197		15			61	119		2	387			
p	How pleased and blest was I						497	563	10					
p	I rejoiced to hear them say										6			
er	Glorious things of thee/you are spoken	172	362	494	158	173	817	560	480	421	435	35	205	173
g	Bright the vision that delighted / Round the Lord	96	343	578	70		445	665	71	353	392	29	86	
g	Exult, archangels bright										402			
g	God our Father and Creator			562										
g	Immortal Love, for ever full	133	378	105	243	328	392	267	198	306	475	176	315	328
g	Jesus shall reign where'er the sun	143	388	516	277	379	239	269	313	413	490	45	359	379
g	My song is love unknown	63	86	136	346	478	173	207	204	224	112	384	463	478
g	Thine arm, O Lord, in days of old	285	324		502		397			214		671		

Year B
Dedication Festival

Genesis **28**: 11-18 or Revelation **21**: 9-14; Psalm **122**; 1 Peter **2**: 1-10; John **10**: 22-29

		AMS	NEH	HTC	HON	MP	H&P	R&S	BPW	CH3	CP	SG	ONC	MPC
s	Be thou my vision / Lord be my vision	343	339	545	56	51	378	489	521	87	386	669	70	51
s	Come, build the church											111		
s	Father, Lord of all creation	356			122				620		418		163	
s	God is here! As we his people	464		560			653				301			
s	Here within this house of prayer			563										
s	Lord, we thank you for the promise											424		
s	Now thank we all our God	205	413	33	354	486	566	72	128	368	530	54	474	486
s	O praise the Lord, ye servants of the Lord		426											
s	Our Father, by whose servants									550				
s	The Church of God a kingdom is	169	483		472						325		635	
s	The Church's one foundation	170	484	501	473	640	515	566	393	420	585	581	636	640
s	Thy/Your hand, O God, has guided	171	485	536	518	705	784	567	398	424	606	649	689	705
s	We have a gospel to proclaim	431	486	519	532	728	465		585		612		716	728
s	Who are we who stand and sing	529												
s	Ye that know the Lord is gracious	175	477								628			
r	For all the saints	305	197	567	134	148	814	658	478	534	232	636	177	148
r	Glorious things of thee/you are spoken	172	362	494	158	173	817	560	480	421	435	35	205	173
r	There's a place where the streets shine										457		1011	
r	Wake, O wake / Sleepers, wake	32	16	199	529		249	132		315	39		703	
o	As Jacob with travel was weary one day	435			36		444				378		775	
o	Lord, your voice in Eden's garden											426		
o	O God of Bethel / O God of Jacob	216	416	35	364		442	71	599	72	536	241	491	907
o	O happy band of pilgrims	208	418	530	368								497	
o	Prayer to a heart of lowly love								601					
pr	Jerusalem the golden	184	381	573	259			662	312	537	482		340	

continued on next page

		AMS	NEH	HTC	HON	MP	H&P	R&S	BPW	CH3	CP	SG	ONC	MPC
p	Before Jehovah's aweful/awesome throne / Sing to the Lord	197		15			61	119		2	387			
p	I joyed when to the house of God / Pray that Jerusalem		441				510	727		489				
es	Here on the threshold of a new beginning										506	280		
e	Christ is made the sure foundation / Blessed city, heavenly Salem	283/ 332	204-5	559	76	73	485	559	474	10	208	572	97	73
e	Christ is our corner-stone	161		564	77						395		98	
e	Church of God, elect and glorious			504					406			592		
e	Each of us a living stem											793		
e	Forth in the peace of Christ we go	458	361	542	142			602	607	589	429	594	187	
e	Hail to the Lord's anointed	142	55	190	193	204	125	127	142	317	87		259	204
e	Here in this place the new light is streaming										4			
e	How firm a foundation			430	216	243		589	380				292	243
e	Through all the changing scenes of life	209	467	46	516	702	73	685	544		604	654	686	702
e	To him we come			518		709			547			679		709
g	Loving Shepherd of thy/your sheep	134		305	325					93	517		424	

Year C
Dedication Festival

1 Chronicles 29: 6-19; Psalm 122; Ephesians 2: 19-22; John 2: 13-22

		AMS	NEH	HTC	HON	MP	H&P	R&S	BPW	CH3	CP	SG	ONC	MPC
s	Be thou my vision / Lord be my vision	343	339	545	56	51	378	489	521	87	386	669	70	51
s	Come, build the church											111		
s	Father, Lord of all creation	356			122				620		418		163	
s	Forth in thy/your name, O Lord	239	235	306	143	159	381	521	526	463	430	623	188	159
s	Glorious things of thee/you are spoken	172	362	494	158	173	817	560	480	421	435	35	205	173
s	God is here! As we his people	464		560			653				301			

continued on next page

		AMS	NEH	HTC	HON	MP	H&P	R&S	BPW	CH3	CP	SG	ONC	MPC
s	Here within this house of prayer			563										
s	Lord, we thank you for the promise											424		
s	O praise the Lord, ye servants of the Lord		426											
s	Only-begotten, Word of God eternal		210											
s	Our Father, by whose servants									550				
s	Rejoice in God! Let trumpets sound										60			
s	The Church of God a kingdom is	169	483		472						325		635	
s	The Church's one foundation	170	484	501	473	640	515	566	393	420	585	581	636	640
s	Thy kingdom come! on bended knee	178	500		520					323	608		690	
s	Thy/Your hand, O God, has guided	171	485	536	518	705	784	567	398	424	606	649	689	705
s	We have a gospel to proclaim	431	486	519	532	728	465		585		612		716	728
s	Who are we who stand and sing	529												
o	Eternal God, we bring our praise FF p80													
o	Holy, holy, holy, Lord God almighty	95	146	7/594	212	237	594	34	51	352	202	290	286	237
o	Immortal, invisible, God only wise	199	377	21	242	327	9	67	383	32	474	44	314	327
o	Prodigal Father, here we stand FF p109													
o	This is the day the Lord hath/has made	22	257	379			577	376			9	70	677	
p	All people that on earth do dwell	100	334	14	17	20	1	712	2	1	369	77	21	20
p	How pleased and blest was I						497	563	10					
p	I joyed when to the house of God / Pray that Jerusalem		441				510	727		489				
p	Jerusalem the golden	184	381	573	259			662	312	537	482		340	
p	Jerusalem! How glad I was LUTR251													
es	Here on the threshold of a new beginning										506	280		
e	Christ is made the sure foundation / Blessed city, heavenly Salem	283/332	204-5	559	76	73	485	559	474	10	208	572	97	73
e	Christ is our corner-stone	161		564	77						395		98	
e	Christ is the world's light	440		321			455	600	34		213	591	99	
e	City of God, how broad and far	173	346		85		809			422	400		106	
e	Light's abode, celestial Salem	185	401		305						502		398	
e	Sing together on our journey										580			
e	Ye that know the Lord is gracious	175	477								628			
g	I danced in the morning	375	375		228			195			468		305	
g	Lead us, heavenly Father, lead us	224	393	595	293	400	68	543	597	90	496	640	379	400
g	We love the place, O God	160	471	558	533	731				15	211		718	731

Years A, B, C

All Saints' Day (Seasonal material)

		AMS	NEH	HTC	HON	MP	H&P	R&S	BPW	CH3	CP	SG	ONC	MPC
s	Behold what witnesses unseen									531				
s	Blest be the everlasting God						669	588		530	139			
s	By every nation, race and tongue			579								30		
s	For all the saints	305	197	567	134	148	814	658	478	534	232	636	177	148
s	For all thy saints, O Lord	308	224								2115		179	
s	For those we love within the veil									538				
s	Give me/us the wings of faith	324	225		156		815	664			216		202	
s	Glory to thee, O God, for all thy saints	363			163						217		209	
s	God we praise you! God we bless you		341								450	38		
s	Hark how the adoring hosts									532				
s	Hark! the sound of holy voices	304	226		200								267	
s	Here from all nations, all tongues, and all peoples			571					309		462	455		
s	How bright these glorious spirits shine	306	227	572						533	221			
s	Jesu, Son of Mary/Think, O Lord, in mercy	281	329		263							356		
s	Joy and triumph everlasting		229											
s	Let saints on earth / Come let us join our friends above	182	396	574	297	409	812	472		543	222	578	384	409
s	Light a candle for thanksgiving											396		
s	Lo, round the throne a glorious band	303												
s	Lord God, we give you thanks for all your saints	488												
s	Lord, in our lonely hours										641			
s	O heavenly Jerusalem	322												
s	O what their joy / What of those sabbaths	186	432					659		535	225		550	
s	Once to every generation										605			

continued on next page

		AMS	NEH	HTC	HON	MP	H&P	R&S	BPW	CH3	CP	SG	ONC	MPC
s	Praise to God for saints and martyrs											571		
s	Rejoice in God's saints	508									227	675		
s	Sing alleluia forth in duteous praise / ye saints on high	188	446							542	568			
s	Sing for God's glory											598		
s	Sing we the song of those who stand						821	666						
s	Soldiers, who are Christ's below	302	450		450						228		607	
s	Ten thousand times ten thousand	189		576										
s	Thanks be to God for his saints										64			
s	The saints in Christ are one in every place										629			
s	The victory of our God is won										68			
s	There is a land of pure delight	190	460	575			822	668	323	536	597			
s	We are called to stand together										607			
s	We praise, we worship thee/you, O God						443	755	490			258		
s	We sing for all the unsung saints									614				
s	Who are these, like stars appearing	323	231		555						229		746	
s	Ye watchers and ye holy ones	532	478		567						230		758	
e	Now from the heaven descending										314	439		

Year A
All Saints' Day (Lectionary material)

Revelation **7**: 9-17; Psalm **34**: 1-10; 1 John **3**: 1-3; Matthew **5**: 1-12

		AMS	NEH	HTC	HON	MP	H&P	R&S	BPW	CH3	CP	SG	ONC	MPC
o	Father, if justly still we claim						299							
o	Help us, O Lord, to learn	373	370	493			474				460	226		
p	God will I bless at all times									391				
p	Tell his praise in song and story			41					563				630	
p	Through all the changing scenes of life	209	467	46	516	702	73	685	544		604	654	686	702
er	There is a louder shout to come										444			
e	Behold the amazing gift of love						666	587		396	389			

continued on next page

		AMS	NEH	HTC	HON	MP	H&P	R&S	BPW	CH3	CP	SG	ONC	MPC
g	Blessed are the humble souls who see PR807													
g	Blest are the pure in heart	238	341	110	63	58	724		588	113	391	372	77	58
g	Happy are those who acknowledge their need										667			
g	How blest the poor who love the Lord								197					
g	Seek ye first the Kingdom of God				442	590	138	512	357				590	590
g	Show me thy ways, O Lord									74				

Year B
All Saints' Day (Lectionary material)

Wisdom **3**: 1-9 or Isaiah **25**: 6-9; Psalm **24**: 1-6; Revelation **21**: 1-6a; John **11**: 32-44

		AMS	NEH	HTC	HON	MP	H&P	R&S	BPW	CH3	CP	SG	ONC	MPC
p	The earth belongs unto the Lord									566				
e	Christ is made the sure foundation / Blessed city, heavenly Salem	283/ 332	204-5	559	76	73	485	559	474	10	208	572	97	73
e	City of God, Jerusalem			187										
e	Father of everlasting grace						300				420			
e	Jerusalem on high			565										
e	Jerusalem the golden	184	381	573	259			662	312	537	482		340	
e	Jerusalem, my happy home / thou city blest	187	225	569	258						481		339	
e	Now from the heaven descending									314	439			
e	O holy City, seen of/by John	409						628		509				
e	Songs of praise the angels sang	196	451	350			512	667		38	574		608	
e	Then I saw a new heaven and earth					669						456		669
g	God who created light										288			

Year C
All Saints' Day (Lectionary material)

Daniel **7**: 1-3, 15-18; Psalm **149**; Ephesians **1**: 11-23; Luke **6**: 20-31

		AMS	NEH	HTC	HON	MP	H&P	R&S	BPW	CH3	CP	SG	ONC	MPC
o	Immortal, invisible, God only wise	199	377	21	242	327	9	67	383	32	474	44	314	327
o	O worship the King all glorious above	101	433	24	393	528	28	47	63	35	546	90	551	528
o	The head that once was crowned with thorns	141	134	182	480	647	209	257	274	286	172	442		644
p	All praise to our redeeming Lord					19	753		401		371			19
p	Bring to the Lord a glad new song			336					30			78		
p	O praise our mighty Lord PR149													
p	Rejoice! the Lord is King	139	443	180	432	575	243	657	317	296	563	440	580	575
el	Jesus invites his saints						612	434	438					
e	And he shall reign: LPB 237													802
e	At the name of Jesus	148	338	172	46	41	74	261	370	300	380	317	54	
e	Christ from whom all blessings flow			491			764	561						
e	Come, Holy Ghost, our souls inspire	93	138	589	92	90	283	751		342	178	555	118	90
e	Come, thou/most Holy Spirit, come / Come, thou Holy Paraclete	92	139	227	97		284	297		105		180	127	
e	Head of the Church, our risen Lord						547	562						
e	How deep the Father's love for us										193		988	
e	O King enthroned on high	158	421		373		311	296			180		504	
e	Our blest/great Redeemer	151		241	410	548	312	330		336	193	448	543	548
e	Ride on Jesus, all-victorious						272							
e	See where our great High Priest						622							
e	Spirit of wisdom, turn our eyes						385							

Year A
CLC: The Fourth Sunday before Advent
RCL: Proper 26

Micah **3**: 5-12; Psalm **43**; 1 Thessalonians **2**: 9-13; Matthew **24**: 1-14

		AMS	NEH	HTC	HON	MP	H&P	R&S	BPW	CH3	CP	SG	ONC	MPC
og	God of all human history											223		
o	Judge eternal, throned in splendour		490	329	285	395	409	626	627	519	356	600	372	395
o	Lord of all hopefulness	394	239	101	313		552	531	517	92	507	509	413	882
o	Now that the daylight fills the sky		151							45				
o	O Christ the Lord, O Christ the King		496				406	630						
o	O Spirit of the living God			513			322	577	579	496	190	605		
o	The Kingdom of God is justice and joy			333		651	139	200	321		591	184	646	651
o	The voice of God goes out to all the world						140	131						
o	Thy/Your kingdom come, O God	177	499	334	519		783	638	644	322	607	269	691	949
p	God defend me! Traitors rise PR43													
p	O send thy/your light forth						537	690	18	7				
p	Send out your light, Lord										231			
el	Author of life divine	258	274	395	48		596	440		587	281		56	
e	Brother, sister, let me serve you				73			474	473		393	619	88	
e	Christ from whom all blessings flow			491			764	561						
e	God is love, and where true love is / Here in Christ we gather	465	513				757	473			441			
e	Head of the Church, our risen Lord						547	562						
e	Jesus, Lord, we look to thee	380	481				759	564			489			
e	Jesus, where'er thy people meet / Lord Jesus, when your people	162	390	371	282		549	476			492	16	367	
e	Love divine, all loves excelling	131	408	217	321	449	267	663	559	437	516	179	428	449
e	My God, how wonderful thou art / you are	102	410	369	343	468	51	408		356	523	202	457	468
e	My spirit longs for thee	57	299					333			99			
e	The Church's one foundation	170	484	501	473	640	515	566	393	420	585	581	636	640
e	We are your people	519						483						
e	Ye/You servants of God, your Master proclaim	149	476	520	565	784	278	293	76	372	627	75	784	756
g	All my hope on God is founded	336	333	451	15	16	63	586	327	405	368	525	19	16
g	Christ is coming! Let creation									313				
g	Hark what a sound, and too divine for hearing						236	660		314	28			
g	Jesus, priceless treasure			461	262		259				484	535	344	
g	Lo, he / Jesus comes with clouds descending	28	9	196	307	424	241	656	185	316	31	438	405	424
g	The day of the Lord shall come							637						
g	The king shall come when morning dawns								320					
g	We have a gospel to proclaim	431	486	519	532	728	465		585	.	612	331	716	728

Year B
CLC: The Fourth Sunday before Advent
RCL: Proper 26

Deuteronomy **6**: 1-9; Psalm **119**: 1-8; Hebrews **9**: 11-14; Mark **12**: 28-34

		AMS	NEH	HTC	HON	MP	H&P	R&S	BPW	CH3	CP	SG	ONC	MPC
s	Join all the glorious names			214		392	78	280	557	304	493	46		392
s	Now that the daylight fills the sky		151							45				
o	Father of all, whose laws have stood			539				335			664			
o	God has spoken — by his prophets			248			64		100			225		831
o	O Lord my / Thee will I love, my strength, my tower			485			40			678				
o	Spirit of God, descend upon my heart						313	305			108	575		
o	The prophets spoke in days of old	513									327			
o	Thee will I love, my God and King			485			40			678				
e	All praise to thee/Christ, for thou / our Lord and King divine	337	335	204	18		253	750		297	372		22	
e	Come, my soul, thy suit prepare						546				404			
e	Come, thou everlasting Spirit						298	315						
e	Eternal Light! Eternal Light!			454			458	83	85	357	414	527		
e	Glory be to Jesus	66	83	126	159						108	146	206	
e	Praise to Christ, the Lord incarnate										327			
e	Priest and victim, Jesus dies										328			
e	Souls of men / Restless souls / There's a wideness	251	461	443	501	607, 683	230	353	573	218	598	188	662	607
e	Victim divine, thy grace we claim		309				629							
e	What offering shall we give			439										
e	With joy we meditate the grace	530				774	235	206	275		624			774
g	Can we/man by searching find out God	438					76	80			201	496		
g	Come, let us to the Lord our God						33	81		69	402			
g	Fill thou/now my/our life	200		541	129	146	792	406	569	457	424	665	171	146

Year C
CLC: The Fourth Sunday before Advent
RCL: Proper 26

Isaiah **1**: 10-18; Psalm **32**: 1-7; 2 Thessalonians **1**: 1-12; Luke **19**: 1-10

		AMS	NEH	HTC	HON	MP	H&P	R&S	BPW	CH3	CP	SG	ONC	MPC
o	I'll praise my Maker while I've breath			20		320	439	734	127		473	84		320
o	O day of God, draw near/nigh In beauty	405						632	635	511	33			
p	Happy are those, beyond all measure blessed										172			
e	Head of thy Church triumphant						818							
e	Lo, he / Jesus comes with clouds descending	28	9	196	307	424	241	656	185	316	31	438	405	424
e	Lord, save thy world; in bitter need	397					425							
e	O thou/Lord who came[st]	233	431	552/ 596	392	525	745	433	355	110	191	560	541	525
gl	Deck thyself/yourself, my soul, with gladness	257	280	400	108		606	446		567	295		146	
gl	I come with joy to meet my Lord	473		408	227		610	447	437		365	469	304	
gl	Let all mortal flesh keep silence	256	295	61	295		266	454	441	577	309	472	381	
g	All ye who seek a comfort / for sure relief	64	63		22						101		26	
g	Almighty God, we come to make confession											27		
g	God makes his rain to fall: SS96													
g	God who came in Jesus FF p86													
g	He gave his life in selfless love			405		214			435			467		214
g	I heard the voice of Jesus say	247	376		231	275	136	349		212	469		310	275
g	Jesus who walked beside the lake: SS81													
g	Jesus, whose all-redeeming love	383							215					
g	Just as I am, without one plea	246	294	440	287	396	697	364	346	79	308	507	374	396
g	Little Zacchaeus: SS64													
g	Long ago you taught your people FF p99													
g	Lord of all life and power											414		
g	My Lord, you wore no royal crown			118								628		
g	O for a closer walk with God	231	414	368	360	494		551		663	532		483	494
g	This is the day the Lord hath/has made	22	257	379			577	376			9	70	677	
g	When Christ was lifted from the earth	525		335				655					142	
g	Zacchaeus was a wealthy man FF p115													

Remembrance: also National, Peace, Justice; seasonal

		AMS	NEH	HTC	HON	MP	H&P	R&S	BPW	CH3	CP	SG	ONC	MPC
s	'I have a dream,' a man once said								625					
s	Almighty Father, who for us thy Son didst give	338					401	621			374			
s	Beneath the shade of our vine and fig tree							622						
s	Christ is the world's light	440		321			455	600	34		213	591	99	
s	Christ is the world's true light	346	494	323	78		456	601	618	505	396	432	100	
s	Creator of the earth and skies	351		320			419	82			410	296		
s	Eternal Ruler of the ceaseless round	353	355		115			623	477	514	181		154	
s	Father eternal, Ruler of creation							624		507				
s	For the healing of the nations	361			139		402	620	621		427	261	186	
s	God as with silent hearts we bring to mind											210		
s	God enthroned in majesty											490		
s	God of freedom, God of justice							625	623		447		224	
s	God of grace and God of glory	367		324	174	192	712	344	572	88	448	574	225	192
s	God of love and truth and beauty	368					403					5		
s	God save and bless our nation			325										
s	Gracious God in adoration											244		
s	Grant us your peace: SS14													
s	In a world where people walk in darkness									476				
s	It is God who holds the nations						404					304		
s	Judge eternal, throned in splendour		490	329	285	395	409	626	627	519	356	600	372	395
s	Lead me from death to life							627	628					
s	Let there be peace on earth							629						
s	Light a candle for thanksgiving											396		
s	Lord of lords and King eternal	396									357			
s	Lord, save thy world; in bitter need	397					425							
s	Lord, while for all mankind we pray		491			.				518				
s	Make me a channel of your peace			S19	328	456	776	629	634		519	691	437	456
s	O Christ the Lord, O Christ the King		496				406	630						
s	O day of God, draw near/nigh In beauty	405						632	635	511	33			
s	O day of peace that dimly shines											259		

continued on next page

		AMS	NEH	HTC	HON	MP	H&P	R&S	BPW	CH3	CP	SG	ONC	MPC
s	O God of hope											493		
s	O God we bear the imprint of your face										250			
s	O holy City, seen of/by John	409						628		509				
s	O let us spread the pollen of peace							633						
s	O Lord our God, arise		497					631		495				
s	Pray for the Church, afflicted and oppressed						556	634			559	267		
s	Sing for God's glory											598		
s	Son of God, eternal Saviour	132	498	102				605	639	454	573			
s	The Church of Christ in every age						804	636	613					
s	The Kingdom of God is justice and joy			333		651	139	200	321		591	184	646	651
s	The Saviour's precious blood						410							
s	The universe was waiting											669		
s	This we can do for justice and for peace							639						
s	Thy love, O God, has all mankind created						411			503				
s	Thy/Your kingdom come, O God	177	499	334	519		783	638	644	322	607	269	691	949
s	We bring you, Lord, our prayer and praise									611	262			
s	We pray for peace						413	641			613			4
s	We turn to you, O God of every nation	522					412	654	641				725	
s	We utter our cry: that peace may prevail							642						
s	What does the Lord require	432					414							
p	O/Our God, our help in ages past	99	417	37	366	498	358	705	389	611	537	542	494	498

Year A
CLC: The Third Sunday before Advent
RCL: Proper 27

Wisdom **6**: 12-16 and (Canticle) Wisdom **6**: 17-20 or Amos **5**: 18-24 and Psalm **70**; 1 Thessalonians **4**: 13-18 and Matthew **25**: 1-13

		AMS	NEH	HTC	HON	MP	H&P	R&S	BPW	CH3	CP	SG	ONC	MPC
o1	Be thou my vision / Lord be my vision	343	339	545	56	51	378	489	521	87	386	669	70	51
o1	Happy the man that finds the grace						674							
o1	Thou hidden love of God						544			96	602			
o1	Your words to me are life and health						482	321						
o2	Command thy blessing from above						488	385		117				
o2	Great Shepherd of thy/your people, hear	164		363			490	387			454	238	250	
o2	O Christ the Lord, O Christ the King		496				406	630						
o2	O day of God, draw near/nigh In beauty	405						632	635	511	33			
o2	O Lord our God, arise		497					631		495				
o2	O worship / Worship the Lord in the beauty of holiness	49	52	344	394	529	505	187	22	40	89	204	552	529
o2	What shall we bring											730		
e	Come with the sound of trumpet										15			
e	Leader of faithful souls and guide						819							
e	Let saints on earth / Come let us join our friends above	182	396	574	297	409	812	472			543	222	578	384	409
e	Lord, it belongs not to my care	242	402				679	545			679	224			
e	Love divine, all loves excelling	131	408	217	321	449	267	663	559	437	516	179	428	449
e	Rejoice! the Lord is King	139	443	180	432	575	243	657	317	296	563	440	580	575
e	Shepherd divine, our wants relieve	228					558				566			
e	That priceless gift, what tongue can tell										329			
e	The Lord will come and not be slow	29	15		489		245	128		321	37		655	
e	The universe was waiting											669		
e	Thou Judge of quick and dead						247							
e	Ye faithful souls who Jesus know						751							
g	Here, O my Lord, I see thee/you	274		406		230	608		436	573	304	468	279	230
g	The day of the Lord shall come							637						
g	Wake, O wake / Sleepers, wake	32	16	199	529		249	132		315	39		703	
g	Ye/You servants of the Lord	150	18	598	566		248			319	40		757	

For seasonal hymns see Remembrance, page 216

Year B
CLC: The Third Sunday before Advent
RCL: Proper 27

Jonah **3**: 1-5, 10; Psalm **62**: 5-12; Hebrews **9**: 24-28; Mark **1**: 14-20

		AMS	NEH	HTC	HON	MP	H&P	R&S	BPW	CH3	CP	SG	ONC	MPC
I	Christ, whose glory fills the skies	4	234	266	82	79	457	380		114	2	170	105	79
I	Thy/Your hand, O God, has guided	171	485	536	518	705	784	567	398	424	606	649	689	705
o	Come, let us to the Lord our God						33	81		69	402			
o	Forgive our sins as we forgive	362	66	111	141		134	84	83		428	145	180	
o	God, who stretched the spangled heavens						86				625			
o	The love of God comes close							107				186		
o	When all thy/your mercies	109	472	39	544	751	573	109		150	617	73	732	751
p	Almighty God, my Redeemer										102			
p	Only on God do thou, my soul									25				
p	Put thou thy trust / Commit thou all thy griefs	223			429		672	550		669	562		576	
el	And now, O Father, mindful of the love	260	273	392	32		593			580	279	459	34	
el	Lord, enthroned in heavenly splendour	263	296	416	309	431	616			583	311	52	408	
el	Once, only once, and once for all	261	304		404								522	
e	Alas! and did my Saviour bleed			124										
e	Lord your voice in Eden's garden											426		
e	Priest and victim, Jesus dies										328			
e	See, Christ was wounded for our sake			137					229					
e	We sing the praise of him who died	138	94	146	536	738	182	229	231	258	125	390	723	738
e	When God almighty came to earth				545								733	
g	And can it be			588	30	33	216	136	328	409	376	168	32	
g	Christ who called disciples to him										620			
g	Come, living God, when least expected							354			403			
g	From heaven you came (The servant King)				148	162		522	529		432	632	195	16

continued on next page

		AMS	NEH	HTC	HON	MP	H&P	R&S	BPW	CH3	CP	SG	ONC	MPC
g	Here comes Jesus: SS79													
g	I want to walk with Jesus Christ			S16		302		367						302
g	James and Andrew, Peter and John				257								338	
g	Jesus who walked beside the lake: SS81													
g	Love is the only law											430		
g	O happy day that fixed my choice			442	369	499	702	359	539				498	499
g	O Jesus, I have promised	235	420	531	372	501	704	509	352	434	538	676	503	501
g	O thou/Lord who came[st]	233	431	552/ 596	392	525	745	433	355	110	191	560	541	525
g	Take my life, and let it be	249		554	464	624	705	371	358	462	581	678	625	624
g	We are your people	519						483						
g	When the Son of Mary: SS80 HSN82													
g	Will you come and follow me?				560			558	363		622	634	752	

For seasonal hymns see Remembrance, page 216

Year C
CLC: The Third Sunday before Advent
RCL: Proper 27

Job **19**: 23-27a; Psalm **17**: 1-9; 2 Thessalonians **2**: 1-5, 13-17; Luke **20**: 27-38

		AMS	NEH	HTC	HON	MP	H&P	R&S	BPW	CH3	CP	SG	ONC	MPC
o	I know that my Redeemer lives, and ever prays						731							
o	I know that my Redeemer lives, what joy			169	232	278	196	278	251			406	311	278
o	Jesus Christ, our great Redeemer					356								
o	Led like a lamb / You're alive, you have risen				294		402	241	254					402
o	My God, how wonderful thou art / you are	102	410	369	343	468	51	408		356	523	202	457	468
o	Walking in a garden	518	123					334					705	
p	Be thou / O Lord, my/our guardian	217	64	374	55	385		68			385		68	
e	Father almighty / Wherefore O Father, we thy/your humble servants	275	313	402							332			
e	With glorious clouds encompassed round						184				623			
gl	Come, let us with our Lord arise	449	254	375			575	383			142			
gl	Forth in the peace of Christ we go	458	361	542	142			602	607	589	429	594	187	
g	Christ the Lord is risen today / Love's redeeming work is done / All creation	83	113	150	324	76	193	232	246	275	150	412	433	76
g	Christian people, raise your song	443					601	435	430		289			
g	Come on and celebrate				95	99								99
g	My Lord, I did not choose you			107										
g	Now is eternal life	402	114		351		203	432			152		470	
g	The universe was waiting											669		
g	You, living Christ, our eyes behold	533	487								333			

For seasonal hymns see Remembrance, page 216

Year A
CLC: The Second Sunday before Advent
RCL: Proper 28

Zephaniah **1**: 7, 12-18; Psalm **90**: 1-8 [9-11] 12; 1 Thessalonians **5**: 1-11;
Matthew **25**: 14-30

		AMS	NEH	HTC	HON	MP	H&P	R&S	BPW	CH3	CP	SG	ONC	MPC
o	Be thou / O Lord, my/our guardian	217	64	374	55	385		68			385		68	
o	The day of the Lord shall come							637						
p	Lord, thou hast been our dwelling-place									102				
p	O/Our God, our help in ages past	99	417	37	366	498	358	705	389	611	537	542	494	498
e	Almighty Lord, the holy one			273										
e	As sons of the day and daughters of light			490								570		
e	Be thou my vision / Lord be my vision	343	339	545	56	51	378	489	521	87	386	669	70	51
e	Captains of the saintly band / Christian soldiers	299	215							539	212		91	
e	From heaven you came (The servant King)				148	162		522	529		432	632	195	16
e	Help us to help each other / Jesus, united by thy grace	374		540	208		773	500			461		275	
e	Jesus lives! Thy/Your terrors now	82	112	156	272	373	198	239	253	605	148	409	354	373
e	Let us talents and tongues employ	481		414	301			453					391	
e	No weight of gold or silver			138								181		
e	O Holy Ghost, thy people bless / O Holy Spirit, come to bless	155		238	370						187		500	
e	Soldiers of Christ, arise	219	449	533	449	604	719	370	580	441	571	643	606	604
e	Soldiers of the cross, arise			534						478				
e	When circumstances make my life										540			
g	God makes his rain to fall: SS96													

Year B
CLC: The Second Sunday before Advent
RCL: Proper 28

Daniel **12**: 1-3; Psalm **16**; Hebrews **10**: 11-14 [15-18] 19-25; Mark **13**: 1-8

		AMS	NEH	HTC	HON	MP	H&P	R&S	BPW	CH3	CP	SG	ONC	MPC
s	And can it be			588	30	33	216	136	328	409	376	168	32	
l	From glory to glory advancing	276	286		147			462		325	299		194	
l	The first day of the week	424					576							
o	Christ, the fair glory	321	190		79						246		102	
o	For all the saints	305	197	567	134	148	814	658	478	534	232	636	177	148
o	Who are these, like stars appearing	323	231		555						229		746	
p	Christ, whose glory fills the skies	4	234	266	82	79	457	380		114	2	170	105	79
p	Forth in thy/your name, O Lord	239	235	306	143	159	381	521	526	463	430	623	188	159
p	Holy Spirit, Truth divine			235			289	301	292	106	184		289	
p	O God, my refuge, keep me safe PR16													
el	Father almighty / Wherefore O Father, we thy/your humble servants	275	313	402							332			
el	O God of our forefathers, hear / With solemn faith		314				554							
e	Come, ye faithful / Alleluia, raise the anthem	145	351	205	99	103			269		409	25	131	103
e	Crown him with many crowns	147	352	174	103	109	255	262	37	298	166	321	137	109
e	God has promised many things										503			
e	Happy the souls to Jesus joined						816							
e	Jesus, our hope, our hearts' desire	86		178							169			
e	Praise, my soul, the King of heaven	192	436	38	422	560	13	104	65	360	555		565	560
e	The head that once was crowned with thorns	141	134	182	480	647	209	257	274	286	172	442		644
e	The Lord ascendeth up on high		135				210			287	173			
e	Where high the heavenly temple stands	130		184				259		295	75			
g	All my hope on God is founded	336	333	451	15	16	63	586	327	405	368	525	19	16
g	Christ is our corner-stone	161		564	77						395		98	
g	Fight the good fight	220	359	526	128	143	710	496	524	442	423	635	169	143
g	Glorious things of thee/you are spoken	172	362	494	158	173	817	560	480	421	435	35	205	173
g	Head of thy Church triumphant						818							
g	Oft in danger, oft in woe / Christian soldiers, onward go	210	434	524	396	533	715				547		487	533
g	Souls of men / Restless souls / There's a wideness	251	461	443	501	607, 683	230	353	573	218	598	188	662	607
g	Through all the changing scenes of life	209	467	46	516	702	73	685	544		604	654	686	702
g	Through the night of doubt and sorrow	211	468	466	517		441		546	423	605	544	687	948
g	When the stars in their flight										445			

Year C
CLC: The Second Sunday before Advent
RCL: Proper 28

Malachi **4**: 1-2a; Psalm **98**; 2 Thessalonians **3**: 6-13; Luke **21**: 5-19

		AMS	NEH	HTC	HON	MP	H&P	R&S	BPW	CH3	CP	SG	ONC	MPC
o	Christ, your glory fills the heavens										272			
o	Hills of the north, rejoice	470	7		209		237		311		29		282	
o	Judge eternal, throned in splendour		490	329	285	395	409	626	627	519	356	600	372	395
o	Sometimes a light surprises	108					571	595			572			
o	The race that long / The people that in darkness	52	57	71	491		89	129		168	38		656	
o	Thou/God whose almighty / Father your mighty word	180	466	506	514	699	29	38	591	494	267	684	597	699
p	Joy to the world, the Lord is come			197	283	393	77	135	315		57	340	370	393
p	New songs of celebration render	498		343	350		491	709			527	87	468	
p	Sing a new song to Jehovah									348				
el	Lord, as we rise to leave the shell of worship	385							608		209			
el	Now let us from this table rise	403		419	352		619	463	451		315	475	472	
el	Strengthen for service, Lord, the hands	421	306	423	460		626	461	453	588	323	473	619	
e	Christ from whom all blessings flow			491			764	561						
e	God of love and truth and beauty	368					403					5		
e	Help us to help each other / Jesus, united by thy grace	374		540	208		773	500			461		275	
e	My gracious Lord, I own thy right						741	535					459	
e	What does the Lord require	432					414							
gl	Christ, whose glory fills the skies	4	234	266	82	79	457	380		114	2	170	105	79
g	Christ is our comer-stone	161		564	77						395		98	
g	For the healing of the nations	361			139		402	620	621		427	261	186	
g	O Christ the Lord, O Christ the King		496				406	630						
g	The Saviour's precious blood						410							
g	We turn to you, O God of every nation	522					412	654	641				725	

Year A
CLC: Christ the King
RCL: Proper 29

Ezekiel 34: 11-16, 20-24; Psalm 95: 1-7a; Ephesians 1: 15-23; Matthew 25: 31-46

		AMS	NEH	HTC	HON	MP	H&P	R&S	BPW	CH3	CP	SG	ONC	MPC
s	'The Kingdom is upon you!'	512									590			
s	Christ is the King!	345	345	492				571	475	474	165	31		
s	The Kingdom of God is justice and joy			333		651	139	200	321		591	184	646	651
s	Thy/Your kingdom come, O God	177	499	334	519		783	638	644	322	607	269	691	949
oe	God is our strength from days of old				171								220	
o	Praise the Lord! rise up	416			424						319		569	
o	The King of love my shepherd is	126	457	44	484	649	69	552	394	388	589	205	649	649
o	Thou Shepherd of Israel and mine						750							
p	Let us sing to the God of salvation								15			86		
p	O come, and let us to the Lord						567	707		19				
el	Rejoice! the Lord is King	139	443	180	432	575	243	657	317	296	563	440	580	575
e	At the name of Jesus	148	338	172	46	41	74	261	370	300	380	317	54	
e	Crown him with many crowns	147	352	174	103	109	255	262	37	298	166	321	137	109
e	God of love and truth and beauty	368					403					5		
gl	Deck thyself/yourself, my soul	257	280	400	108		606	446		567	295		146	
gl	Let all mortal flesh keep silence	256	295	61	295		266	454	441	577	309	472	381	
gl	Lord, as we rise to leave the shell of worship	385							608		209			
g	Glorious the day when Christ was born							263						
g	God is love: his the care			311	169		220	274	45	416			216	
g	He is Lord, he is Lord			S7	204	220	256	264	378				274	220
g	Heaven shall not wait				207								272	
g	Help us to help each other / Jesus, united by thy grace	374		540	208		773	500			461		275	
g	I cannot tell why/how he whom angels worship			194	226	266	238	265	381		54	437	303	266
g	Jesus Christ is waiting				268				534			624	349	
g	Jesus, my Lord, how rich thy grace / Fountain of good	381					147			459				
g	Lord Christ, who on thy heart	388			308		394						407	
g	Lord, to you we bring our treasure	495												
g	O King enthroned on high	158	421		373		311	296			180		504	
g	Ride on Jesus, all-victorious						272							
g	Son of God, eternal Saviour	132	498	102				605	639	454	573			
g	The day of the Lord shall come						637							
g	The universe was waiting											669		
g	We find thee, Lord, in others' need	430												
g	When I needed a neighbour	433			548								736	
g	Where love and loving-kindness dwell	528												

225

Year B
CLC: Christ the King
RCL: Proper 29

Daniel **7**: 9-10, 13-14; Psalm **93**; Revelation **1**: 4b-8; John **18**: 33-37

		AMS	NEH	HTC	HON	MP	H&P	R&S	BPW	CH3	CP	SG	ONC	MPC
s	'The Kingdom is upon you!'	512									590			
s	Christ is the King! O friends rejoice	345	345	492				571	475	474	165	31		
s	The Kingdom of God is justice and joy			333		651	139	200	321		591	184	646	651
s	Thy/Your kingdom come, O God	177	499	334	519		783	638	644	322	607	269	691	949
oe	God is our strength from days of old				171							220		
o	Great God, what do I see and hear			189										
o	Immortal, invisible, God only wise	199	377	21	242	327	9	67	383	32	474	44	314	327
o	Jesus came — the heavens adoring			195										
o	Let all the world in every corner sing	202	394	342	296	404	10	114	54	361	497	47	382	404
o	O worship / Worship the Lord in the beauty of holiness	49	52	344	394	529	505	187	22	40	89	204	552	529
o	O worship the King all glorious above	101	433	24	393	528	28	47	63	35	546	90	551	528
o	The God of Abraham praise	331	148	9	478	645	452	121	131	358	586	66	642	645
p	The Lord doth reign and clothed is he									140				
p	The Lord Jehovah reigns						59							
e	At the name of Jesus	148	338	172	46	41	74	261	370	300	380	317	54	
e	Come, wounded healer											130		
e	God the source and goal of being											233		
e	Let all mortal flesh keep silence	256	295	61	295		266	454	441	577	309	472	381	
e	Lo, he / Jesus comes with clouds descending	28	9	196	307	424	241	656	185	316	31	438	405	424
e	To God be the glory			584	522	708	463	289	566	374	609	71	695	708
g	Ah, holy Jesus, how hast thou offended		62	123	8		164	215	215	251	100		5	
g	Alleluia, Jesus is Lord											7		
g	Great Son of God, you once on Calvary's cross				187							251		

continued on next page

		AMS	NEH	HTC	HON	MP	H&P	R&S	BPW	CH3	CP	SG	ONC	MPC
g	Hark what a sound, and too divine for hearing						236	660		314	28			
g	He stood before the court			129										
g	Heaven shall not wait				207								272	
g	Jesus in the olive grove						169							
g	Lord of the boundless curves of space	493	405				335	44			210			
g	Lord, enthroned in heavenly splendour	263	296	416	309	431	616			583	311	52	408	
g	Man of sorrows			130	330	458	228		350	380		383	439	458
g	Mine eyes have seen the glory				336		242			318			449	
g	My song is love unknown	63	86	136	346	478	173	207	204	224	112	384	463	478
g	Nature with open volume stands	497	87				174	219			113			
g	Praise to the living God						56	118						
g	Rejoice! the Lord is King	139	443	180	432	575	243	657	317	296	563	440	580	575
g	The head that once was crowned with thorns	141	134	182	480	647	209	257	274	286	172	442		644
g	Unto us a Child / boy/ Jesus Christ the Lord is born		39	83	526	714	127	169	181	187	73	355	700	714
g	Ye/You choirs of new Jerusalem	73	124	168	563		823				162	419	754	

Year C
CLC: Christ the King
RCL: Proper 29

Jeremiah 23: 1-6; Psalm 46; Colossians 1: 11-20; Luke 23: 33-43

		AMS	NEH	HTC	HON	MP	H&P	R&S	BPW	CH3	CP	SG	ONC	MPC
s	'The Kingdom is upon you!'	512									590			
s	Christ is the King! O friends rejoice	345	345	492				571	475	474	165	31		
s	The Kingdom of God is justice and joy			333		651	139	200	321		591	184	646	651
s	Thy/Your kingdom come, O God	177	499	334	519		783	638	644	322	607	269	691	949
œ	God is our strength from days of old				171								220	
o	All hail the power of Jesus' name	140	332	587/ 203	13	13	252		29	382	163	24	16	13

continued on next page

		AMS	NEH	HTC	HON	MP	H&P	R&S	BPW	CH3	CP	SG	ONC	MPC
o	O come, O come, Emmanuel	26	11	66	358	493	85	126	144	165	32	338	480	493
p	A safe stronghold/fortress/refuge	114		523		2	661	585	375	406/7				2
p	Be still and know that I am God				52	48		347	280			18, 242	66	
p	God is our refuge and our strength								691		24			
eg	So dies this man, this carpenter: SS41													
e	From glory to glory advancing	276	286		147			462		325	299		194	
e	How shall I sing that majesty	472	373				8	661			466		296	
e	Lord, enthroned in heavenly splendour	263	296	416	309	431	616			583	311	52	408	
e	Lord, teach us how to pray aright	227	406	367	316		551				98		418	
e	O Christ the same, through all our story's pages		258	263									477	
e	Praise be to Christ, in whom we see		220											
e	Praise to God the Father LUTR162													
e	Soldiers of Christ, arise	219	449	533	449	604	719	370	580	441	571	643	606	604
g	He gave his life in selfless love			405		214			435			467		214
g	Heaven shall not wait				207								272	
g	It was on a Friday morning: SS43													
g	Jesus, prince and saviour				274	377						410	358	377
g	Meekness and majesty				335	465			58			395	448	465
g	O sacred head	68	90	139	389	520	176	220	223	253	120	385	535	520
g	There is a green hill far away	137	92	148	499	674	178	223	230	241	123	388	657	674
g	Were you there	523	93		540	745	181	227	232		126		721	

The Naming and Circumcision of Jesus

Numbers 6: 22-27; Psalm 8; Galatians 4: 4-7; Luke 2: 15-21

		AMS	NEH	HTC	HON	MP	H&P	R&S	BPW	CH3	CP	SG	ONC	MPC
sp	Tell out, my soul, the greatness of the Lord	422	186	42	467	631	86	740	391	164	362	62	631	631
s	I'm not ashamed to own/name my Lord			448	240	323	677	428	343	591		532	316	323
s	Jesus, good above all other	378	387	96	269		732	528		111	487		350	
s	The name of the Lord is a strong tower										136		809	
o	God of mercy, God of grace	179	366	293	175			575	48	497	449		227	
p	O Lord my God, when I in awesome wonder [How great thou art]				380	506		117	62		262	56	511	506
p	O Lord of every shining constellation	411		314					130	141	263		512	
e	All hail the power of Jesus' name	140	332	587/ 203	13	13	252		29	382	163	24	16	13
e	At the name of Jesus	148	338	172	46	41	74	261	370	300	380	317	54	
e	God of love, you freely give											226		
e	How sweet the name of Jesus sounds	122	374	211	220	251	257	277	339	376	467	42	297	251
e	Jesus! the name high over all			213		385	264					323		385
e	Name of all majesty			218		481					525	324	465	481
e	O for a thousand tongues to sing	125	415	219	362	496	744	285	59	371	534	55	485	495
e	To the Name of our / that brings salvation	121	470	222	523		80	291		373	610	72	698	
e	To us a child of royal birth	45		64										
g	Jesus, what a beautiful name										334			
g	Unto us a Child / boy/ Jesus Christ the Lord is born		39	83	526	714	127	169	181	187	73	355	700	714

See also New Year, page 24

The Conversion of St Paul

Jeremiah **1**: 4-10, Psalm **67** and Acts **9**: 1-22
or Acts **9**: 1-22, Psalm **67** and Galatians **1**: 11-16a; Matthew **19**: 27-30

		AMS	NEH	HTC	HON	MP	H&P	R&S	BPW	CH3	CP	SG	ONC	MPC
s	Children of the heavenly King	213	344	566	63									
s	Christ is made the sure foundation / Blessed city, heavenly Salem	283/ 332	204-5	559	76	73	485	559	474	10	208	572	97	73
s	Disposer supreme and judge of the earth	298	216		110						214		149	
s	Eternal Spirit of the living Christ							300						
s	Give praise for famous men			568										
s	It is a thing most wonderful	70	84	131	255	346	224	503	219	385	109	557	333	346
s	The eternal gifts of Christ the King	297	213		476					540			639	
s	Thy/Your hand, O God, has guided	171	485	536	518	705	784	567	398	424	606	649	689	705
s	To God be the glory			584	522	708	463	289	566	374	609	71	695	708
s	Who would true valour / He who would valiant / Who honours courage	212	372	537, 590	205	224	688	557	362	443	621	639	281	224
s	Ye/You servants of God, your Master proclaim	149	476	520	565	784	278	293	76	372	627	75	784	756
l	Captains of the saintly band / Christian soldiers	299	215							539	212		91	
l	We sing the glorious conquest	313	155								237			
o	All my hope on God is founded	336	333	451	15	16	63	586	327	405	368	525	19	16
o	My Lord, I did not choose you			107										
p	God of mercy, God of grace	179	366	293	175			575	48	497	449		227	
æ	At the name of Jesus	148	338	172	46	41	74	261	370	300	380	317	54	
æ	Christ is the world's light	440		321			455	600	34		213	591	99	
a	Fight the good fight	220	359	526	128	143	710	496	524	442	423	635	169	143
a	Just as I am, without one plea	246	294	440	287	396	697	364	346	79	308	507	374	396
a	Lord of glory, in our darkness										603			
a	Saul of Tarsus planned it LUTR116													
e	Amazing grace			28	27	31	215	92	550		375	26	29	
e	And can it be			588	30	33	216	136	328	409	376	168	32	
e	Light of the minds that know him		400	477				529			501	626	397	
e	Lord of all power, I give you my will / Lord of creation, to you be all praise	395		547		440	699	532		428	508			
e	Lord, speak to me, that I may speak			510		444	553	613	611	485	512			444
e	Stand up, stand up for Jesus	221	453	535	457	617	721			481	578	644	617	617
e	Will you come and follow me?				560			558	363		622	634	752	
g	Take my life, and let it be	249		554	464	624	705	371	358	462	581	678	625	624

The Blessed Virgin Mary

Isaiah **61**: 10, 11 or Revelation **11**:19 — **12**:6, **12**:10; Psalm **45**: 10-17;
Galatians **4**: 4-7; Luke **1**: 46-55

		AMS	NEH	HTC	HON	MP	H&P	R&S	BPW	CH3	CP	SG	ONC	MPC
s	Alleluia, alleluia, give thanks to the risen Lord			S3	24	30	250	234	31		136	398	8	30
s	Blest are the pure in heart	238	341	110	63	58	724		588	113	391	372	77	58
s	Hail, O star that pointest		180		190								254	
s	Her Virgin eyes	310	182								239			
s	Mary, blessed grieving mother				331								441	
s	Mary, blessed teenage mother				332								442	
s	O glorious Maid, exalted far		183											697
s	Sing we of the blessed Mother		185		448								605	
s	The Lord/God whom earth and sea and sky	309	181								243			
s	Virgin-born, we bow before thee	311	187		527						244		701	
s	We thank you, God almighty										365			
s	When Mary sang her gladness AFJ33													
s	Who better than Mary: SS73													
s	Ye who own the faith of Jesus		188		568						231		759	
o	He brought me to his banqueting table												837	
o	O Christ the Lord, O Christ the King		496				406	630						
p	My heart is full of Christ, and longs						799							
p	The Church's one foundation	170	484	501	473	640	515	566	393	420	585	581	636	640
e	Of the Father's love/heart begotten / God of God	33	33	56	395		79	181	145	198	64,65		486	
e	To the Name of our / that brings salvation	121	470	222	523		80	291		373	610	72	698	
gs	Mary blessed teenage mother				352								442	
g	For Mary, Mother of our/the Lord	360	161		136					238			182	
g	Mary, blessed grieving mother				331								441	
g	Sing we a song of high revolt	419							638		241		604	
g	Tell out, my soul, the greatness of the Lord	422	186	42	467	631	86	740	391	164	362	62	631	631
g	The angel Gabriel from heaven came				471		87	139	177		242		634	
g	When our God came to earth				552								740	
g	Who would have dreamed it										366			

Rogationtide Years A, B, C

Deuteronomy **8**: 1-10; 1 Kings **8**: 35-40; Job **28**: 1-11; Philippians **4**: 4-7;
2 Thessalonians **3**: 6-13; 1 John **5**: 12-15; Psalms **104**: 21-30, **107**: 1-9 or
121; Matthew **6**: 1-15; Mark **11**: 22-24; Luke **11**: 5-13

		AMS	NEH	HTC	HON	MP	H&P	R&S	BPW	CH3	CP	SG	ONC	MPC
s	As the light upon the river PR920													
s	By the rutted roads we follow									619				
s	For the beauty of the earth	104	285	298	137	152	333	41	121	367	253	298	184	152
s	God of light and life's creation			561										
s	God of mercy, God of grace	179	366	293	175			575	48	497	449		227	
s	God, whose farm is all creation	370		282	179		344	612	124		271	302	236	
s	God, you have / who hast given us power	469					345				256			
s	Great God, we sing that mighty / your guiding hand						356	63	552	613				
s	Great is thy/your faithfulness			260	186	200	66	96	553		453	39	249	200
s	Lord of the changing year			261								303		
s	Lord, in thy name thy servants plead		126											
s	Morning has broken		237	265	337	467	635	45	132		260		450	467
s	O Lord of every shining constellation	411		314					130	141	263		512	
s	O Lord of heaven and earth and sea	287	422	287			337		387	145	540	306		
s	Praise to the Lord, the Almighty	207	440	40	427	564	16	74	68	9	558	59	573	564
s	The earth is yours, O God			290								313		
s	To thee, our God, we fly	330	127								274		698	
s	We bring you, Lord, our prayer and praise									611	262			
p	All creatures of our God and King	105	263	13	9	7	329	39	28	30	250	23	6	7
p	All people that on earth do dwell	100	334	14	17	20	1	712	2	1	369	77	21	20
p	All things bright and beautiful	116	264	283	21	23	330		116	154	251	294	25	23
p	Before Jehovah's aweful/awesome throne / Sing to the Lord	197		15			61	119		2	387			
p	Forth in thy/your name, O Lord	239	235	306	143	159	381	521	526	463	430	623	188	159
p	Immortal, invisible, God only wise	199	377	21	242	327	9	67	383	32	474	44	314	327
p	Judge eternal, throned in splendour		490	329	285	395	409	626	627	519	356	600	372	395
p	O worship the King	101	433	24	393	528	28	47	63	35	546	90	551	528
p	Unto the hills around			48										
e	Within the busy rush of life										648			
g	For the fruits of his/all creation	457		286	138	153	342	42	123		254	299	185	153
g	God, the source and goal of being											233		
g	Lord, teach us how to pray aright	227	406	367	316		551				98		418	
g	O God of Bethel / O God of Jacob	216	416	35	364		442	71	599	72	536	241	491	907
g	Rejoice, O land, in God thy might / your Lord	296	493	331	431						227		579	
g	We plough the fields and scatter	290	262	292	534	732	352	124	135	620	275	311	719	732

See also Sixth Sunday of Easter

Harvest Years A, B, C

Year A: Deuteronomy **8**: 7-18 or **28**: 1-14; Psalm **65**; 2 Corinthians **9**: 6-15;
Luke **12**: 16-30 or **17**: 11-19
Year B: Joel **2**: 21-27; Psalm **126**; 1 Timothy **2**: 1-7 or **6**: 6-10;
Matthew **6**: 25-33
Year C: Deuteronomy **26**: 1-11; Psalm **100**; Philippians **4**: 4-9
or Revelation **14**: 14-18; John **6**: 25-35

		AMS	NEH	HTC	HON	MP	H&P	R&S	BPW	CH3	CP	SG	ONC	MPC
s	All people that on earth do dwell	100	334	14	17	20	1	712	2	1	369	77	21	20
s	All that I am, all that I do				19							23		
s	All things bright and beautiful	116	264	283	21	23	330		116	154	251	294	25	23
s	All things praise thee, Lord most high				24		331							24
s	Come, ye/you thankful people, come	289	259	284	101	106	355	40	120	627	270	34	133	106
s	Dance and sing, all the earth				105								139	
s	Fair waved the golden corn		260		116					629			155	
s	Fill your hearts with joy and gladness			30	147			40				80	172	147
s	For the beauty of the earth	104	285	298	137	152	333	41	121	367	253	298	184	152
s	For the fruits of his/all creation	457		286	138	153	342	42	123		254	299	185	153
s	Fountain of mercy, God of love									628				
s	Glory, love, and praise, and honour	461	287		160		35				436		207	
s	God in his love for us lent us this planet						343	85				300		832
s	God of all ages					190								190
s	God of mercy, God of grace	179	366	293	175			575	48	497	449		227	
s	God, whose farm is all creation	370		282	179		344	612	124		271	302	236	
s	Great is thy/your faithfulness			260	186	200	66	96	553		453	39	249	200
s	In humble gratitude, O God	377												
s	Let us, with a gladsome mind / Let us gladly with one mind	204	397	23	302	415	27		56	33	498	312	392	415

continued on next page

		AMS	NEH	HTC	HON	MP	H&P	R&S	BPW	CH3	CP	SG	ONC	MPC
s	Lord, by whose breath all souls and seeds	486												
s	My father was a wandering Aramean: SS54													
s	Now thank we all our God	205	413	33	354	486	566	72	128	368	530	54	474	486
s	O Father, whose creating hand						349							
s	O Lord of heaven and earth and sea	287	422	287			337		387	145	540	306		
s	O Lord, all the world belongs to you				378			90	136				509	
s	O worship the King all glorious above	101	433	24	393	528	28	47	63	35	546	90	551	528
s	Praise and thanksgiving, Father, we offer	415					350	48			272		558	
s	Praise God for Harvest-Time										307			
s	Praise God for the harvest of farm and of field			288			351					308	559	
s	Praise God from whom all blessings flow	1	232	586	417	557	632	21	113	658	1	57	560	557
s	Praise, O praise our God and King	288			423		359				273		566	
s	See the farmer sow the seed									621				
s	The earth is yours, O God			290								313		
s	To thee/you, O Lord, our hearts we raise	291	261	291	524		362	53				310	696	
s	We are not our own							484					510	
s	We plough the fields and scatter	290	262	292	534	732	352	124	135	620	275	311	719	732
p	Praise the Lord of heaven						507						568	
eA	The gifts we bring express our love										278			
eC	Within the busy rush of life										648			
g	Cry 'freedom' in the name of God				104								138	

Christian Initiation

Infant Baptism

	AMS	NEH	HTC	HON	MP	H&P	R&S	BPW	CH3	CP	SG	ONC	MPC
At the dawning of creation							424					52	
Eternal God, we consecrate	452									336			
Eternal God, we praise your love AFJ29													
Glory and praise to God who loves						581	464						
God the Father, name we treasure	466		385							337			
In the name of God the Father NSC3													
Lord Jesus, as you came NSC5													
Lord Jesus, once a child						585	417						
Lord, bless and keep this little child										493			
Now in the name of him who sent						590	425						
Sing to the Lord glad hymns of praise		316											
This child from God above						589							
We bring our children, Lord, today									339				
We praise you, Lord, for Jesus Christ	521						418			340			
Word of the Father, the life of creation							419						

Adult or Family Baptism

	AMS	NEH	HTC	HON	MP	H&P	R&S	BPW	CH3	CP	SG	ONC	MPC
At the dawning of creation							424					52	
Awake, awake, fling off the night	342		49				404			334		57	
Baptized in water for our Lord PR634													
Christ, when for us you were baptized	442					129		405		92			
Come, Father, Son and Holy Ghost						580							
Come, Holy Spirit, come inflame			93							179		119	
God of all human history											223		
Lord, here is one to be baptized						584							
Praise and thanksgiving be to our creator	506												
Praise to God, almighty Maker						582	430	414					
Spirit of God, come dwell											611		
Stand, soldier of the cross						591							
The servants of God are baptized PR638													
Waken, O sleeper, wake and rise											702		
We bring our children, Lord, today NSC10													
Baptized in water			381								492		

Re-affirmation of Baptismal Faith
(see also Confirmation)

	AMS	NEH	HTC	HON	MP	H&P	R&S	BPW	CH3	CP	SG	ONC	MPC
A mighty mystery we set forth								403					
All who believe and are baptized							421	402		373			
By the sacrifice of Jesus										571			
Come, Lord, to our souls	345					470	361			335		122	
Jesus, we follow thee						583							
Light of the minds that know him		400	477				529			501	626	397	
This is the truth which we proclaim			388								494		
We believe in God almighty			10								285		
We believe in God the Father									363	286			
We know that Christ is raised and dies no more			389				426						

Confirmation

	AMS	NEH	HTC	HON	MP	H&P	R&S	BPW	CH3	CP	SG	ONC	MPC
Forth in thy/your name, O Lord	239	235	306	143	159	381	521	526	463	430	623	188	159
God be in my head	236	328	543	166		694	498	592	433	439	666	211	
I bind unto myself / myself to God today / Christ be with me		159	5	225		695	36		402	203		302	
I'm not ashamed to own/name my Lord			448	240	323	677	428	343	591		532	316	323
Jesus, our Lord and King							429						
Lift high the cross	72		508	303	417	170	422	575	550	499	601	394	417
Lord of all power, I give you my will / Lord of creation, to you be all praise	395		547		440	699	532		428	508			
Lord of the love that in Christ							431						
Lord, for the years			328	310	428		603	535		51	602	409	428
Lord, let your grace descend on those						587		412					
My God, accept my heart this day	279	318	551	341		701			429	338	559	455	
Now is eternal life	402	114		351		203	432			152		470	
O happy day that fixed my choice			442	369	499	702	359	539				498	499
O Jesus, I have promised	235	420	531	372	501	704	509	352	434	538	676	503	501
O thou/Lord who came[st]	233	431	552/ 596	392	525	745	433	355	110	191	560	541	525
Take my life, and let it be	249		554	464	624	705	371	358	462	581	678	625	624
Thine/Yours for ever	234	463	556	504						599		673	992
Will you come and follow me?				560			558	363		622	634	752	